ETHICS FOR ADVERSARIES

ETHICS FOR ADVERSARIES

THE MORALITY OF ROLES IN PUBLIC AND PROFESSIONAL LIFE

ARTHUR ISAK APPLBAUM

PRINCETON UNIVERSITY PRESS

PRINCETON, NEW JERSEY

Library of Congress Cataloging-in-Publication Data

Applbaum, Arthur Isak.
Ethics for adversaries : the morality of roles in public and
professional life / Arthur Isak Applbaum.
p.   cm.
Includes bibliographical references and index.
ISBN 0-691-00712-8 (cloth : alk. paper)
1. Ethics.   2. Professional ethics.   3. Political ethics.
4. Adversary system (Law).   I. Title.

BJ1031.A65   1999   172—dc21   98-32010

This book has been composed in Palatino

The paper used in this publication meets the minimum
requirements of ANSI/NISO Z39.48–1992 (R1997)
(*Permanence of Paper*)

http://pup.princeton.edu

Printed in the United States of America

10 9 8 7 6 5 4 3

For Sally

CONTENTS

ACKNOWLEDGMENTS

THIS BOOK was not written in haste, and over time I have been helped by many good people. Thank you.

Jean Dombrowski, Greg Dorchak, and Shari Levinson, professionals all, prepared uncounted drafts and tracked down shadowy sources with skill, dedication, and good cheer.

I have benefited from substantial comments on particular chapters—in some cases, on more than one—from Miriam Avins, Daniel Bell, Susan Cleary, Robert Darnton, Linda Emanuel, Richard Fallon, Robert Fullinwider, Michael Hardimon, Frances Kamm, John Kleinig, Frederick Kraus, Martha Minow, Lynn Peterson, Robert Rosen, T. M. Scanlon, Tamar Schapiro, Maureen Scully, James Sebenius, Seana Shiffrin, Daniel Wikler, Lloyd Weinreb, and Richard Zeckhauser. Elizabeth Kiss and Simon Schama each pointed me toward important sources. A number of my former graduate fellows in Harvard's Program in Ethics and the Professions—now colleagues and friends—were especially generous with their red ink: Deborah Hellman, Stephen Latham, Karl Lauterbach, Petr Lom, Daniel Markovits, and Alec Walen. Though only a couple of pentimenti show, my earliest efforts on the ethics of adversaries were written with Harold Pollack, then a precocious graduate student, now a friend and peer.

I spent a memorable year working on this book at the Princeton University Center for Human Values as a Laurance S. Rockefeller visiting fellow. I am grateful to George Kateb and Amy Gutmann for assembling a cohort of colleagues whose influence on my work has been deep and enduring: Christine Korsgaard, Avishai Margalit, Arthur Ripstein, Jeff Spinner-Halev, and Michael Thompson.

I have presented parts of the book at various times to audiences at Harvard's John F. Kennedy School of Government, New York University, Harvard Business School, Harvard Law School, and Princeton University, and at meetings of the American Political Science Association, the Association for Practical and Professional Ethics, the Office of Government Ethics, and the American Medical Association. On these occasions I have learned much from the commentary of Robert Bennett, Harry Frankfurt, Amy Gutmann, Mark Kleiman, Sandra Lynch, Bernard Nussbaum, Arthur Ripstein, and David Wilkins.

Mark Moore, Frederick Schauer, and Kenneth Winston, my colleagues at the Kennedy School of Government, have read and perceptively commented on almost all of the chapters at one time or another. Michael Aronson, Mark Kleiman, Jane Mansbridge, Brian Mac-

Donald, and Alan Strudler read the entire draft with care, and their wise advice helped with both unity and clarity. I am especially grateful to David Estlund both for many fruitful conversations along the way and for expert advice on the final draft. Working with Ann Himmelberger Wald, editor in chief at Princeton University Press, and her able staff has been a joy.

Howard Raiffa taught me by example that honesty and charity are intellectual virtues. Chapter 6 begins to make good on a long-standing promise to him to write about the ethics of negotiation.

Alan Wertheimer has fixed my arguments and prose so many times at so many different stages that he shares the blame for the result. In thinking about professional roles, I turn often to Montaigne. In thinking about Alan's friendship, I do the same.

To Dennis Thompson, I owe my calling. He took a chance when he picked me for the first class of faculty fellows in Harvard's Program in Ethics and the Professions. My fellow fellows, from whom I learned so much—Ezekiel Emanuel, Robert Massie Jr., and Robert Rosen—left at year's end, but I did not. The standing joke, stale but not without truth, is that Dennis would keep leaving me back until I got it right. Dozens of faculty and graduate fellows in ethics have now come and gone from Harvard on my watch, and most of them have read one chapter or another of this book in some form. Though I cannot name them all, I am grateful for their invigorating fellowship. Many of those whom I have already mentioned I know because of this rare intellectual community that Dennis directs with exacting standards and generous spirit. Without his deliberative engagement and steadfast encouragement, argument by argument and year after year, I could not have written this book.

Like the prospect of a guillotining, the expectation of twins succeeds marvelously in concentrating the mind. Each time Sophie and Emma kicked in their Mom's belly, they kicked their Dad in the pants as well. Now in early toddlerhood, they have utterly convinced me that William Godwin is wrong. There *is* magic in the pronoun "my."

Sally Louise Rubin has borne the trials of marriage to a ruminant writer with characteristic grace. Sally was my guide on all matters French, from the translation of sources to the navigation of Paris archives. More important, I have relied on her sound judgment and refined ear for matters large and small. She is my one true love, and to her I dedicate this book.

Little Deer Isle, Maine
August 1998

PART I

NECESSARY OFFICES

Likewise in every government there are necessary offices which are
not only abject but also vicious. Vices find their place in it and are
employed for sewing our society together, as are poisons for the
preservation of our health. If they become excusable, inasmuch as we
need them and the common necessity effaces their true quality, we still
must let this part be played by the more vigorous and less fearful
citizens, who sacrifice their honor and their conscience, as those
ancients sacrificed their life, for the good of their country. We who are
weaker, let us take roles that are both easier and less hazardous. The
public welfare requires that a man betray and lie and massacre; let us
resign this commission to more obedient and suppler people.

Michel de Montaigne, "Of the Useful and the Honorable"

Chapter One

ARGUMENTS FOR ADVERSARIES

ETHICS FOR ADVERSARIES is a philosophical inquiry into arguments that are offered to defend adversary roles, practices, and institutions in public and professional life. The adversary professions in law, business, and government typically claim a moral permission to harm others in ways that, if not for the role, would be wrong. I shall argue that the claims of adversary institutions are weaker than supposed and do not justify much of the harm that professional adversaries inflict. Institutions and the roles they create ordinarily cannot mint moral permissions to do what otherwise would be morally prohibited.

Adversary institutions are pervasive, and the arguments offered to justify such arrangements cut across professional boundaries. The most vivid example is the adversary legal system, in which lawyers are permitted, within its rules, to make the case for what they know to be false and to advance causes they know to be unjust. But many other practices invoke some sort of adversary argument for their justification: competitive markets for goods and services, for labor and capital, and for corporate control; internal competition among managers; electoral politics, interest-group pluralism, constitutionally separated powers, and bureaucratic competition; commercial and political advertising, investigative and advocacy journalism, and the marketplace of ideas. The practice of medicine in a for-profit and managed health care system is becoming an adversary institution too. Though the details of these practices and the nuances of the arguments of practitioners vary, I believe that these adversary settings have more in common than is commonly supposed. Though I shall illustrate my view with specific examples drawn from law, business, government, and medicine, my purpose is to develop a general account of "necessary offices" in politics and the professions.

Adversaries can line up a phalanx of arguments to defend their sharp practices, but not all arguments are good ones. For concreteness, consider the claims that might be made by a political candidate and his campaign strategist who, as James Madison puts it, "practice with success the vicious arts," and willfully distort an opponent's record to smear her reputation in the eyes of voters.[1] The claims are

---

[1] *The Federalist*, no. 10 (1787), in *The Founders' Constitution*, ed. Philip B. Kurland and Ralph Lerner (Chicago: University of Chicago Press, 1987), 1:130.

presented in pairs. The members of each pair are easily conflated, but that would be a mistake.

EXPECTATION: Political opponents expect to be slandered, and voters expect to be deceived.
CONSENT: Political opponents consent to be slandered, and voters consent to be deceived.

RULES OF THE GAME: The rules of the game of politics permit slandering opponents and deceiving voters.
FAIR PLAY: Fairness to players in the game of politics morally permits slandering opponents and deceiving voters.

INCREASED NET BENEFIT: More benefit than burden is caused by political slander and deception.
PARETO SUPERIORITY: No one on balance is burdened, and some benefit, from political slander and deception.

NO DIFFERENCE: If I don't slander my opponent and deceive the voters, someone else will.
SELF-DEFEAT: If I don't slander my opponent and deceive the voters, someone else will slander and deceive them even more viciously.

ROLE OBLIGATION: The rules of the role of campaign strategist require engaging in the vicious arts by any legal means.
MORAL OBLIGATION: Morality requires that campaign strategists obey the rules of the role of campaign strategists.

SELFLESSNESS: A professional strategist serving a candidate should filter out her own self-interest.
PERSON NEUTRALITY: A professional strategist serving a candidate should filter out her own moral judgments.

Now, in each pair, the first claim might hold, but does not justify much. The second claim would justify much, but does not hold. In no pair does the second proposition follow from the first. Substitute claims about other adversary practices, and the upshot is the same. If you need convincing, this book is for you.

RESTRICTED REASONS AND PERMISSIBLE VIOLATION

Adversaries act for by acting against. The way that adversaries act *for* poses a problem about good reasons: how to justify adopting the partial aims and point of view of the partisan, thereby restricting the range of moral reasons that count in one's deliberations, so that some good moral reasons are excluded or discounted, and others are given priority or magnified. What justifies such a division of moral labor?[2] Call this the problem of restricted reasons. The way that adversaries act *against* poses a problem about right action: how to justify engaging in adversary tactics that harm others, especially actions that, if performed outside of one's adversary role, would wrongfully violate persons or their rights?[3] Call this the problem of permissible violation. Adversaries offer arguments in defense of their practices that appeal to restricted reasons and that assert permissions to violate.

The Problem of Restricted Reasons

Professional and political actors occupy roles that often instruct them to work at cross-purposes, furthering incompatible ends and trying to thwart each other's plans. Prosecuting and defending attorneys, Democratic and Republican candidates, secretaries of state and national security advisers, industrial manufacturers and environmental regulators, investigative journalists and official sources, and physicians and insurance companies often are pitted against one another by their missions, jobs, and callings.

Sometimes, when adversaries further conflicting moral ends, one is thought to be right and the other wrong; or, one is thought to act for the better, and the other for the worse. But sometimes the actions of both actors are thought to be for the good; indeed, observers often believe that both actors ought to act as they do, though what one ought to do conflicts with what the other ought to do. But how can two political or professional actors facing the same situation be required to act in opposing ways? How can two adversaries who act to further conflicting purposes both have good enough reasons to do so? Why are the reasons the one has to act not reasons, or not good enough reasons, for the other?

One reply is pervasive in both casual and considered talk in support of adversary institutions. Although the form of the argument varies from practice to practice, the heart of it looks something like this: actors occupying professional or public roles are not to make all-things-considered evaluations about the goodness or rightness of

---

[2] The expression "ethical division of labor" comes from Thomas Nagel, "Ruthlessness in Public Life," in his *Mortal Questions* (Cambridge: Cambridge University Press, 1979), p. 85. See also his *Equality and Partiality* (New York: Oxford University Press, 1991); Virginia Held, *Rights and Goods* (Chicago: University of Chicago Press, 1984), pp. 21–39; and David Luban, *Lawyers and Justice* (Princeton, N.J.: Princeton University Press, 1988), pp. 78–81. Each usage is somewhat different.

[3] As developed in Chapter 7, persons are violated when their capacity for moral agency is either denied or damaged.

their actions, but rather, they are to act on restricted reasons for action, taking into account only a limited or partial set of values, interests, or facts. Reasons for action are restricted in two ways. First, the professional is exempted from the broadest, most inclusive of deliberative concerns, allowing for specialized moral aims across roles—*role relativity*. Second, when acting on behalf of others, the professional is precluded from counting the most local of deliberative concerns, requiring uniformity within role—*person neutrality*. Each adversary actor ought to do so (or, more modestly, is permitted to do so) because, in the aggregate, the institution of multiple actors acting from restricted reasons properly takes into account the expansive set of reasons, values, interests, and facts. The competitive market, the system of legal representation, and electoral politics—each turns for justification to a version of this division-of-moral-labor argument. Adam Smith and James Madison, in different ways, appeal to such a division. Some arguments in support of freedom of expression—notably, that of John Stuart Mill—take a similar form.

These arguments rely on some notion of a favorable equilibrium that will result if adversaries restrict their concerns to narrow aims. The mechanism by which a system is to arrive at this equilibrium varies, and at least three evocative images are used to describe it. The division-of-moral-labor image itself suggests not necessarily conflict between professionals or professions, but rather, selective attention to interests, values, and reasons by specialized actors, whose efforts result in the efficient and possibly harmonious manufacture of social value. The adversary-equipoise image adds to this specialization a contest between identified opponents, in which the aims and efforts of one are poised against the contrary aims and efforts of the other in careful balance, so that if one shirks her part, the favorable equilibrium will be upset. In contrast, Adam Smith's famous invisible-hand image, though it too seeks to justify restricted reasons, suggests the opposite of both specialization and individual importance of actors. In the face of competitive pressure and market reaction, actors are interchangeable, no *one* has room for successful discretion, and no one's actions make a difference to the outcome.

The favorable claims made for the resulting equilibria also vary. The strongest versions of equilibrium arguments in the professions unconditionally claim that it is better that all actors narrow their reasons for action than if all actors tried to take the broadest range of reasons for action into account. Such first-best claims are often made for competitive markets and for the moral doctrine known as ethical egoism. The conditional division-of-labor argument claims that if some actors pursue restricted or partisan aims, then it is for the best that all do (though it might be better still if none did). The conditional argument often is invoked to justify the training and deployment of soldiers and lawyers. The weakest version claims only that adversary institutions adequately anticipate and neutralize the bad effects of partisan action. Madison, whose arguments for separation of powers and representative government are often misread as championing the strong argument, actually subscribes to the weakest form.[4]

Arguments for divided moral labor in public and professional life face both a factual and a conceptual challenge. Factually, the equilibrium mechanism by which partial actions are said to serve impartial goods must be specified, and the conditions necessary for a good equilibrium outcome must be shown to hold. What precisely is the route by which manipulative and misleading commercial or political advertising is supposed to lead to market efficiency or legitimate government? Conceptually, it must be shown why a prescription to act from filtered and partial reasons follows from the evaluation that it would be a good state of affairs if practitioners did so. It may be good that diverse, conflicting beliefs are held in the marketplace of ideas, but that doesn't give any actor a good reason to adopt a false belief, and it doesn't justify circulating information one believes to be false. Good forms of social organization do not by themselves dictate the forms of moral reasoning particular actors within institutions ought to employ. The gap between what an institution may allow and what an actor within an institution may do is especially great when the action in question deceives, coerces, or violates persons in other ways.

The Problem of Permissible Violation

Imagine a society, Badland, where people are motivated by self-interest alone, and where everyone pursues his or her own advantage in every interaction with intense vigor. In those pursuits, no one avoids harming another unless there are penalties discouraging such harm, and all craftily engage in manipulation and deception if doing so will advance their ends. In Badland, Avarice talks Bully into buying a worthless painting, Bully dumps toxic waste near Cutthroat's backyard, and Cutthroat refuses to repay the loan borrowed from Avarice. Now, if there are stringent enough rules in place to govern the pursuit of self-interest, Badland *might* be a just society. Kant held that just laws could be written even for a nation of devils. But Badland would

---

[4] See *The Federalist*, no. 10, in Kurland and Lerner, 1:128–31, and no. 51 (1788), ibid., 1:330–31.

not be a *good* society—its inhabitants would be vicious, not virtuous, and we would not admire such people or their character.

Across the border, in Roland, people have the same motivations, but do not pursue their own advantage. Rather, each appoints a trustee who pledges to advance the trustor's interests through a blind trust, and each trustor also is someone else's trustee. Exactly the same conflicts are fought, the same manipulations occur, the same harms inflicted, but each actor is acting as a faithful professional in fulfilling obligations to a client. In Roland, Comity sells Arista's worthless painting to Bono, and thinks that she has a duty to Arista to get the best price; Arista lobbies the legislature to pass a law permitting the expeditious disposal of Bono's poisons despite the risk to Comity's health, and believes that it would be wrong not to seek a rule most favorable to the polluter; Bono is required by the rules of his profession to extricate Comity from her debt to Arista through the skillful manipulation of Roland's legal system. The people of Roland believe that it would be wrong not to meet their fiduciary responsibilities, distasteful as they are. Because they devote their days to fulfilling their professional obligations, they pride themselves on their virtue.

The puzzling self-understanding of the inhabitants of Roland (which perhaps is no more puzzling than the self-understanding of our marketers, lobbyists, and litigators) raises what we might call the problem of hired hands: how can a professional have an obligation to do on a client's behalf what would be wrong if done on the professional's own behalf? The answer cannot simply be that the professional has promised. Whether the promissor is a contract killer or a contract liar, a promise to wrong another has no moral force. One response is to redescribe the doing, so that the action of the professional is said to be "fulfilling professional responsibilities" or "realizing social values served by the division of moral labor," rather than "lying," "poisoning," or "stealing." Another is to redescribe the actor so that it is the professional role that performs the nasty acts, not the person who occupies the professional role—a response to the hired-hands problem we might call the no-hands solution.

The problem of hired hands is an instance of a more general problem. How can acts that ordinarily are morally forbidden—violence, deception, coercion—be rendered morally permissible when performed by one who occupies a professional or public role? Occupants of adversary roles claim such a moral permission when the rules of their profession permit, and claim to be morally required to exercise these permissions when the rules of their profession require. But why do the conventional rules of a practice have the power to create moral permissions and requirements? True, adversary roles direct practitioners to filter out moral reasons that count against harming others, but why are practitioners morally allowed, let alone morally required, to follow such directions?

Précis

To begin, I examine in some detail a professional role that Montaigne counts among his necessary offices: the executioner of Paris.[5] Charles-Henri Sanson is appointed by Louis XVI, and serves the punitive needs of the *ancien régime* for decades. What becomes of the King's Executioner come the French Revolution? He becomes Citizen Sanson, the king's executioner. Sanson adapts seamlessly to the Revolution and its new technology, the guillotine, and ministers with professional detachment to each defeated political faction throughout the Terror and its aftermath. First, the historical record of what is known about Sanson, how he was viewed, and how he wished to be viewed is reconstructed. Then, the most plausible arguments that might have been made in his defense are constructed. The claims that can be made on Sanson's behalf strikingly resemble the claims made by politicians, bureaucrats, lawyers, business executives, and journalists to justify their commitments to their professional roles when the roles ask them to act in ways that ordinarily would be wrong. By exploring one extraordinary professional career and the arguments from the morality of roles that can be offered in its defense, unsettling doubts are raised about arguments in defense of less sanguinary professions and their practices. These doubts are explored more systematically in subsequent chapters.

The three chapters of Part II, "Roles and Reasons," assess arguments in defense of adversary practices that invoke role as an important moral concept. Roles claim to change the morally apt descriptions of actions (lawyering isn't lying) and to restrict the moral reasons that properly enter into a roleplayer's deliberations (defense attorneys are not to consider the consequences of setting a dangerous offender free). Do these bids to filter descriptions and reasons succeed?

  Chapter 3, "Doctor, Schmoctor," introduces the concept of a social and professional role and discusses the various ways that roles can

---

[5] "Of the Useful and the Honorable," in *The Complete Essays of Montaigne*, 3:1 (1588), ed. Donald M. Frame (Stanford, Calif.: Stanford University Press, 1958), p. 606.

generate moral obligations and permissions. I argue for *practice positivism*, the idea that the rules of practices, roles, and institutions do not have any necessary moral content—they simply are what they are, not what they morally ought to be. There is nothing incoherent about a role that can be performed well only by being bad, as Sanson demonstrates. Practice positivism has two upshots: first, roles can demand too little, because a practitioner might not have acquired a moral obligation to comply with a good role. This, I argue, is the challenge new institutional arrangements for the delivery of medical expertise, such as health maintenance organizations, present to the traditional doctor-patient relationship. Second, roles can permit too much, because a practitioner can acquire a moral obligation to comply with a bad role—or so it might seem.

Roles characteristically claim to generate moral prescriptions that vary from professional role to role (role-relative prescriptions) but that do not vary by the personal attributes of those who occupy the role (person-neutral prescriptions). Chapter 4, "The Remains of the Role," explores the argument, often heard from British civil servants, that the demands of person neutrality properly filter out the substantive moral objections that persons occupying roles might have to what the role requires. The standard view of the civil service is compared with a butler's view of private service in Ishiguro's novel, *The Remains of the Day*. I argue that public servants must make political philosophical judgments about both the justice and legitimacy of public policies, and that sometimes those judgments will justify disloyalty and disobedience. The political actor must not defer to the authority of his role obligations without exercising judgment about the legitimacy of the role or of the content of the actions it prescribes.

Chapter 5, "Are Lawyers Liars?" examines the claim that professional practices create new ways of acting that can be judged only by the rules of the practice. If this strategy of redescription succeeds, then the central question of this book is misposed. To the question, How can a professional role morally permit actions that otherwise would be morally wrong? the response is, There is no otherwise. The argument of redescription seeks to short-circuit the moral evaluation of both actions and actors by redescribing them in practice-defined terms. But the argument does not work, because act and actor descriptions persist. Whichever way a practice describes an action, preconventional descriptions do not disappear, and so actions can always be evaluated under multiple descriptions. The rules of the practice of business might claim to redescribe the breaking of a promise so that it is no longer the breaking of a promise, but merely the nonperformance of a contract, and the practice of lawyering might claim to redescribe lying so that willfully causing beliefs one knows to be false is no longer a lie, but merely zealous advocacy. Still, these claims fail.

The harms that adversaries cause cannot be redescribed away or filtered out—the claims of the target not to be mistreated pierce the masks that role players wear. The three chapters of Part III, "Games and Violations," consider arguments that address directly the complaints of those harmed by adversary practices and institutions.

In Chapter 6, "Rules of the Game and Fair Play," I assess several arguments claiming that presumptively wrong actions, if permitted by the rules of a game, for that reason are no longer wrong, and so become morally permitted. Arguments from consent and tacit consent are explored, and shown either to fail to justify sharp tactics or to require stringent conditions that are unlikely to be met in practice. The most promising argument in support of at least some deceptive, coercive, and violent practices is grounded, surprisingly, on the principle of fair play, which obligates us to do our fair share in schemes of social cooperation from which we willingly benefit, and not to free-ride on the burdens shouldered by others. The fair-play argument is here employed in a new way, to establish a moral permission that otherwise would not exist, rather than to establish a moral obligation that otherwise would not exist. Necessary and sufficient conditions for the fair-play argument to work in establishing a permission are developed, and the question of whether various games in business, legal practice, and politics meet these conditions is explored.

If some ways of treating others never are morally permissible, however, then arguments in defense of some adversary permissions cannot get off the ground. Chapter 7, "Are Violations of Rights Ever Right?" establishes the conceptual possibility of morally permissible violations. I distinguish violating persons from violating the rights of persons not to be violated. Though it may be a contradiction to violate a right in order to express the inviolable status of rights, persons, not rights, have that status, so it is no contradiction to violate a right in order to express the inviolable status of persons. I explore a number of conditions under which the violation of persons could meet a test of reasonable acceptance—for example, when constraints against violation are self-defeating or Pareto-inferior. But adversary professions and practices typically do not meet these conditions, and so the violations they inflict typically do not meet the test of reasonable acceptance.

Chapter 8, "Ethics in Equilibrium," assesses appeals to the overall good of a system of adversaries pursuing partial and partisan purposes. A few pages ago I sketched the forms that such appeals take—

to an invisible hand, to a division of labor, or to equipoise. In this chapter, I examine both the claim that harmful actions taken under an equilibrating mechanism produce good consequences and the claim that such actions pass the test of reasonable acceptance. Adversaries in equilibrium might argue that, because of the institutional structure in which they act, the harms they cause fall on the easier-to-justify side of two distinctions: the difference between intentional and accidental harm and the difference between doing and allowing harm. Both moves fail. The adversary cannot redescribe his aims in a way that makes the violation he inflicts an accidental effect of the overall good aims of the institution. Invisible hands don't violate people— people violate people. And, though the designers and rule makers of an adversary institution can be understood to allow certain activities, practitioners do them, and actions that are not wrong to allow might be wrong to do. Failure to note this asymmetry leads to the conflation of justified forms of social organization with justified forms of moral reasoning by practitioners within institutions.

If institutions may permit or even require actions that practitioners within those institutions ought not to do, then a different sort of adversary relation arises—not one designed by governments, markets, or professions, but one that follows from the conflict between the authority of these institutions and the judgment of practitioners. Part IV, "Authority and Dissent," takes up this conflict.

Chapter 9, "Democratic Legitimacy and Official Discretion," considers the conditions under which the occupant of a political role may take adversary action against superiors or constituents in the face of substantive political disagreements. When may government officials create and exercise effective discretion to pursue policies that dissent from the wishes of superiors or of most citizens? I argue that neither the obedient servant nor the catch-me-if-you-can entrepreneur are proper models of official discretion. Criteria for justified discretion are offered, drawing on accounts of legislative representation and civil disobedience. Conclusion: dissenters ought to make judgments about the common bads or injustices at issue and about the legitimate jurisdiction and the legitimate reasons of the sources of political mandates. These conditions of democratic legitimacy are matched with possible strategies of dissent—persuasive, incentive, or deceptive. In the end, it is not the role-relative prescriptions of divided government institutions that justify adversary action by political actors, but rather, dissenting political judgments about justice and legitimacy.

Chapter 10, "Montaigne's Mistake," illustrates the book's main arguments through an analysis of an event important in shaping American views of authority and dissent under a division of *constitutional* labor, the conflict between President Richard Nixon and Special Prosecutor Archibald Cox over the Watergate tapes. I assess various ways that a claim for a division of labor in moral reasoning, given an institutional separation of powers, can be pressed, so that both those who brought about Cox's dismissal and those who refused are justified. I conclude that, under plausible assumptions, to obey the president is to violate political liberties in a way that fails to meet any of the tests of morally permissible violation.

PHILOSOPHICAL COMMITMENTS

I hope that there is something in this book for readers who come to it with a variety of foundational views in moral and political philosophy. Chapter 2 and Part II raise questions and reject answers in a way that travels fairly light. But obviously one cannot be completely ecumenical in one's philosophical commitments and still say something. As will become clear in Parts III and IV, I believe that some version of contractualism owing much to Kant is the right account of moral philosophy, and some version of liberalism owing much to Rawls is the right account of political philosophy. But it is not my project here to demonstrate the correctness of contractualism or liberalism in general. Whatever the correct view is about divisions of moral labor, surely there is room for a division of intellectual labor. I leave those more foundational pursuits to others.[6] Nor is it my purpose to enter into intramural discussions about just which formulation of contractualism or liberalism is most promising—on that, except for occasional lapses, I am intentionally noncommittal. I hope that what I have to say about adversary roles and institutions is sufficiently robust to hold water, with some minor plugging, under any plausible version. Rather than argue for, I argue *from* a contractualist sensibility, in the hope that, if you are not already convinced, you will feel enough of its tug to question whether morality is, at bottom, simply about the summing up of benefits and burdens across persons. If utilitarianism or a straightforward consequentialism is the correct moral theory, then there are no deep moral objections to an adversary profession or

---

[6] See, for example, John Rawls, *A Theory of Justice* (Cambridge, Mass.: Harvard University Press, 1971), and *Political Liberalism* (New York: Columbia University Press, 1993); Thomas Nagel, *The View from Nowhere* (New York: Oxford University Press, 1986), and *Equality and Impartiality*; Christine M. Korsgaard, *Creating the Kingdom of Ends* (Cambridge: Cambridge University Press, 1996); and T. M. Scanlon, *What We Owe to Each Other* (Cambridge, Mass.: Harvard University Press, 1998).

institution that, all things considered, breaks even on benefits and burdens.[7] If, instead, moral justification is about giving reasons to each person burdened that she, if reasonable, would accept, an appeal to good consequences alone is not likely to meet the test of reasonable acceptance. This book is a search for acceptable reasons adversaries could give to those they deceive, coerce, and otherwise violate. Though there is truth in many arguments for adversaries, these truths are far more limited in scope and setting than is often claimed. The task ahead is to draw these limits.

[7] I say straightforward consequentialism to exclude versions that attempt to account for nonconsequentialist intuitions. See, for example, Amartya Sen, "Rights and Agency," *Philosophy and Public Affairs* 11 (1982): 3–39, and "Evaluator Relativity and Consequential Evaluation," *Philosophy and Public Affairs* 12 (1983): 113–32.

Chapter Two

PROFESSIONAL DETACHMENT:
THE EXECUTIONER OF PARIS

> Saviours of the homeland, hereafter do not make such a hasty end of criminals who fall into your clutches. Put it to those extreme patriots of excess that it is no service to their fellow citizens to eradicate, by their slapdash zeal, the only way to come at the root of the catastrophes that were then being prepared. Put it to them that they owe me compensation for the executions of which they have deprived me. Each of the heads of the four scoundrels, if my sword had put them off their shoulders, would have been worth twenty *écus* to me. Put it to them that the work would have been much more neatly done and that a great many spectators would have enjoyed the spectacle of the sacrifice of these vile victims, if the tragedy had been played at my theatre. . . .
>
> . . . And let these usurpers consider that they, much more than I, deserve that ignominy with which I am myself visited. For it is not I who kill the criminals who die beneath my blows; it is Justice that sacrifices them, it is Justice that makes me the avenger of society. Should not this appellation rather honour than abase me? . . . *Will philosophy not succeed in making my profession a glorious one?*
>
> > *Complaints of the Public Executioner against Those Who Have Exercised His Profession without Having Served Out Their Apprenticeship*

T HE EXECUTIONER of Paris did not write these words, though the satirist who did captured with dead-on accuracy and prescience much of what can be reconstructed about how Charles-Henri Sanson, perhaps the least understandable figure of the French Revolution, understood himself and was understood by his contemporaries.[1]

At the risk of causing squeamishness, I invite you to explore with me one extraordinary professional career and the arguments from the

---

[1] This anonymous, satirical pamphlet (emphasis added) was published in reaction to the *lanterne* lynchings and the parading of heads on pikes that followed the storming of the Bastille in July 1789.

morality of roles that can be offered in its defense. The uneasiness this will cause is not merely an affront to delicate feelings, for the claims that can be made on Sanson's behalf strikingly resemble the claims about role morality that have been offered for the less sanguinary professions. By entertaining arguments in Sanson's defense, we might learn much about what sorts of claims about roles succeed. If these arguments are perverse when offered by Sanson, why are they not perverse when offered by lawyers, politicians, bureaucrats, journalists, and business executives in defense of actions that, if performed outside of their roles, would be morally wrong? If Sanson's defense fails, so might the defenses of other professional roles. The point of this chapter is to unsettle. The contradictory reactions that are stirred up are assayed in later chapters.[2]

THE "ARGUMENT OF THE GUILLOTINE"

Sanson's grandfather's father was appointed Louis XIV's headsman in 1688. The professional calling, with its art and science of torture, dismemberment, and death, was handed down through apprenticeship and regal reappointment to Charles-Henri. He began doing his father's work in 1751 and was formally appointed in 1778 by Louis XVI (who would come to observe his appointee's handiwork up close). Sanson formally passed the commission on to *his* son in 1795 (though the son clearly was active on the scaffold, and may have taken the lead, before then). All six of Sanson's brothers, along with uncles and cousins, were also executioners, holding commissions in Tours, Dijon, Provins, Versailles, Blois, Montpellier, Rheims, and Genoa around the time of the Revolution. The Paris post stayed in the family until 1847.[3]

For decades, Sanson and his assistants conscientiously attended to the punitive needs of the *ancien régime*: the lesser sentences of public exposure, branding, and various mutilations; the rare beheading of nobles, the more common hanging of commoners, the breaking of robbers at the wheel, the burning of heretics at the stake, and, for attempted regicide, one quartering (botched, because the lore had

---

[2] Several mentions in Simon Schama's cornucopian *Citizens: A Chronicle of the French Revolution* (New York: Random House, 1989) aroused my curiosity about Sanson. Professor Schama generously responded to my request for further references.

[3] See G. Lenôtre, *The Guillotine and Its Servants* (1893), trans. Mrs. Rodolph Stawell (London: Hutchinson, 1929), pp. 72–84, 134–35, 140. Lenôtre is a pseudonym for Louis Léon Théodore Gosselin.

been lost).[4] But Sanson seamlessly adapted to both the Revolution and its new technology, the humane and ennobling machine proposed by the good Doctor Guillotin. He ministered with professional detachment to, in turn, common criminals under the constitutional monarchy, royalist "plotters" at the direction of the Paris Commune, the king upon conviction by the National Convention, the moderate Girondins when purged by the Jacobins, the extremist Hébertistes at the instigation of Danton, the indulgent Dantonistes after their denunciation by Robespierre, and Robespierre himself when finally outmaneuvered by the Thermidorians.

After the Terror, the possibility of a Sanson fired the imagination of many writers, and he has been posed, alternately, as both grotesque and tragic. In 1795, the writer and onetime Girondist legislator Louis-Sébastien Mercier wonders in horror about the man he calls "that monster":[5]

> I should love to know what goes on in that head of his, and whether he considers his appalling duties simply as a profession . . . How does he sleep after receiving the last words and the last glances of all those severed heads? . . . He sleeps well enough, we are told, and it may well be that his conscience is untroubled . . . It is said that the queen apologized to him when, on the scaffold, she accidentally placed the tip of her foot on his. What were his thoughts then? The coins of the royal treasury were for a long time his living. What a man this Sanson is! He comes and goes just like anyone else. Sometimes he goes to the Théâtre du Vaudeville. He laughs, he looks at me. My head escaped him, but he knows nothing of that.[6]

---

[4] See Daniel Arasse, *The Guillotine and the Terror*, trans. Christopher Miller (1987; London: Penguin Books, 1989), p. 13. Though it often required exceptional cruelty, capital punishment did not demand much of the Paris executioner's time in the *ancien régime*. Diderot estimated that 300 executions a year occurred in all of France. See Alister Kershaw, *A History of the Guillotine* (London: John Calder, 1958), p. 8. About 160 public executioners held commissions throughout France before the Revolution. See Lenôtre, *The Guillotine and Its Servants*, p. 13. Out of a French population of about 25 million, some 600,000 lived in Paris. See B. R. Mitchell, *International Historical Statistics: Europe, 1750–1988* (New York: Stockton Press, 1992), pp. 10, 74. Even with generous allowances for the higher concentration of political cases tried in the capital, it is unlikely that Sanson inflicted the death penalty more than a couple of dozen times a year before the Revolution.

[5] Louis-Sébastien Mercier, *Le Nouveau Paris* (1795), vol. 3, ch. 88, reprinted in Louis-Sébastien Mercier, *The Picture of Paris before and after the Revolution*, trans. Wilfrid Jackson and Emilie Jackson (London: George Routledge and Sons, 1929), p. 220.

[6] *Le Nouveau Paris*, vol. 3, ch. 97, quoted in Arasse, *The Guillotine and the Terror*, p. 129 (translating all quoted text except the last sentence) (omissions in original), and reprinted in *The Picture of Paris*, p. 223 (translating the last sentence of the quotation).

But others, creating grotesqueries of their own, present him as a man of humane sensibilities in the fashion of the cult of Rousseau, a tragic figure caught between duty and sentiment, and beset by undeserved social stigmatization for doing what must be done. Such a portrayal is entirely consistent with the high-minded hopes of Guillotin and the penal reformers of 1789. More than two years before the first guillotine was built, two engravings, almost mirror images of one another, envision an execution scene. One shows the face of a delicate executioner turning his head away in sadness or pain as he cuts a rope to drop the blade.[7] In the other, we see the back of a dramatically posed and shaded executioner, head turned away from both us and the victim, one hand raised to cover his mouth or face as the other cuts the rope.[8] This same averted gaze is reproduced, fancifully, in a German engraving of the guillotining of Louis XVI, thereby turning hope into historical fact.[9] By 1804, Joseph Joubert in his notebooks can cuttingly lampoon this attribution of sensitivity with the following anecdote: " 'Where have you been, young misses?' 'Mummy, we went to see a guillotining; oh, my goodness, how that poor executioner suffered.' "[10] Apocryphal memoirs were written humanizing the monster, one penned in part by Balzac. Some of these tales, with a royalist bent, show an executioner who has more compassion for his victims and their loved ones than do his murderous masters.[11]

Mercier spent thirteen months in prison. See H. Temple Patterson, *Poetic Genesis: Sébastien Mercier into Victor Hugo*, vol. 11 of *Studies on Voltaire and the Eighteenth Century*, ed. Theodore Besterman (Geneva: Institut et musée Voltaire, 1960), p. 35.

[7] *Machine Proposed to the National Assembly by Monsieur Guillotin for the Execution of Criminals*, Musée Carnavalet, Paris; reproduced in Arasse, *The Guillotine and the Terror*, following p. 116.

[8] Reproduced in Schama, *Citizens*, p. 620; see his description, p. 621.

[9] *Execution of Louis XVI, King of France, 21 January 1793*, Musée Carnavalet, Paris; reproduced in Arasse, *The Guillotine and the Terror*, following p. 116.

[10] Arasse, *The Guillotine and the Terror*, p. 128 (quoting Joseph Joubert, *Carnets* [1804]); see Joseph Joubert, *The Notebooks of Joseph Joubert*, trans. and ed. Paul Auster (1938; San Francisco: North Point Press, 1983), pp. 101–2.

[11] Balzac had a hand in writing *Mémoires pour servir à l'histoire de la Révolution française, par Sanson, exécuteur des arrêts criminels, pendant la Révolution* (1829). See Lenôtre, *The Guillotine and Its Servants*, p. 72. Henri-Clément Sanson, Charles-Henri's grandson and the last in the dynasty, was paid to permit another of these memoirs to be written under his name, but there is no evidence that he provided any material for it. The six-volume work was published in Paris as *Sept générations d'exécuteurs (1688–1847): Mémoires des Sanson mis en ordre, rédigés et publiés par H. Sanson, ancien exécuteur des hautes oeuvres de la Cour de Paris* (1862–63). Though a source for popular histories, it is at best historical fiction, and my account does not depend on it. The work was later abridged, translated, and published as *Memoirs of the Sansons*, ed. Henry Sanson (London: Chatto and Windus, 1876).

Despite the literary portrayals, neither Sanson the monster nor Sanson the sensitive heart accounts for what is known about how Sanson presented himself and how the political factions of the Revolution viewed him. Any reconstruction must offer a coherent explanation of two facts: first, every revolutionary faction that gained momentary ascendancy viewed Sanson as a practitioner of a necessary profession; second, Sanson viewed himself precisely that way.

Let us begin with how Sanson was viewed. In a climate of continual unmasking, where charges of betraying the Nation and the Revolution could be made to stick on the slightest pretext, where thousands were shaved by the "national razor" either to sate the mob's appetite for conspirators, to eliminate political rivals, or to exercise sincere revolutionary zeal, Sanson was the only citizen of Paris safely beyond the reach of his machine. Consider how extraordinary this is: the king's functionaries swing from the *lanternes*, the king's Swiss guard is hacked to bits, but the King's Executioner becomes Citizen Sanson, the king's executioner. More than 2,500 heads later, the remnant of moderates succeeds in deposing Robespierre, and the final purge begins, but not of Sanson. One hundred more heads fly off in the first three days of the Counter-Terror, but Sanson is still on the right side of the blade. Fouquier-Tinville, the Revolutionary Tribunal's prosecutor through the Terror, is reviled as a monster even by fellow Jacobin prisoners, but the question of Sanson's responsibility does not arise.[12] At trial, the prosecutor pleads in vain, "I am the axe! One does not punish the axe!"[13] The only blameless tool, however, is Sanson. He officially retires in September 1795, over a year after the end of the Terror, and applies for a government pension. His son, "whose name is on the list of candidates capable of carrying out the duties"—indeed, his capabilities have been well demonstrated—is appointed to succeed the father without further comment.[14]

That Sanson would be immune from the virulent politics of his day—the only Parisian who could answer "the argument of the guillotine"—was not obvious at the outset. In December 1789, he was denounced by republican journalists, who reported that a royalist press was operating in the house of the executioner. Camille Desmoulins, one of the accusers, mischievously called Sanson a *bourreau*, a derogatory term connoting brutishness, whose use was banned by

---

[12] See Schama, *Citizens*, p. 851.

[13] Kershaw, *History of the Guillotine*, p. 97.

[14] Lenôtre, *The Guillotine and Its Servants*, p. 103–4. Eyewitness accounts of the execution of Marie-Antoinette in October 1793 and of one of the last batches to be dispatched in *Thermidor*, Year II (July 1794), describe a young man in charge of the scaffold. See Arasse, *The Guillotine and the Terror*, p. 128.

royal decree at Sanson's request. "I call a cat a cat, and Sanson the *bourreau*," Desmoulins taunted.[15] How much truth was in the charge of royalism is unknown, but, in any case, Sanson successfully sued for libel and extracted a public retraction.[16] (He would renew his acquaintance with Desmoulins on the scaffold when luck ran out for the Dantonistes; there is no mention of recusal due to conflict of interest.)

The failed attempt to discredit Sanson is to be viewed in light of the heady legislative activity that brought scrutiny to the office of the public executioner that winter. On December 1, 1789, Doctor Guillotin reintroduced his egalitarian and humane revisions of the penal code, which, if adopted, would transform Sanson's job.[17] Guillotin's egalitarian principle, that like crimes be punished alike, without regard to rank or estate, was approved at once. Other provisions that protected the families of criminals from dishonor, eliminated confiscation of the property of the condemned, and returned the body to the family for burial were intensely debated and adopted the following month. The provision that called for decapitation in all capital crimes, and by means of "a simple mechanism,"[18] met with less success. Argued one doubting representative, "Rather than elevate the masses to the dignity of the block, we should reduce the nobility to the modesty of the gibbet."[19] Guillotin oversold his innovation in a breathless speech— "The mechanism falls like a thunderbolt, the head flies off, the blood spurts forth, the victim is no more"—and was met by laughter in the Assembly.[20] The press lampooned Guillotin's enthusiasm but nonetheless was favorably disposed toward his idea.[21]

[15] Camille Desmoulins, *Révolutions de France et de Brabant*, no. 9 (circa January 1790), p. 392.

[16] See Lenôtre, *The Guillotine and Its Servants*, pp. 92–93. Desmoulins attributed to Sanson "spite against street-lanterns and M. Guillotin" (ibid., p. 92, and Desmoulins, *Révolutions de France*, no. 7 [circa January 1790], p. 307). Gorsas, the journalist who lost the libel suit (and later, too, his head), quipped that "an executioner was not qualified to bring an action, except against the lantern at the corner of the Rue de la Vannerie" (Lenôtre, p. 94). Perhaps the pamphlet quoted as our epigraph was known to them; indeed, one or the other may have been the author. But see Arasse, *The Guillotine and the Terror*, p. 29 (characterizing the pamphlet as "clearly royalist in tendency").

[17] When the revisions were first introduced in October, the reception was ecstatic, and some legislators demanded, irregularly, immediate action; but procedure prevailed and adoption was delayed. See Kershaw, *The History of the Guillotine*, p. 13.

[18] Ibid., p. 14.

[19] Arasse, *The Guillotine and the Terror*, p. 16 (quoting Verninac de Saint-Maur, *Le Moniteur universel*, December 1789).

[20] Ibid., p. 17 (quoting *Journal des Etats généraux*, December 1789).

[21] One wag had Guillotin saying: "The form of death I have invented is so gentle that, were one not expecting to die, one would scarcely know what to say of it, for one feels no more than a slight sensation of coolness at the back of the neck." Arasse, *The*

Then, in late December 1789, a lingering question about the Assembly's Declaration of the Rights of Man and Citizen was debated: were even Jews and Protestants to count as citizens? Could they vote, stand for election to the Assembly, participate in the Communes? Debate spread to other customary outcasts, the profession of actor and—now that a humane penal code was in the air—the profession of executioner. The citizen-aristocrat the comte de Clermont-Tonnerre argued for the rehabilitation of the executioner:

> Professions are either harmful or not. Those that are constitute a habitual infraction that the law should prohibit. Where they are not, the law must be consistent with justice, on which it is based . . . We have simply to overcome a prejudice . . . Whatever the law requires is good. It requires the death of a criminal. The executioner simply obeys the law. It is absurd that the law should say to a man: do that, and if you do it, you will be abhorrent to your fellow men.[22]

The abbé Maury disagreed:

> The exclusion of public executioners is not founded on a mere prejudice. It is in the heart of all good men to shudder at the sight of one who assassinates his fellow man in cold blood. The law requires this deed, it is said, but does the law command anyone to become a hangman?[23]

The Assembly settled the matter with a broad but oblique proclamation on December 24: "the eligibility of any citizen cannot be combated on any grounds for exclusion but those which arise from constitutional decrees."[24] Because executioners had never been legally excluded, they were, by implication, entitled to full citizenship.

Sanson, smarting from charges of royalism in the printing press affair, wanted a more explicit affirmation. He engaged a lawyer to lobby the Assembly with a petition on behalf of his profession. Worth quoting at some length, this extraordinary claim of civil rights for an ordinary civil servant is a marvelous tour through the republican sensibility—reason, triumphing over prejudice, will recognize the delicate virtues of an honorable profession:

Guillotine and the Terror, p. 17 (quoting *Le Moniteur universel*, Dec. 18, 1789). But see Kershaw, *The History of the Guillotine*, pp. 15–16 (providing positive press accounts).

[22] Jacques Delarue, *Le Métier de bourreau* (Paris: Fayard, 1979), pp. 49–50 (quoting *Le Moniteur universel*), quoted in Arasse, *The Guillotine and the Terror*, p. 120 (omissions in Arasse). Clermont-Tonnerre became one of the casualties of the August 10, 1792 massacre: he was shot and tossed from a window. See Schama, *Citizens*, p. 679.

[23] Delarue, *Le Métier*, p. 50, quoted in Arasse, *The Guillotine and the Terror*, p. 120 n. 3.

[24] Lenôtre, *The Guillotine and Its Servants*, p. 219.

The words that are about to be read . . . express the just complaints of a body of men whom a blind prejudice has marked with the seal of infamy, and whose life is a perpetual endurance of humiliations, shame, and opprobrium—offences which in themselves demand suppression; they tell the grievances of men who are unfortunately indispensable, and who now, before the fathers of their country, bewail the injustice of their fellow-citizens and claim the imprescriptible rights that are derived from nature and the law. . . .

There is no question—whatever may be said to the contrary by an *obscure journalist*, who makes a habit of calumniating the members of the National Assembly, and its decrees, and the public—of deciding whether the Executioners of Criminal Judgments shall take their seats beside the mayors, or shall fill the places of the generals in command of National Guards in the different towns of the kingdom: irony dishonours the person who employs it, when his business is to discuss the status of a citizen and to combat the prejudice that disgraces him unjustly; but the questions to be decided are whether executioners be eligible for places in the Communes, whether they have consultative or deliberative votes in assemblies; and in short whether they have any status as citizens. That the question should be answered in the affirmative can only be a matter of doubt in those feeble minds whose judgment is subservient to the tyrannical empire of prejudices.

Executioners practise their profession *by right of office*; they hold it directly from the King; their commissions are sealed with the Great Seal; and, like those of officers, are only to be obtained on *a good and laudable report* of the individuals receiving them. . . .

There is certainly nothing to be found, differing from other offices, in the commissions of executioners; and in the formalities that precede their acceptance there is nothing to be found that dishonours them, or proves a lack of delicate feeling on their part.[25]

Once the prejudice against executioners dies out, the appeal continues, "society would no longer be deprived of their enlightenment, their patriotism, and the example of their virtues."[26]

Sanson requested an explicit declaration of citizenship for these honorable, enlightened, and virtuous professionals of delicate feeling; ever sensitive to his dignity, he also wanted reaffirmation of the royal decree banning the use of the term *bourreau*. What began after the summer lynchings as a pamphleteer's farce had become, by January 1790, a serious argument. Indeed, philosophy was making Sanson's calling into a glorious profession.

The executioner's argument did not convince the ironists, of course.

---

[25] Ibid., pp. 220–22. Sanson is debunking a legend that the commission of the executioner is thrown at his feet, symbolizing an untouchable status.

[26] Ibid., pp. 222–23.

Marat, whose incendiary journalism would later divert even more of Sanson's business to the *lanternes*, took a parting shot:

> We cannot resist our desire to call the attention of our readers to a master-piece of *sensibility*, taste, and learning. . . . The prejudice that dooms execu-tioners to infamy is absolutely demolished in this Memorial, which cannot be read without *emotion*; and the National Assembly, to whom it is ad-dressed, cannot fail to give a good reception to demands that have for their foundation the imprescriptible rights of man, and reason, and philosophy.[27]

The Assembly, for its part, simply allowed its previous decrees on citizenship to stand.

With the press plot quashed and his full citizenship established, the executioner did not have his political impartiality publicly questioned again. From then on, Sanson projects the sensibility and self-image of a professional civil servant. He gives expert opinions about new tech-nologies, takes care to clarify instructions with his superiors, and frets with increasing intensity about his budget as the demands of his of-fice increased.

Having settled on decapitation as the method of execution for all, the National Assembly asked Sanson for his professional opinion about the need for a "simple mechanism." Sanson is insightful as only an expert can be. Freestyle beheading requires not only a skilled headsman, but a courageous victim. He worries that democratic citi-zens may not have the bearing that could be counted on in aristo-crats, so if beheading is to be democratized, some mechanical stan-dardization is advisable:

> For the execution to arrive at the result prescribed by the law, the execu-tioner must, with no impediment on the part of the condemned man, be very skilful, and the condemned man very steadfast. . . .
>
> . . . How can one deal with a man who cannot or will not hold himself up?
>
> With regard to these humane considerations, I am bound to issue a warn-ing as to the accidents that will occur if this execution is to be performed with the sword. It would, I think, be too late to remedy these accidents if they were known only from bitter experience. It is therefore indispensable, if the hu-mane views of the National Assembly are to be fulfilled, to find some means by which the condemned man can be secured so that the issue of the execu-tion cannot be in doubt, and in this way to avoid delay and uncertainty.[28]

---

[27] Ibid., p. 226 (quoting Jean-Paul Marat, *L'Ami du peuple*).

[28] Report of Sanson to the minister of justice on the mode of decapitation, reprinted in Arasse, *The Guillotine and the Terror*, app. 1, pp. 184–85. At least one contemporary observer, however, found some irony in the headsman becoming the technician. A crude cartoon has the executioner proclaim, "I am not changing my occupation," as he operates the new machine (*Essai de la Guillotine*, musée Carnavalet, Paris).

Sanson was summoned to use the new machine on his former king and employer in January 1793. Much apocrypha has grown around this ironic reversal, but the reliable historical record reveals but two clues about Citizen Sanson's deportment. The day before the execution, he asks for clarification about his duties with bureaucratic precision and formality that betray neither emotion nor recognition of the transformative importance of the deed he is to perform the next morning:

CITIZEN,

I have just received the orders you sent me. I will adopt all the measures necessary to prevent any delay in carrying them out. The carpenter has been informed of the position required for the machine, which will be set up at the spot indicated.

It is absolutely necessary that I should know how Louis will leave the temple. Will he have a carriage, or will it be in the vehicle ordinarily used for executions of this kind? After the execution, what will become of the dead man's body?

Is it I or my assistants who must be at the temple at eight o'clock, as is stated on the order?

In the case of it's not being myself who must bring him from the temple, what is the place and the exact point at which I am to be?

Since all these things are not mentioned in the order it would be well if the citizen acting for the *procureur-sindic* [*sic*] of the department would supply me as quickly as possible with this information, while I am engaged in giving all the orders necessary to ensure that everything shall be punctually carried out. . . .

Citizen SANSON,
Executioner of Criminal Sentences[29]

After the execution, a jubilant crowd is reported to have scrambled for scraps of cloth dipped in the king's blood and other souvenirs of regicide.[30] In a notice to the newspapers, Sanson huffily defends the propriety of his office against hopeful gossip that he could provide such mementos:

I have this moment learnt that there is a rumour abroad to the effect that I am selling Louis Capet's hair, or causing it to be sold. If any of it has been sold, the infamous trade can only have been carried on by knaves: the truth is that I did not allow anyone connected with me to take away or appropriate the smallest vestige of it.[31]

[29] Lenôtre, *The Guillotine and Its Servants*, pp. 104–5 (endnote omitted). The *procureur-général-syndic* was the legal agent of the state—roughly the public prosecutor.
[30] See ibid., pp. 105–6.
[31] Ibid., p. 106 (quoting *Le Thermomètre du jour*, Jan. 29, 1793).

Sanson will neither hint at any sympathy for his victim nor pander to the patriotic zeal of the mob: he fulfills the duties of his position with utter professional detachment.

But not without complaint. Our anonymous satirist's charge about lost *écus* notwithstanding, the executioner had not been paid on a per capita basis. Until Turgot's tax reforms of 1775, he was supported through the right of *havage*, a toll on the city's merchants. In the last years of the *ancien régime*, he received a fixed sum plus expenses. The Revolution eliminated reimbursement for most variable expenses.[32] As the case load picked up, Sanson complained with increasing bitterness to his superiors that he was being driven into personal ruin.

Early on, he thought the logic of a simple accounting would move the authorities. Here are some of his expenses, detailed in a letter to the National Assembly in June 1790:

Expenses of the Executioner
    Two of his brothers to whom he gives 600 *livres* each, to answer the magistrates and give orders to the servants when there are executions to be carried out at several places on the same day 1,200
. . . .
The building of three carriages and a tumbril 300
. . . .
For the rent of a house large enough for his family, his servants, his horses, carriages, and the utensils necessary to his position, the said house being situated so that he is able to carry out orders promptly 4,800

Incidental Expenses
    The expenses on the days when there are executions.
    The utensils to be used at executions, which have to be constantly renewed.
. . . .
    If the executioner were expected to put the torture, or to act as carpenter, the following expenses would result from the work:
    For putting the torture, one extra servant; . . .[33]

A year later, his financial situation worsening, he writes the public prosecutor:

The method of execution that is practised to-day is at least three times as expensive as the old method, over and above the increase in cost of all the necessaries of life.

The service of the numerous criminal tribunals forces me to employ a number of persons capable of fulfilling the orders I receive. Since I cannot

[32] See ibid., pp. 16–17, 27, 127.
[33] Ibid., pp. 96–98.

personally be everywhere at once I must have people that I can depend upon. For the public still demands decency. It is I who pay for that. . . .

. . . I can only have recourse to yourself, Monsieur, to give orders that I may be paid the money due to me, otherwise it seems that the sacrifices I have made up to the present time, in order that the duties of my office might be correctly performed, will result in the total wreck of my life in this place and my inevitable ruin, by forcing me to abandon my post and my family after twenty-four years of such employment.[34]

Finally, in April 1794, at the height of the Terror, he writes an extraordinarily revealing letter to the minister of justice:

Neither the executioner of Paris, nor those in any part of the Republic, are expected to supply their own equipment, and the law is so clear and has so plainly intended to give them no expense that it enjoins upon the Government to pay their assistants.

The executioner in Paris, who is supplied with four assistants, employs seven, and has not too many of them in the present circumstances, in view of the immense amount of unremitting work that is laid upon him and his assistants. Day and night on their feet, whatever the weather may be, and not a single day of rest—work that might well disable the most robust! Is it possible for a man to live on 1,000 francs, especially in these days?

The executioner gives his four chief assistants 1,800 francs and lodging, which things they insist upon having; otherwise he would secure no one at all. Their duties must be taken into consideration, as well as the expenses in upkeep caused by their work; and it must be remembered that nothing but the desire of gain induces anyone to adopt this calling. . . .

. . . This post is supposed to be worth 17,000 *livres*—but when the cost of his assistants has been deducted, as well as all the different and numerous expenses that he pays out of his own pocket, it will be seen that he is very unlucky to have such a post. And indeed the executioner cares little for the post. He has fulfilled its duties for forty-three years. The overwhelming work that it entails makes him wish to bring his services to an end. . . .

. . . If it be found possible to get the work done more cheaply, that another man shall be entrusted with it, since he cannot undertake it any

---

[34] Ibid., p. 99–100. The more expensive method cannot refer to the guillotine, which was first built and used in April 1792. The National Assembly adopted decapitation, method unspecified, in June 1791. See Arasse, *The Guillotine and the Terror*, p. 20. Perhaps Sanson is anticipating the high costs of sword work, though there is no evidence that the sword replaced the gibbet in practice between June 1791 and April 1792. But see Kershaw, *The History of the Guillotine*, pp. 29–31 (suggesting that beheadings occurred); Lenôtre, *The Guillotine and Its Servants*, p. 99 n. 1 (same).

longer, and can do nothing but give it all up if he be not reimbursed, and if he fail to obtain justice.[35]

Sanson is not resigning, mind you—just demanding of the minister of justice a budget increase. This, just days after chopping off the head of a former minister of justice. Danton quipped on the scaffold to his quondam subordinate, "But do not forget, do not forget to show my head to the people: it is worth seeing."[36] The king, we see, was not Sanson's only bossicide, and this could not have been lost on his current boss. At the depths of the revolutionary spiral of political paranoia, Sanson shows no fear that he himself may be the target of revolutionary unmasking. Rather, he conveys a strong sense of injustice at being overworked and underpaid—somewhat like a physician newly subjected to cost-containment measures complaining that the terms of the profession have been unilaterally changed. What he does not show is a hint of revulsion at the carnage, a question about its evil, or a doubt about the political legitimacy of whatever faction has gained control of the machinery of justice that supplies his machine. With Mercier, we too wonder, what goes on in that head of his?

Something must go on in that head of his, because Sanson is forced to explain himself. The Terror was unmistakably both public and political, and was intended to be so. The scaffold was theater, the dripping head held aloft the main prop, and the Terrorists did not seek to hide the performance. Euphemistic distance was not possible for Sanson, who was wet with his deeds. We may conclude that his arguments, and the best arguments that can be made for him, are tendentious, but he cannot be oblivious to the need for justification.

What, then, is the best case that can be made in defense of Sanson and his role? In the tradition, until this moment disreputable, of penning fictional memoirs in his name, we take up his cause. Perhaps philosophy *will* succeed in making his profession a glorious one.

CIRCA 1799

> LOUIS-SÉBASTIEN MERCIER: Ah, Monsieur Sanson. Taking in the theater, I see. Coming and going, just like everyone else. I hope you don't find my forwardness rude, but I have always wondered: what goes on in that head of yours?[37]

---

[35] Lenôtre, *The Guillotine and Its Servants*, pp. 124–26 (footnote omitted). Here, Sanson must be counting his years of service from when he began assisting his father.

[36] Arasse, *The Guillotine and the Terror*, p. 113.

[37] Compare the opening scene of Joseph de Maistre's *Les Soirées de Saint-Pétersbourg*:

CHARLES-HENRI SANSON: My, you look familiar . . . Of course! Mercier the writer. One of the fortunate ones. Too bad about Desmoulins, no? I am so relieved that the past is past. Naturally, it was not to my liking, but we cannot always choose our professional assignments.

I take it that you are wondering how I can detach people's heads for a living? I will tell you. It is my profession. The role of the Paris executioner has been handed down, father to son, from my grandfather's father to me, and will be passed on to my grandson. It is not, strictly speaking, a hereditary position, but one into which each successive generation has been initiated and that each has adopted as its vocation. There are families with a tradition of doctoring, families with a tradition of soldiering, families that have handed down cheese making and wine making and all manners of art and trade. We are a family of professional executioners: that is what we do, and each generation seeks to do it better. It is our calling.

MERCIER: A professional calling! I suppose you are a professional in the loose way that "professional" can mean anything done for pay, so that there are professional beggars and gamblers. And nasty ways of earning a living may run in families, from thievery to tyranny. But to justify your horrible work, you must mean by "profession" and "tradition" more than a mere description of customary employment. You must make a moral claim: that the role of executioner is justified because executioners are committed to some ideal that is an interpretation of a valuable tradition of professional practice. But where are the ideals? What is valuable about your bloodstained lineage? You are simply hired killers! Madame Roland was right about you: "He does his job and he earns his money."[38]

Without openly sharing our feelings, we were enjoying the pleasures of the beautiful spectacle that surrounded us, when abruptly Chevalier de B*** broke the silence, exclaiming: "I would like to have here in this boat with us one of those perverse men born for society's misfortune, one of those monsters that weary the earth . . .

And what would you do if he accommodated you? This was the question the two friends asked, speaking at the same time. 'I would ask him,' the Chevalier replied, 'if the night appeared as beautiful to him as it does to us.'" Joseph de Maistre, *St. Petersburg Dialogues* (1821), trans. Richard A. Lebrun (Montreal: McGill-Queen's University Press, 1993), p. 5.

[38] Barbara Levy, *Legacy of Death* (Englewood Cliffs, N. J.: Prentice Hall, 1973), p. 101 (quoting Manon Philipon Roland).

SANSON: This charge of avarice is unseemly and unfair. Yes, I expect to get paid for what I do, and yes, I expect that the expenses I incur in my work will be reimbursed. But that does not distinguish the executioner from the lawyer or the physician, and I take it you do not deny that law and medicine are professions. I am much less a hired blade than the surgeon or lawyer. Money never enters into any decision of *mine* about whom to serve and how to provide service. Indeed, I have incurred large out-of-pocket losses because I refuse to compromise on quality. The Ministry of Justice may have been negligent in paying my expenses, but I would not work with a dull blade or stained baskets—that would have been unprofessional.

I agree that if a claim of professionalism is to have any moral force it has to refer to ideals and commitments, and that a claim of tradition must involve more than mere habit. But the role of executioner meets both requirements. We take great pride in our craft and hold ourselves to the highest ethical and technical standards that apply to our work. We have learned from our predecessors and teach our apprentices to value excellence in the practice, which reflectively adapts to both new technologies and new political sensibilities. I realize that from the outside you cannot always appreciate our commitments, so we must appear rather ghoulish, but that is either ignorance or prejudice on your part. I have come to expect such reactions: you know, one of the marks of a true profession is that excellent practice can only be judged by fellow practitioners. You are not an expert judge of a court opinion or of a surgical procedure; why do you think that you can appreciate the niceties of the executioner's craft? For example, you may have thought from his scream that it was cruel to rip Robespierre's bandage from his shattered jaw, but I assure you it was a mercy—the consequences of an obstructed blade are far worse than the moment of pain he suffered. To carry out the judgments of law with dependable precision, the executioner worries about dozens of similar details that are designed to treat the condemned, the spectators, and the law with precisely the respect that each is owed, in light of the circumstances. Another example: in the days when violent criminals were broken at the wheel, the judges in their wisdom would direct us in cases meriting leniency to secretly strangle the victim after the first blows. A deft maneuver, which even the judges did not fully appreciate: to give to the crowd the edifying spectacle that they wanted and, more to the point, needed, but also to spare the victim unnecessary pain. If the punishment is to fit the crime, we are the tailors.

How to transport the victim to the scaffold? How and when to bind and shear? How much time to allow for leave-taking and last words? Who is to be handled roughly? Firmly? Gently? In short, how, in my stagecraft, to satisfy the competing demands of impartiality and particularity? I trust that Madame Roland, in the end, revised her disparaging opinion of me. I was foil to her much-noted grace and dignity on the tumbril and scaffold, and I even granted her brave and compassionate request to go after the trembling Simon François Lamarche, contrary to the standing rule of women first. But I neither expect you to understand my commitments nor to share them. You are not an executioner.

MERCIER: No doubt you possess a horrible expertise of sorts, and as a onetime torturer you must have exquisite sensitivity to pain and suffering. Those who call you brutal are mistaken: you are cruel, which requires thoughtfulness. But I fail to see why the employment of expert cruelty is a virtue. Yes, on occasion you employ your expertise to relieve indignity and suffering, but on other occasions you do the opposite—slapping Charlotte Corday's cheek . . .

SANSON: The assistant who pandered to the mob by insulting the head of Marat's assassin acted unprofessionally. He was severely reprimanded.

MERCIER: . . . And always, you are methodically killing another human being. You will answer that I cannot understand because I am not one of you. But you cannot expect that your appeal to inaccessible knowledge will persuade me. How else can I evaluate your claims, except on grounds that we can share?

SANSON: You have not yet convinced me that my reasons must be reasons for you too, but for now I will grant your premise and, as I did before the National Assembly, appeal to Reason. Since I see that I will not succeed, just yet, in showing you that the profession of executioner is rich with its own goods and virtues, I will start from the outside, so to speak, and show why my role is a socially useful and necessary one. A just society requires laws and their enforcement, including criminal laws and punishments. Punishments are not self-inflicting—someone must impose them. A just society also requires that the enforcement of laws not be arbitrary or capricious. People may disagree about whether criminal judgments are just, including the executioner called upon to carry them out. These disagreements may be about the justice of the outcome in a particular case, about the justice of a proceeding, about the justice of a law, or about the justice of a form of punishment. But if law is to rule, the executioner must obey a division of labor between his office and the office of the tribunal. To allow personal views about the sentences I execute to interfere with my duty is to substitute arbitrariness for the rule of law. Whatever you think of my character for having chosen this work, whether or not you cringe at the prospect of shaking my hand, you must grant that I do not act unjustly.

MERCIER: Was it not unjust to mutilate human beings with hot pincers and burning sulphur? To apply bone-mangling tortures to extract confessions? To behead the political scapegoats of a tyrant? And was it not unjust to slaughter a few thousand Parisians convicted of imaginary offenses in sham proceedings?

SANSON: The best way to untangle the thicket of charges you make against me is to distinguish the several phases of my career. As you note, I have been torturer and headsman for a now despised monarchy and the instrument of summary justice for a now despised revolutionary government. But I have also applied the death penalty in the most humane way that we know in ordinary criminal cases tried fairly under the laws of a democratically elected republic. Permit me to begin with this easiest case, and then perhaps I will be able to persuade you of the harder ones.

Recall the comte de Clermont-Tonnerre's eloquent defense of my rights as a citizen: whatever the law requires is good. The law requires the death of a criminal. By putting the criminal to death, the executioner simply obeys a good law. How can that make him bad? The penal code that established death by decapitation was enacted by a democratically elected legislature, and so has the force of law. The court that imposed this penalty on the violent robber Pelletier, the guillotine's first victim, rendered an impartial and fair reading of that law. How, then, can there be any moral stain on my hands and character for executing the judgment of the court? Would that not be unreasoned prejudice?

MERCIER: But Clermont-Tonnerre's argument is mistaken at almost every step. Whatever the law requires is not necessarily good, for even democratic lawmakers can enact horribly bad and unjust laws. The death penalty is arguably an example of an unjust law.[39] And even if the punishment is not unjust to its victim, to

[39] Mercier urged the sparing use of capital punishment, but not outright abolition: "Kindly philosophy has for some time past commended to magistrates an economy of bloodshed." Louis-Sébastien Mercier, *Tableau de Paris* (1789), vol. 10, ch. 799, reprinted

use one's hands to kill another human being is immoral. The abbé Maury was right: the law may require executions, but the law does not require anyone to be an executioner. What sort of man chooses such a gruesome trade?[40]

SANSON: As for the first step, I concede that laws may be bad or unjust. If the revolutionary idea of *Vox populi, vox Dei* is taken to mean that democracy is by definition infallible, the idea is patently false. But the National Assembly did not err in maintaining the death penalty: to kill those who kill is both just retribution and necessary deterrence.

But what if one believes that the death penalty is not just? After all, the Milanese reformer Cesare Beccaria urged its abolition, and our great Voltaire, much to my dismay, agreed.[41] Marie Antoinette's brother, the Habsburg emperor Leopold, followed Beccaria's advice in Tuscany (and put some honest men out of work). One of the great ironies of the Assembly debates over the penal code is that Robespierre himself argued for an end to the practice. Still, one would need to acknowledge that enlightened philosophers and statesmen of our time have taken both sides. Our own legislature, of course, saw fit to retain the death penalty, and this German fellow Kant has recently written that, were a society to disband, justice would demand that it first execute its condemned prisoners.[42] So there is considerable disagreement

---

in *The Picture of Paris*, p. 148. In Mercier's futuristic utopian novel, capital punishment survives as a rare ritual of voluntary reconciliation with humanity: a condemned murderer, the first in thirty years, is given the choice between dying with honor or living in shame. Louis-Sébastien Mercier, *L'An deux mille quatre cent quarante* (1772), ch. 16, reprinted in Louis-Sébastien Mercier, *Memoirs of the Year Two Thousand Five Hundred*, trans. W. Hooper (Richmond, Va.: N. Pritchard, 1799), pp. 72–85.

[40] In *L'An deux mille quatre cent quarante* Mercier writes, "I have frequently heard it debated, whether the person of an executioner be infamous. I have always been concerned when they have given it in his favour, and could never have a respect for those who ranked him with the class of other citizens. I may be wrong, but such is my opinion" (ch. 16, reprinted in Mercier, *Memoirs*, p. 83 n.*).

[41] See Cesare Beccaria, *On Crimes and Punishments* (1764), ed. and trans. David Young (Indianapolis: Hackett Publishing, 1986), pp. 48–53. In his commentary on Beccaria, Voltaire writes: "It hath long since been observed, that a man after he is hanged is good for nothing, and that punishments invented for the good of society, ought to be useful to society. It is evident, that a score of stout robbers, condemned for life to some public work, would serve the state in their punishment, and that hanging them is a benefit to nobody but the executioner." Voltaire, *Commentaire sur le livre Des Delitis et des peines* (1766), reprinted in Cesare Beccaria, *An Essay on Crimes and Punishments* (1766; Charleston, S.C.: David Bruce, 1777), p. 128.

[42] See Immanuel Kant, *The Metaphysics of Morals* (1797), trans. Mary Gregor (Cambridge: Cambridge University Press, 1991), p. 142 (Prussian Academy edition, p. 333).

among democratic lawmakers and lovers of liberty about the justice of capital punishment. Am I then to appoint myself tyrant and substitute my own view about what the law should be for the view of the people? No. Let us revise Clermont-Tonnerre's first step: though whatever the law requires is not necessarily good or just, at least when there is reasonable disagreement about what is good or just, what the law requires is The Law. So interpreted, *Vox populi, vox Dei* is true: the decrees of the National Assembly, and the judgments of courts in accordance with those decrees, have legitimate authority.

Before the Revolution, you argued that magistrates should be lenient in imposing the death penalty.[43] I have no objection, so long as they exercise no more discretion than allowed them by law. But the law allows no discretion for those of us who enforce the judgments of those magistrates. Even impartial judges under good and just laws can mistakenly render bad or unjust judgments. Are you suggesting that the jailer refuse to take custody of a mistakenly convicted prisoner? That the officer of the court refuse to enforce payment when the judge has erred in deciding a lawsuit? Surely not. What is the difference if the error has occurred at the point of legislation, rather than judgment? Either way, does the legitimate authority of the state not morally bind me to carry out its sentences?

As for the abbé Maury's view that, though I carry out the law, I am abhorrent because I have chosen to do so, it is a deeply confused position. True, the law does not prohibit all immoral behavior, so claiming an action is legal is not enough to show that it is moral. Those disreputable actresses in the Palais-Royal deserve their reputation. But the profession of executioner is not simply permitted by law; the law *requires* of the government that the tasks of the executioner be performed. It is incoherent to desire that capital punishment be executed and condemn the executioner.

MERCIER: Have you not desired those disreputable actresses, Monsieur de Paris?

---

[43] "Out of a hundred malefactors condemned to the galleys, thirty at least owe their lives and exemption from execution to the humanity of magistrates. Such magistrates date from our own day; and without fear of prevarication they know how to lessen the cruelty of the law. To spare the guilty man a violent death, to restore the proportion between punishment and crime, to weigh circumstances which may diminish punishment, this is what their humanity and wisdom may now effect. They obey the spirit of the law which is for the good of society and not for its torture." *Tableau de Paris*, vol. 10, ch. 799, reprinted in *The Picture of Paris*, p. 149.

SANSON: Touché. I was too quick to disparage my sister-citizens of the stage. Though I may consistently want them to be free of legal restriction and still condemn them, I cannot approve of my patronage but disapprove of their performance.

MERCIER: But why not? You, after all, are not putting on an immodest spectacle, you are merely enjoying those who do. You are not devoting a life to the frivolity of the theater, merely an evening. (As a playwright, I am far more vulnerable on this score than you!) So, too, citizens may with consistency applaud your performance on the scaffold, but damn *you* for what you have done with your hands, and abhor *you* for building a career out of the bones of your victims.

SANSON: Consistency? It strikes me as irrational prejudice. I act *for* the people in every sense of the word: in their name, for their benefit, and upon their direction. My actions are their actions. Every time I cut off a head, every citizen—or at least every citizen who approves of the death penalty—does so as well. If they are blameless, so am I. If I am blameworthy, so are they.

MERCIER: If I must choose, I choose the latter: the people share in your evil. If the abbé Maury is mistaken, it is not because the comte de Clermont-Tonnerre is correct, but because Diderot is. You left the great encyclopedist off your list of worthies who oppose the death penalty, perhaps because his reasoning is so damaging to your case. Remember what he thought of your profession: "The odious name of hangman is now, as it was in other days, a stigma upon the man who bears it, and so it will be as long as it denotes one who publicly strangles another man, or breaks him on the wheel. This fact is not now founded on public opinion, but on the overwhelming force of the instinct that abhors every murderer except the man who murders in self-defence; which proves incidentally that the death-penalty is contrary to nature and beyond the jurisdiction of society."[44]

Diderot does not argue that the death penalty treats the criminal unjustly (though it might). Rather, he argues that the wrongness of capital punishment follows "incidentally" from something else: the death penalty turns men into killers, and killers are abhorrent. Because, Monsieur Sanson, *you* are made morally odious by your profession, *we* may not ask you to practice it on our behalf. The act of execution is wrong, even if the consequence—dead criminals—is good. If Diderot is correct, your attempts to justify your work from the outside, by appeal to the social utility of what you do, are to no avail. Even if we grant your usefulness, and even if we grant that the criminal can claim no right to be spared, killing is odious *from the inside* (to use your terms), so we may not ask you to kill for us.

SANSON: I see now why you are called Diderot's ape, Monsieur Mercier. *Unjustified* killing is odious, I agree. But even your idol Diderot grants that killing in self-defense is justified, and so, the hands of one who so kills are *not* morally tainted. You and Diderot need to show why the killing of a criminal, if such a killing is both justly retributive and socially useful, is nonetheless unjustified. Do you consider abhorrent the courageous soldiers who defend the Nation against our enemies from without?[45] Of course not. Well, I defend the Nation against enemies from within. You cannot sustain the view you attribute to Diderot. If killing is always immoral, then killing in self-defense or war is also immoral. Pacifism is a consistent doctrine, but you are no pacifist. If killing in self-defense or in a just war is justified, you need to show why the death penalty is not justified. You cannot argue from some essential odiousness of the act, for you concede that the act is not always odious.

MERCIER: Monsieur Sanson, such concessions do not help you very much. Let us not forget that we have spoken of the easiest case only, where the death penalty is enacted by a democratic legislature and imposed by fair courts. Even if I grant that conditions can be stipulated under which your profession is not monstrous, those conditions held for a year or so at best during the constitutional monarchy and the first few months of the Republic. Enough of easy cases. One cannot forget that before the Revolution you were the instrument of a tyrannical monarchy. Despite the efforts of judicial reformers like Montesquieu and Males-

[45] Compare Joseph de Maistre, who imagines asking a visitor from another planet to guess how the executioner and soldier are viewed on earth: "The one brings death to convicted and condemned criminals, and fortunately his executions are so rare that one of these ministers of death is sufficient for each province. As far as soldiers are concerned, there are never enough of them, because they kill without restraint and their victims are always honest men. Of these two professional killers, the soldier and the executioner, one is highly honored and always has been by all the nations who have inhabited up to now this planet to which you have come; but the other has just as generally been regarded as vile. Try to guess on which the obloquy falls." Joseph de Maistre, *Les Soirées de Saint-Pétersbourg* (1821), in *The Works of Joseph de Maistre*, trans. Jack Lively (New York: Schocken Books, 1971), p. 246.

herbes, the state and its various tribunals were often arbitrary in the administration of punishment. And until Louis XVI abolished the *question extraordinaire*, you and your assistants extracted confessions through grotesquely inhumane methods.

In some other time or place, one of your calling might have invoked loyalty to the king in defense. But such a claim in your case is preposterous, since you beheaded your king. You then promiscuously lent your services to every revolutionary faction that held sway in Paris, mechanically carrying out the purges of each against its predecessors—and then had the effrontery to officiate throughout the Counter-Terror. If the king's justice was often rough, the Terror's justice was perverse: you murdered a few thousand innocents under changing cloaks of legality.

Obedience is no excuse for immorality, but you cannot even claim to have been obedient. You cannot hide behind authority when you show no allegiance to authority. At least that wretched public prosecutor, Fouquier-Tinville, was a loyal Jacobin. We reject his defense, "Je suis la hache! On ne punit pas la hache!" not because we deny that he indeed was the tool of others, but because following orders does not absolve an actor of moral responsibility. But whose tool are you? Better you should say, "I am the whore! One does not punish the whore!"

SANSON: Please, Monsieur Mercier, some civility. Have you forgotten that I too have all the rights of an active citizen? The axe defense is not one I claim. You have recently wondered about me, "What an instrument—what a man!"[46] But that question misunderstands me in two ways. On the job, I am neither an instrument nor a man. Let me explain.

I am not a mere instrument, if by that you mean one who takes no responsibility for what his superiors demand of him. Indeed, I roundly reject any simple appeal to authority to justify my career, if such an appeal takes the form of "One must follow orders; I was ordered to kill; therefore, I must kill." I am not an instrument devoid of mind or conscience, but a *professional*. Professions are committed to the realization of important values. My profession is the guardian of a political value that is of utmost moral importance. Although the good sought by my profession is valuable for all of society and capable of being recognized as valuable by all subjects and citizens, this good cannot be pursued except from within my professional role or roles like it. To this good I have dedicated my life, and my practice as executioner has aimed at

---

[46] *Le Nouveau Paris*, vol. 3, ch. 97, reprinted in *The Picture of Paris*, p. 221.

it through all the changing regimes to which you accuse me of whoring. My devotion is not to any one regime or political ideology, but to the good of *social order* and the stability and security it brings. By stability, I do not mean the stability of any regime or form of government, but of civilized life itself; and by security, I mean security from the random horror of murderous mobs. To realize the good of social order, my profession is committed to a simple principle: the state must maintain its monopoly over violence.

Danton understood this principle quite well, and was compelled by its necessity. Now remembered most for his heroic efforts to stop the Terror, as minister of justice and founder of the Committee on Public Safety he had as big a hand in starting the bloodletting as anyone. Recall his argument for the establishment of the Revolutionary Tribunal: "Let us be terrible so that the people will not have to be."[47] If the National Convention was to control the retributive violence of the mobs and the neighborhoods, it would have to use organized violence to do so. So those who condemn me for my *sang-froid* should consider the alternative: hot-blooded and hot-headed vigilante justice. It is not I who fret about losing business to the *lanternes*; all who fear murderous disorder do, or ought to. Desmoulins punned that I was "le représentant du pouvoir exécutif," the representative of the executive power.[48] Though he meant this to be yet another joke at my expense, he spoke an important truth. In a time of great unrest and danger, my steadfastness on the scaffold projected to the people that there was always a government, and that it was in control. So, what you see as a life of murderous prostitution, I see as a life spent preserving order. As long as the people could depend on me to work my machine, Paris would continue to trust that the machinery of social organization, at the deepest level, would not break down. Were there serious failures of justice in the *ancien régime*? Of course. Was the Terror a perversion of justice? Of course. But basic social order, though less inspiring, is a precondition for justice. I have been the humble guardian of order all these years.

MERCIER: So you are actually a reactionary authoritarian, like that Savoyard exile we have been hearing about, Joseph de Maistre? He is said to think that the horror of you holds up the world![49]

---

[47] Schama, *Citizens*, p. 707.

[48] Desmoulins, *Révolutions de France*, no. 9, p. 389.

[49] "And yet all grandeur, all power, all subordination rests on the executioner: he is the horror and the bond of human association. Remove this incomprehensible agent

SANSON: You seriously misunderstand me. The profession, as I have described it, takes no stand about the Revolution and its legitimacy. Nothing that I have said supports any particular form of government, but government simply. We fear social disintegration and the murderous fear it produces. I have heard that Maistre has likened my powers of retribution to God's. If I have heard rightly, this is both obscurantist poppycock and simplistic social science. My profession sustains order neither by acting as an agent of divine retribution nor by repressing crime through the fear of temporal punishment. If these were the primary purposes of our work, we would not be justified in enforcing sentences against the innocent. We serve order, not by deterring lawlessness through threat, but more subtly, by deterring the lawless punishment of lawlessness through trust.

MERCIER: You would massacre innocents in the name of order?

SANSON: In my official capacity, I would execute innocents condemned to death by a judicial process authorized by the existing regime, so long as the practice of execution contributed to the maintenance of the rudiments of social order. If it came to pass that the regime I served was incapable of preventing chaos, or that the practice of execution within such a regime made widespread social disorder more, rather than less, likely, then the continued practice of execution under such conditions would fail to provide the good to which it is committed. My work would no longer be justified, and conscience would force me to step down from the scaffold. But such invalidating conditions did not hold in the *ancien régime*. One could imagine the Terror progressing to the point where the machinery of state execution itself became destabilizing, but revolutionary politics reversed its disastrous course on the ninth of *Thermidor*. All of Paris (but the Robespierristes) were thankful that I was in place on the tenth to administer order-preserving justice. To be clear: I was not needed to *kill* Robespierre—any number of vengeful citizens were prepared to

---

from the world, and at that very moment order gives way to chaos, thrones topple, and society disappears. God, who is the author of sovereignty, is the author also of chastisement: he has built our world on these two poles." Maistre, *Les Soireés de Saint-Pétersbourg*, in *Works*, p. 192. Although Maistre's anti-Enlightenment and counterrevolutionary *Considérations sur la France* (1797) was well known, these words would not be published in *Les Soirées de Saint-Petersbourg* until his death in 1821, after the deaths of Mercier in 1814 and Sanson in 1806. But perhaps our interlocutors have already heard Maistre's views on the intimate connections between God, King, and Executioner from returning émigrés.

do that—but only I could *execute* him. So you see, I am a professional who mindfully practices his calling so long as such practice is valuable. I am no blind obedient or mere instrument.

MERCIER: And dare I ask how you are not a man?

SANSON: I knew that you would not let that pass. My detractors have attributed inhuman qualities to me, but I mean something else, of course. (Anyone who doubts my capacity for human feeling need only recall my tears on that sorrowful day when my youngest son fell to his death from the scaffold.) What I mean by saying that on the job I am not a man is that I do not act as a man simply. In exercising my professional duties I must set aside personal considerations. I naturally have views, held at varying degrees of certainty, about the guilt or innocence of my victims. I may personally admire or loathe those who come before me. I have my own views about the politics of the day. These are the views of Charles-Henri, man and citizen. But the executioner must set aside the reasons of Charles-Henri, for it is not Charles-Henri acting on the scaffold, but the Executioner of Criminal Sentences of Paris.

I do not mean simply that the executioner *may* not take personal considerations into account, but that the executioner *cannot*, and still be the executioner. Charles-Henri can commit murder, can massacre, as you put it. But only the executioner can perform an *execution*. The act of execution that the executioner performs on the scaffold does not exist apart from his professional role—it is constituted by it. You would not describe what a surgeon does as stabbing, what a lawyer does as robbing, or what a prosecutor does as kidnapping, would you?

MERCIER: No, not when acting as proper surgeons, lawyers, or prosecutors. But they are capable of failing to act properly, and then they may become villains. I don't doubt that when you act as a proper executioner what you do is described as execution. But you are also capable of employing your expertise and the trappings of your office to murder, just as a surgeon is capable of murder. That is precisely what you did in the Terror.

SANSON: Though I agree that it is possible for one with the name of a professional to violate the criteria that confer upon an action the description constituted by the professional practice, those criteria are *professional* criteria. *Medical* judgment distinguishes surgery from butchery. *Carnificial* judgment distinguishes executions from murder. I am tempted to say that only physicians are capable of exercising medical judgment, and likewise executioners, but I will refrain—I don't need to go that far to make my point. All that I need to establish is that, on the scaffold, to be a good executioner, I must employ the reasons of the Executioner of Criminal Judgments, not of Charles-Henri. And I have already explained that for good executioners, preserving the state's monopoly over violence is reason enough.

MERCIER: Did you think your sleight of tongue about the senses of "good" would slip past me? Why should a person be a "good" professional if "good" professionals commit horribly bad acts? One should be *morally* good, a good man, Charles-Henri. If a good professional must be a bad man, then it is immoral to be a good professional. Why on earth should a man ignore moral reasons that run against professional ones?

SANSON: I do not deny the possibility of a bad professional role that is not worthy of anyone's commitment. But that is a judgment made about the role itself, not particular actions the role requires. I have already explained to you why I believe that the role of executioner is worthy of a person's commitment, and you half-believe it yourself. Having made such a commitment to the role, I cannot then reject the reasons for action the role provides. Only if the overall justification fails is any particular performance no longer an "execution," but a murder. As I said, I am not an instrument. I must judge my role. But the judgment is of a life in a role, not the particular acts the role requires me to perform.

MERCIER: Why should you decide at that level of generality, if you could avoid doing evil by judging the goodness of particular acts?

SANSON: Because in acting on my personal judgments, I step out of my professional role. But only within my role can my actions be described as state execution. You ask me to cease to be the Executioner of Criminal Judgments and become Charles-Henri the serial murderer.

MERCIER: I'm baffled. No one is suggesting that personal morality demands that you kill in cases where the professional role forbids killing, but that personal morality sometimes forbids you from killing in cases where the professional role demands it!

SANSON: Ah, but think of how deciding to refuse a professional assignment transforms the assignments I do *not* refuse. If Charles-Henri may sometimes decide *not* to kill, then when he does perform an execution, Charles-Henri has decided *to* kill. For what reason? Not that it is the executioner's professional duty, for you would have professional duty defer to personal judgment. The reason must be that Charles-Henri personally believes the condemned deserves to die. But for his personal judgment, the prisoner would live (or at least not die by his hand). But who is Charles-Henri to decide who lives and who dies? The person who takes that upon himself is a private assassin, not a public executioner, and so necessarily undermines the good of social order.

When I said before that only an executioner can perform an execution, I was not quibbling about the definitions of words, but saying something important about the meaning of actions. Though all may hope that the good of order the executioner pursues is realized, and though there may be other practices in other positions that contribute to social order, only an executioner can pursue this good through violent means. For anyone other than the executioner to employ violence for the sake of reinforcing the state's monopoly over violence would be self-defeating. If I were to act on reasons that the role requires the executioner to ignore, I would cease to be the executioner. My performance would no longer be an act of the state. The purpose of my profession would be undermined, and I would become a murderous butcher. Therefore, Charles-Henri and his judgments must stay off the scaffold.

But all this talk after the theater has made me hungry. I know of a little place that serves the best Alsatian sausages in all of Paris. Will you dine with me? . . . You've turned green, my dear Louis-Sébastien. Are you a vegetarian?

––––––––––

The record breaks off here. Whether Mercier dined at the executioner's table is not known. Left on our table are a number of claims Sanson has made in defense of his professional role that deserve closer attention. We should attend, for Sanson's arguments do not look all that different from the arguments offered by lawyers, business executives, politicians, bureaucrats, journalists, and soldiers to justify their commitments to their professional roles when those roles ask them to act in ways that, if not for the role, would be wrong. If versions of these arguments do indeed justify the moral permissions to harm others that are claimed by these professions, why do they not work for Sanson? And if we are sure that they do not work for Sanson, should we not reconsider whether they work to justify less sanguinary professional roles?

Lawyers are not serial murderers, but Maistre's visitor from another planet might be forgiven if he described them as serial liars and thieves. He would observe that lawyers—good lawyers—repeatedly try to induce others to believe in the truth of propositions or in the validity of arguments that they themselves do not believe, and he would observe that lawyers—again, good lawyers—often devote their skills to advancing the unjust ends of rapacious clients. "Liar" and "thief," the good lawyer would retort, are either ignorant or malignant misdescriptions. But the arguments lawyers invoke to defend zealous advocacy echo all of the executioner's claims. Does "murderer" misdescribe Sanson?

PART II

ROLES AND REASONS

KO-KO: Pooh-Bah, it seems that the festivities in connection with my approaching marriage must last a week. I should like to do it handsomely, and I want to consult you as to the amount I ought to spend upon them.

POOH-BAH: Certainly. In which of my capacities? As First Lord of the Treasury, Lord Chamberlain, Attorney-General, Chancellor of the Exchequer, Privy Purse, or Private Secretary?

KO: Suppose we say as Private Secretary.

POOH: Speaking as your Private Secretary, I should say that as the city will have to pay for it, don't stint yourself, do it well.

KO: Exactly—as the city will have to pay for it. That is your advice.

POOH: As Private Secretary. Of course you will understand that, as Chancellor of the Exchequer, I am bound to see that due economy is observed.

KO: Oh! But you said just now "Don't stint yourself, do it well."

POOH: As Private Secretary.

KO: And now you say that due economy must be observed.

POOH: As Chancellor of the Exchequer.

KO: I see. Come over here, where the Chancellor can't hear us. Now, as my Solicitor, how do you advise me to deal with this difficulty?

POOH: Oh, as your Solicitor, I should have no hesitation in saying "Chance it—"

KO: Thank you. I will.

POOH: If it were not that, as Lord Chief Justice, I am bound to see that the law isn't violated.

KO: I see. Come over here, where the Chief Justice can't hear us. Now, then, as First Lord of the Treasury?

POOH: Of course, as First Lord of the Treasury, I could propose a special vote that would cover all expenses, if it were not that, as Leader of the Opposition, it would be my duty to resist it, tooth and nail. Or, as Paymaster-General, I could so cook the accounts that, as Lord High Auditor, I should never discover the fraud. But then, as Archbishop of Titipu, it would be my duty to denounce my dishonesty and give myself into my own custody as First Commissioner of Police.

KO: That's extremely awkward.

POOH: I don't say that all these distinguished people couldn't be squared; but it is right to tell you that they wouldn't be sufficiently degraded in their own estimation unless they are insulted with a very considerable bribe.

W. S. Gilbert, The Mikado

Chapter Three

DOCTOR, SCHMOCTOR:

PRACTICE POSITIVISM AND ITS COMPLICATIONS

> For it is, after all, with men and not with parchment that I quarrel.
> *Henry David Thoreau, "Resistance to Civil Government"*

SANSON THE EXECUTIONER appeals to various arguments from roles to justify the gravest violations of the humanity of persons. Through his apologia to Mercier, he asks us to take his institutional role seriously: to understand it to have independent moral force and, perhaps, independent moral grounding. When professional adversaries invoke their institutional roles to justify some nasty behavior, they too are asking us, in some way, to take their roles seriously, to grant that acting in a role may change the moral reasons one faces, and so change the way that the role actor should be evaluated.

Should we take roles seriously? Are roles usefully understood to have independent moral force or independent moral grounding? Or, rather, are roles merely shorthand for a nexus of obligations, values, and goods that have moral weight without appeal to role as a moral category? After attending to the valuable consequences of the institution of certain social and professional roles (valuable from outside the role), and after attending to the moral obligations of keeping one's promises and commitments (also, obligations understood and respected from outside the role), is there anything of moral interest left unaccounted for, that requires for its explication taking roles seriously?

For focus, recall the twin puzzles about adversaries introduced in the first chapter. The problem of restricted reasons asks how it can be that two actors are both morally justified in aiming at and devoting their energies to realizing partial and conflicting moral ends. The problem of permissible violation asks how it can be that one who takes part in an adversary institution is permitted to violate the humanity of persons in ways that ordinarily are impermissible. Arguments from roles claim to answer these puzzles by showing how the moral prescriptions faced by role actors change because acting in an institutional role changes either the moral description or the moral evaluation of actions taken within a role. To assess whether roles should be taken seriously, and therefore whether they provide the moral justification adversaries seek, we first need to spell out some of the various forms these claims can take.

Role is not a well-defined and well-developed moral idea, and we will have to make do with some sloppiness around the edges. The term has theatrical origins, referring to the roll of parchment on which an actor's part was written, and so, metonymously, to the part itself. It was pressed into service by anthropologists and sociologists to describe positions in society that come along with expected patterns of conduct related to the social function of those positions.[1] Moral philosophers ask normative questions about the social scientists' descriptive category: when, how, and for what reason are the social prescriptions attached to roles also moral prescriptions? When, how, and for what reason is the evaluation that a person is good at one's role also a moral evaluation, that one is a good person? The theatrical metaphor is inspired, because it vividly calls to mind a determinate script that must be read by anyone who plays that role. But the image may assume too much at the start: perhaps the role player ought to be a method actor, or an improvisationist. Provenance of the term "role" aside, the concept of distinctive positions in social practices and institutions that have distinctive duties, values, and virtues is very old, of course. Indeed, the conventional view of the ancient world, not unchallenged, supposes that what we would now call one's social role comprehensively governed moral life in heroic societies. On this view, Homeric characters and their author thought that different virtues attached to different social roles, the fifth-century dramatists began to recognize conflicts between overlapping social roles but saw no resolution, and the Socratics first asked about the virtues of a good man simply.[2]

[1] Montaigne may well be the first to have used the theatrical term in connection with vocations. See "De l'utile et de l'honneste," in *Les Essais de Michel de Montaigne*, 3:1 (1588), ed. Pierre Villey (1924; Paris: Quadrige/Presses Universitaires de France, 1992), p. 791, and "De mesnager sa volonté," 3:10 (1588), p. 1011. Nietzsche made good use of the metaphor. See *The Gay Science* (1887), trans. Walter Kaufmann (New York: Viking, 1974), sec. 356, and Kaufmann's introduction, p. 24. David Luban, *Lawyers and Justice* (Princeton, N.J.: Princeton University Press, 1988), p. 105, attributes the social scientific coinage to the anthropologist Ralph Linton in his 1936 book, *The Study of Man*. Dorothy Emmet, *Rules, Roles, and Relations* (London: Macmillan, 1966), says that G. H. Mead may have used the term in lectures given from 1904 onward. See also Erving Goffman, "Role Distance," in his *Encounters: Two Studies in the Sociology of Interaction* (Indianapolis, Ind.: Bobbs-Merrill, 1961).

[2] For more nuanced views, see Martha Nussbaum, *The Fragility of Goodness* (Cambridge: Cambridge University Press, 1986), and Bernard Williams, *Shame and Necessity*

There persists a whiff of the premodern in talk about roles, making such talk suspect to liberals who have no nostalgia for societies divided into castes, estates, or classes, and who fear any retreat from the idea of universal humanity. The liberal inclination, therefore, is to decompose any claims about role morality into concepts and categories that are easily digested by a universalistic ethic. On such a view, roles are not primary elements of morality, and if role talk is of any use, it is merely as shorthand. The strange bedfellowship of antiliberals—postmoderns, communitarians, and conservatives—is inclined to embrace precisely what liberals fear. Taking roles seriously is one way for them to challenge the supposed thinness and alienation of liberal selves. Moves to analyze and translate the stuff of roles into more basic elements are likely to be viewed by antiliberals as reductive and desiccated, the mode of analysis itself a symptom of the liberal's deeper misunderstanding of the social world. I mention these political-philosophical stakes in order to set them aside for now. A political philosophy of the professions needs to be worked out, and an account of role morality may play in it an important part. But I defer such work until another day. Some conceptual spadework about roles—call it aeration, not desiccation—must be done first.

Good riddance or not, hierarchical social roles are behind us. This is not to say that class inequality is behind us, but that to be a member of a class is no longer a role. The poor may always be with us, but they have no special script. The main contemporary roles are to be found in the family, in offices, professions, and trades, and in associational undertakings such as churches and clubs and movements. I will reserve the term role for positions with some degree of regularity and durability, and where there are collective expectations, however informal or contested, about the content of the position's duties, values, and virtues. Perhaps one can speak of roles that are more loose, more ephemeral—but I will not. So, here, doctor is a social role, but not patient. Father is a role, but, to use Bernard Williams's example, wife's brother in our society is not.[3] It is not fruitful to label every relationship a role.

The next three chapters explore, by way of particular professions, the structure of moral claims about roles. In "Doctor, Schmoctor," the medical profession is used to map the routes by which role prescriptions might generate moral prescriptions. In "The Remains of the

---

(Berkeley: University of California Press, 1993). Cf. Nietzsche, *The Gay Science*, sec. 356, on role acting in Periclean democracy.

[3] Bernard Williams, *Morality: An Introduction to Ethics* (1972; Cambridge: Cambridge University Press, 1993), p. 49.

Role," the characteristic agent-relative form that role prescriptions take is sketched out through a discussion of civil servants. Then, in "Are Lawyers Liars?" the arguments of act and actor redescription, employed earlier by Sanson, are put on trial.

SCHMOCTORING

The standard role of doctor as a learned professional devoted to the care and healing of the sick currently is under challenge by practices that require medical expertise, but that partially conflict with a commitment to serve the medical needs of each individual patient. Managed care has made some doctors into gatekeepers; clinical trials deny some patients treatment that the doctor-researcher has reason to believe is beneficial; consumer demand has turned some doctors into cosmetic and genetic technicians. The job of expert witness, company doc, public health official, and many would say euthanasist all conflict in some way with the role obligations of standard doctoring.

On what grounds can these conflicting pursuits be criticized? One might say that the practice of medicine is a *natural role*, by analogy to natural law. On this view, the standard role obligations of doctoring follow from some truths about the kind of creatures we are. Doctors who pursue ends that conflict with the end of caring for each patient are making a conceptual mistake, for one cannot occupy the role of doctor and coherently pursue ends incompatible with what doctoring must be. I shall explore this claim about the role of doctor, and propose a different, more plausible, but more troubling way to think about professional roles and their connection to morality.

I'd like to begin with an old chestnut of a law case that is widely used in the teaching of legal ethics, *Spaulding v. Zimmerman*.[4] It is also a medical ethics case of first importance—and one with direct implications for some of the pressing challenges that confront the practice of medicine today. In 1956 John Zimmerman had a serious automobile accident. David Spaulding, a teenaged passenger in the car, sustained a severe crushing injury of the chest with multiple rib fractures, fractures of the clavicles, and severe cerebral concussion. Spaulding sought damages from Zimmerman. Zimmerman's auto insurance company sent the young Spaulding to a doctor in its employ for examination. The insurance company's doctor discovered a life-

---

[4] *Spaulding v. Zimmerman*, 116 N.W.2d 704 (1962). See Luban, *Lawyers and Justice*, pp. 149–53 for a discussion.

threatening aortic aneurysm Spaulding's own doctors had missed and that Spaulding knew nothing about.

What do you suppose the doctor did with such information? He picked up the phone and placed an emergency call to . . . Zimmerman's lawyer. Lawyer, doctor, and insurance company decided to conceal the youth's condition, and Spaulding settled for $6,500.

Sometime after settlement, the aneurysm was detected in the course of a routine medical checkup by Spaulding's own doctor, and Spaulding was rushed into surgery. He survived, and successfully petitioned the trial court to set aside the settlement with Zimmerman, arguing that Zimmerman's lawyer improperly withheld information. The Minnesota Supreme Court upheld vacating the settlement, but took pains to proclaim that "no canon of ethics or legal obligation"[5] required the lawyer to inform Spaulding that without treatment he could drop dead at any moment. "There is no doubt that during the course of the negotiations, when the parties were in an adversary relationship, no rule required or duty rested upon defendants or their representatives to disclose this knowledge."[6] It is this defense of the lawyer's actions that makes *Spaulding v. Zimmerman* a notable case in legal ethics.

Our interest, however, is in the actions of the doctor, not the lawyer. Is there no canon of *medical* ethics that requires doctors—even doctors hired by insurance companies or lawyers—to tell Spaulding that his life is in danger? Now, this condemnation of the doctor might be overdetermined, in that, quite apart from any role obligation the doctor has as a doctor, he (and we) have a common, preprofessional moral duty to warn others of grave danger when we are in circumstances where we can do so at little risk or cost to ourselves. But added to any responsibility he might have simply as a person, doesn't he have a professional responsibility, in his role as doctor, to care for his patient?

There are a number of moves the doctor can make in his defense. He might claim that he did not take Spaulding on as his patient—that no doctor-patient relationship had been formed. You might imagine the doctor warning Spaulding before the examination, "Don't be fooled by the stethoscope. Yes, I am a doctor, but not yours. I have not taken you on as my patient." But the standard role of doctoring doesn't let doctors off so easily. In emergencies and in Good Samar-

---

[5] *Spaulding*, p. 710.

[6] Ibid., p. 709. Why then uphold the trial judge's order to vacate? Using tortured logic, the justices faulted the lawyer for withholding information from the *court* when, acting as an officer of the court, rather than as an adversary, he proposed approval of the settlement.

itan cases it is widely believed that doctors have a professional obligation to treat, whether they wish to take on new patients or not. More generally, the rules of the role of doctoring do not permit just *any* contractual relationship between a doctor employing her medical expertise and a consenting adult, and doctors are morally obligated to follow the rules of their role.

It has been claimed that it is not mere convention that the existing role obligations of doctors require that doctors attend to illness and suffering in a certain way, and prohibit them from employing their medical expertise in other ways. Rather, on this view, the fact that we are the sort of creatures that fall ill and suffer creates a set of natural moral obligations that bind those who have the skills to cure and relieve suffering. On this view, one says in response to the insurance company doctor that he cannot coherently claim to be a doctor and then fail to attend in the right way to Spaulding's condition. No agreement with the insurance company or Zimmerman, and no agreement with Spaulding, can release the doctor from the obligations of his natural role.

Suppose the fellow in the employ of the insurance company responds like this: if doctoring indeed is a practice governed by such stringent rules and exclusive ends, then call what I do *schmoctoring*— a different practice with different ends and different role obligations.[7] It's not merely that Spaulding isn't my patient, but that I am not (at least not in this capacity) a doctor. Why am I not free to fashion some other way of employing my science and skill, as long as I do not violate the law or any preprofessional moral obligations that apply to all occupations? I may not lie, cheat, steal, or coerce, just as plumbers and sales clerks may not. But as long as Spaulding is properly informed that, as a schmoctor, my role obligations commit me to serve the insurance company, not Spaulding, what is wrong with occupying the role of insurance company schmoctor?

Similarly, as long as the customer is properly informed that managed-care schmoctors are under contract not to mention the word "transplant" in front of patients, what is wrong with the role of managed-care schmoctor? For a chance to get an experimental drug, consent to be the subject of a research schmoctor. Overweight? Try a pill-mill schmoctor. If you want a traditional patient-doctor relationship, stick with that other profession, the Doctor®.

Indeed, the insurance company schmoctor might go further and claim exemption from some preprofessional moral obligations that bind plumbers and sales clerks. Perhaps insurance company schmoc-

---

[7] The schmoctor gambit is borrowed from Robert Nozick, *Anarchy, State, and Utopia* (New York: Basic Books, 1974), p. 235n.

toring, like lawyering, is a morally justified adversary role. Lawyers claim permission to advance unjust ends, conceal wrongdoing, and persuade others of matters of fact and law that they themselves do not believe to be true on the grounds that, in equilibrium, good and just ends are served by the adversary system. Perhaps the schmoctor is exempt from the common moral duty to inform Spaulding because he has a fiduciary obligation to advance the interests of his employer in an adversary system where others are advancing the interests of Spaulding.

Let me be clear about schmoctoring: I am not suggesting that the vast majority of physicians in the managed-care setting and the vast majority of clinical researchers are not deeply committed to the standard role of doctoring, and I am not suggesting that they are failing to put the needs of their patients first. Rather, I am imagining practices of schmoctoring that might someday come about as contractual and institutional arrangements such as cost containment, capitation rates, and for-profit ownership continue to press against the standard role. In the practice of schmoctoring that might someday come about, schmoctors do not enter into a fiduciary relationship with patients; rather, they are contract employees of for-profit health care providers who in turn have contractual relationships with consenting adult customers.

In contrast with the natural-role view, call the view that admits the possibility of schmoctoring *practice positivism*, by analogy to legal positivism. On this view, the concept of a practice does not impose any general content requirements or restrictions on the rules of all practices. The rules of a practice simply are what they are, not what they ought to be or what we want them to be. If this view is correct, we cannot criticize the schmoctor on grounds that are internal to the concept of a professional practice or role. We can criticize an entire role or practice from the outside, and ask if it is a morally permissible or worthy pursuit. But if practice positivism is the correct view of roles, then medical expertise can be put in service of a wide range of purposes without internal contradiction. I think practice positivism *is* the correct view of roles. To see why, we need to trace out some connections between roles and morality.[8]

WAYS OF MORALIZING ROLES

Suppose that a social or professional role has some moral force, by which I mean that the fact that a person occupies the role affects what

[8] For an elaboration of practice positivism, see Chapter 5, "Are Lawyers Liars?"

he is morally required, permitted, or forbidden to do, and affects how his character and actions are to be morally evaluated. What is the route by which such roles connect to morality? Consider two ways: call them *direct moralization* and *mediated moralization*. In direct moralization, role prescriptions are themselves moral prescriptions for persons who occupy the corresponding role. So, the professional rule that requires doctors to maintain patient confidences is itself a moral rule for one who is a doctor, and the professional rule that requires lawyers to be the zealous advocates of clients is itself a moral rule for one who is a lawyer. This seems to be an unobjectionable way to account for the moral force of role prescriptions when they have such force, until we look at the implication of direct moralization for evaluation, where the view appears to require that role evaluations be themselves moral evaluations. So, if seeking to maximize shareholder value is a criterion for being a good business manager, then for a person occupying the role of business manager, seeking to maximize shareholder value is a criterion for being a good person. Direct moralization, one might think, is too direct.

In mediated moralization, the prescriptions that a role generates are not in themselves moral prescriptions, and standards for evaluating good role occupants are not in themselves moral evaluations. Rather, if one occupies a role that has moral force, one has one big moral reason to follow the role's nonmoral prescriptions. So, the requirement of patient confidentiality is a professional rule of the role of doctoring, but not in itself a moral rule. Morality enters because, by hypothesis, doctors have a moral obligation to obey the nonmoral rules that apply to doctors. Similarly, maximizing shareholder value makes one a good manager, but not, at least not directly, a good person. Under mediated moralization, "good doctor" and "good manager" are not in themselves moral evaluations, any more than are "good hammer" or "good spy." Rather, if one's role has moral force of a certain sort, part of being a morally good person is to be good at one's role.

Neither scheme of moralization supposes that every role has moral force, or that every prescription and evaluation within a moralized role is morally dispositive. Each scheme still is in need of an account of which roles are moralized, and why, and each is in need of an account of how to act and evaluate action when practical reasons, both within and without the role, conflict. The two ways of moralizing roles amount to much the same thing when both conclude that the role occupant morally ought to follow the prescriptions of the role; but they may not always reach the same conclusion.

Direct moralization seems highly implausible if the role prescriptions that are said to be in themselves moral prescriptions include all the *actual* commands, rules, and customs of the role—the *positive* law of the role, so to speak. Many explicit rules and implicit customs of roles clearly are devoid of direct, substantive moral content: doctors are expected to complete lots of paperwork for insurance companies, and lawyers are expected to wear suits in court, but it seems odd to say that billing patients and dressing up are among the direct moral obligations of doctors and lawyers. If morality has something to say about those activities, it is by a more circuitous route. More important, the rule makers and exemplary practitioners in a role are not infallible—even the American Medical Association's Council on Ethical and Judicial Affairs can err—so the content of actual practices, even in otherwise good roles, can be morally and professionally mistaken. If a doctor ought to comply with monopolistic rules prohibiting advertising and if an army officer ought to comply with policies to suppress homosexuality in the military, the reason is not that these features of the role have acquired substantive moral correctness by virtue of their enactment. That would turn the governing mechanisms of various role-generating institutions—the AMA House of Delegates, the Joint Chiefs of Staff—into legislatures of morality. But beyond the borders of Kant's Kingdom of Ends, morality is not so enacted. We can recognize roles to have moral force without adopting a pure proceduralist view about the moral and professional correctness of actual practices.

There is an apt analogy here to political obligation and the moral force of the laws of the state. We distinguish between what the law of the state is and what the law should be. If, by hypothesis, there is a general obligation to obey the law, it is not because all laws are good laws (that is simply false) or because the law prescribes that the law be obeyed (that is circular) but because there are extralegal moral reasons to obey laws, even, generally, the bad ones. Similarly, we distinguish between what the role is and what the role should be. There may be moral reasons to comply with roles as they are, but that is not to be confused with the claim that all of the reasons for action given by a role, even a good role, are already moral reasons.

On the other hand, mediated moralization, the view that role prescriptions are nonmoral prescriptions that role occupants generally are morally obligated to obey, seems to put too much distance between the substantive content of a role and the sources of moral obligation. Mediated moralization might explain an obligation to defer to authority when the actual demands of the institutional role are in error, and might explain obligations to comply with conventions of practice that have no substantive content themselves, but are useful in coordinating behavior in roles. But many role prescriptions and evaluations *do* have substantive moral content of their own, and not because the role prescription accidentally coincides with an ordinary, nonrole obligation, but because the role shapes or gives moral force to a reason or value. Something important is missed if a physician's commitment to heal the sick or a journalist's commitment to inform the public is accounted for by saying that role occupants are morally obligated to perform the nonmoral commands of their roles. That may be true, but it is not the only moral reason physicians and journalists have for pursuing the goods valued by their roles. A physician reproaching a colleague who does not care for patients properly or a journalist reproaching a colleague who handles the truth carelessly do not simply argue that the wayward colleague is obligated to perform her role. Such an argument would appeal to possible sources of a generic moral obligation to obey role prescriptions: that one ought to do well whatever one does, that one ought to do what one has agreed to do, that one ought to fulfill the reasonable expectations of others, or that one ought to be fair to other role occupants, to mention a few candidates. But a physician will also appeal to the substantive goods particular to medicine, and remind the colleague that she once believed that healing the sick was a valuable pursuit; the journalist will recall shared commitments to supporting a free and educated citizenry.

Perhaps it is like this. All roles put forward actual, nonmoral, substantive prescriptions of the institution—what the role is: "Submit forms in triplicate," "Wear a tie in court," "Don't ask, don't tell," "Be home by ten o'clock, dear." Then there are reasonable constructions of substantive role prescriptions—what the role should be: heal the sick, pursue justice, defend the nation, love your parents. Here, then, is the truth in direct moralization: though actual role prescriptions are not in themselves moral prescriptions, reasonable role prescriptions may be. To the extent that what the role is tracks what the role morally should be, the role is, in this sense, directly moralized.

Similarly, roles put forward, with varying degrees of formality, actual structures of authority, ways of determining what person, group, text, or process gets to say what the actual substantive prescriptions of the role are. The umpire behind the plate gets to call balls and strikes; the first-base umpire gets to call the runner out; there are rules of precedence for making other calls, and the commissioner of baseball gets to decide what these rules are, and how large the strike zone is. The actual authority structures of some roles, such as doctors and lawyers, are by and large collectively self-governing. Others, such as the roles of artist and intellectual, are by and large individually self-governing. Still others, like the role of child or the traditional role of nurse, are governed by those who occupy other roles: parent and physician. A description of what the role *is* includes both the substantive prescriptions of the role and the procedures and structures of authority that generate those substantive prescriptions. There are many descriptive puzzles that this formulation poses: what if authority to generate prescriptions is contested, or if the criteria for who occupies a role are contested, or if the prescriptions of a role are largely violated by role occupants? But descriptive puzzles are not conceptual puzzles. Just as actual substantive role prescriptions (what the role is) can be distinguished from reasonable role prescriptions (what the role should be), actual structures and procedures of authority in a role (who or what in fact says what the role is and who is in it) can be distinguished from reasonable structures and procedures of authority (who or what *should* say what the role is and who is in it). Just as there are reasonable constructions of the substance of role prescriptions, there are reasonable constructions of the authority of role prescriptions. Here, then, is the truth in mediated moralization: there can be moral reasons that obligate a role occupant to comply with the actual substantive prescriptions of roles, even when the content of what the role is does not track the content of what the role should be. So, if one is in a role, one can have two different sorts of moral reasons to obey the actual prescriptions of role authorities: direct reasons, when the actual substantive prescriptions track the reasonable construction of the role's substance, and mediated reasons, when the actual structure of authority in the role tracks the reasonable construction of authority in the role.

This account of the connections between morality and roles is not quite adequate, for in distinguishing between what the role is and what the role should be it leaves room for ambiguity about the senses of "should." There can be reasonable criteria for evaluating a role and its prescriptions that are still nonmoral. Architects should design beautiful spaces that work. When the actual practice of architecture strays from that ideal, as it did, for example, when Brutalism was in fashion, architects are not doing what architects ought to do, they are not being good architects. But "should," "ought," and "good" are here aesthetic prescriptions and evaluations, not moral ones. Excellence in architecture may have nothing to do with morality, and appeals to what the role of architect should be need not be moral appeals. Similarly, reasonable constructions of authority in roles need not be moral constructions. Excellence in teaching English usage to schoolchildren requires having and transmitting a view about what is and is not standard grammar. It is perfectly intelligible to distinguish between what the rules of grammar are and what they ought to be, and it is perfectly intelligible to hold a view about whether, to be a good teacher or writer of English, one should follow the rules that are or the rules that ought to be, all the while using "ought," "should," and "good" in nonmoral senses. William Safire's linguistic prescriptivism is a view about good English, not good ethics, and a position on whether to obediently follow Safire on split infinitives is a position about linguistic authority, not moral authority.

We might stipulate that criteria of excellence in roles must operate within the morally permissible range, so that, though reasonable role prescriptions and evaluations can be nonmoral, they cannot be immoral. But such a stipulation is not conceptually required. Excellence in an executioner is not conceptually constrained by the bounds of what is morally permissible. Though perhaps mistaken, it is not incoherent to say that Charles-Henri Sanson was an excellent executioner but an evil man. The notion of a reasonable construction of a role neither captures all the connections between roles and morality nor reconciles roles with morality.

I have, in a somewhat roundabout way, noted distinctions that are worth emphasizing. A role is not simply whatever role occupants happen to do. Since many actual doctors commit malpractice and many actual parents are negligent and abusive, it would be quite odd to think that prescriptive and evaluative force flows directly from what occupants of the role of doctor and parent actually do. The very notion of a good role occupant who does what is prescribed creates the possibility of a bad role occupant who does not do what is prescribed. Indeed, the concepts of malpractice, negligence, and abusiveness assume both a standard and a failure to meet it. If this seems too obvious to mention, recall how common is the notion that art simply is what artists do. This could be a deep insight about the practice of a role if the emphasis is on the plural, what artists do. Practices are collective enterprises that connect practitioners over time and across space, so standards of excellence are likely to have some relationship to what actual practitioners, if only the best of them, actually do. In contrast, the claim that art is whatever *an* artist does is fatuous. This is not to exclude the possibility of iconoclastic artistic excellence, but to include the possibility of art criticism.

Nor are the actual prescriptions and evaluations of a role necessarily what the role should be. I likened the actual role to the positive law to emphasize that, though an actual role prescription is presented as a practical reason for a role occupant, it is not by itself a practical reason: the role occupant still needs a reason to treat actual prescriptions as action-guiding. The reason might be that the actual prescription adequately realizes substantive practical reasons, moral or nonmoral, that the role occupant already has. A doctor who faces actual role prescriptions on patient confidentiality may find that following them satisfies moral reasons to respect and dignify her patients. Or a cellist may find that the conductor's interpretations accord well with his own aesthetic and historical sensibilities. Or a lawyer who faces the actual role prescriptions on zealous advocacy may find that following them satisfies her prudential reasons to seek out challenge, gratification, and financial reward. Alternatively, some attribute of the actual role prescription unrelated to its substance might provide the practical reason. This can be so if the role occupant has a moral reason to follow actual role prescriptions, regardless of their content— for example, a judge may have acquired a moral obligation to follow the role prescriptions of the court by swearing to do so. Or the role occupant can have a nonmoral practical reason to follow role prescriptions regardless of content—for example, a soldier may have a desire or interest in being good at his role in a role where compliance with actual role prescriptions, ordinarily without regard to their content, is part of being good at it.

An actual role prescription, however, can fail to generate moral reasons for action. Not every role has or claims to have moral force, and there is no conceptual requirement that the actual demands of roles be compatible with the reasonable demands of morality. Less obviously, actual role prescriptions can fail to generate even nonmoral practical reasons. This may be so for unchosen roles. Someone who is conscripted into an army against his will occupies the role of soldier, but may lack any reason to be a good soldier (though threat of punishment gives him a reason to *appear* to be a good soldier). Or this may be so when an actual rule or custom of the role prescribes an action that is inconsistent with being good at the reasonable construction of the role, and the role occupant has a practical reason to be good at *that*.

To show the plausibility of practice positivism, let me offer an example where, unlike schmoctoring, we are likely to applaud, rather than condemn, a professional's refusal to take the rules of a role as his own. Suppose a librarian holds the outmoded notion that excellence in his role involves collecting books. For years, his professional colleagues have been computerizing their holdings and linking their users to the information superhighway while he assembled carefully chosen collections on carefully chosen subjects. He is considered by virtually all professional librarians to be an antique, though he takes great pride in and gets much satisfaction out of what he does. Though he clearly is out of step with what the role has become, this does not yet provide him with a practical reason to give up his notion of excellence, for his commitment is to what he believes the role should be, not to what it is. He has a practical reason to be a good librarian on his criteria of good librarianship, not on the dominant view of the role.

One might say about him that if he is unmoved by the evaluative criteria of the role as it is he is not a good librarian (though he might be a good something else—book collector, perhaps); or one might even say that he is not a librarian at all, that he no longer occupies the role (though, again, he may occupy some other role). But these seem to be purely verbal distinctions, and not much rides on them. The important point to observe is that, if he *is* defined to be a bad librarian or not a librarian at all, that does not obviously give him a practical reason to become a good librarian. It might be that, if confronted with the prospect of having to concede that he is not a good librarian, he would discover that he *does* have a reason to be good at the role as it is: he may become convinced that the world of learning and the needs of library patrons have changed, or that he cares about the approval of his peers. But he may instead revise his account of himself, and rename his commitment "excellence in book collecting," rather than in librarianship. In response to the reproach, "Librarians don't browse the stacks, they surf the net," he might respond, "If so, then I am not a librarian, so I have no reason to be a good one." Similarly, the schmoctor has no reason to be a good doctor.

But our antiquated book lover need not give up his claim to be a good librarian or a librarian at all so quickly: he might have good grounds to argue that his criteria of excellence, because they fit the traditional purposes, functions, and values of librarianship, are authoritative, and the database searchers are usurpers. If he is mistaken about the criteria for good librarianship, it is not simply because he is vastly outnumbered. The doctrine of *role realism*, on the model of legal realism, is wrong: a practice is not simply whatever role occupants in fact do. Recall that malpractice is possible. But if the book collector is going to put up an honest fight for the soul of the practice, his claim must be about what librarianship in fact is and how that in fact is decided, not about what librarianship ought to be and how that ought to be decided. Though role realism is wrong, the doctrine of practice positivism, on the model of legal positivism, is right: a role simply is what it is, and not what it ought to be.

Doctoring

If the content of the role of doctoring is largely conventional, not natural, what difference does it make? It is of course as important as ever that professional groups such as the American Medical Association continue to deliberate about and render collective judgments about what the rules of the role of doctoring are. But if I am right about the limitations of the claims about natural roles, and right about the expansiveness of the claims about positive roles, it is not enough to render judgments. It is not enough because, over time, under various market and institutional pressures, those with medical training may come to question whether they are bound by the rules of doctoring, which they did not shape and did not choose. Instead, they may come to see themselves as schmoctors of various stripes. And if enough of them think so, *it will become so*: a new set of social meanings surrounding a new actual role, the role of schmoctor, will have emerged. For the role of doctoring is not discovered in the natural order of things. It is stitched together from the shared social meanings of those who profess to be doctors and those who call upon their services. To be clear: moral obligations are not legislated by social practice. Morality is a construction of reason, not a convention of society. But positive role obligations *are* conventional, and depend only on what the practice in fact *is*. Insofar as we are morally obligated to comply with positive role obligations simply because they are positive role obligations, it is only when the role that is applies to us.

One way a role applies to us is if we agree to it; another is if we accept the benefits of a role generated by those who have accepted upon themselves the role's burdens.[9] And this may be enough to obligate most current practicing physicians to the standard role of doctoring. But conventions and shared understandings are changing, and if enough doctors act like schmoctors, the time will soon come when it cannot be supposed that most of those with medical training have agreed to the role of doctor, not schmoctor. Once this happens—once medical practitioners fail to identify with and endorse the goods and virtues and commitments internal to the standard practice of doctoring—they indeed are morally free from the collective judgments of a social practice that is not their own and that does not apply to them (which is not to say that they are free from the ordinary moral requirements that apply to all persons).

What can the profession of doctoring do to prevent the emergence of schmoctoring? There always is denial. An organized profession can, wittingly or unwittingly, make claims about the source of its moral authority that are not true, and hope that most practitioners believe them. Just as false claims about the divine right of

---

[9] For an elaboration of how such obligations are acquired, see Chapter 6, "Rules of the Game and Fair Play."

kings served to keep subjects in line for a time, false claims about what the role of a medical practitioner must naturally be might hold sway for a time. But the march of transparency and reflection in our social relations will catch up to the myth of natural roles just as surely as it did to the myth of natural monarchy. The task, then, is to inspire medical students and practicing doctors to choose, upon reflection, to commit or recommit themselves to the standard role of doctoring, though they are free, and know that they are free, to do otherwise— though there are other institutional arrangements for the delivery of medical care that satisfy the constraints of common morality. Schmoctoring can meet the logical requirements of coherence and the minimal moral requirements of justice. The profession of doctoring must therefore understand itself as a calling that could have been otherwise, but argue why it still is a calling worthy of being answered by a reflective practitioner. Insofar as doctors continue to identify with their profession, and look to their colleagues for guidance and support on what counts as good professional practice—that is, insofar as those with medical training wish to subject themselves to the judgment and approval of their peers—they will reject the label of schmoctor. The challenge, of course, is to continue to articulate in a clear and reasoned voice to both doctors and patients what would be lost if the practice of doctoring gave way, in substantial measure, to the various forms of schmoctoring that I have described.

Chapter Four

THE REMAINS OF THE ROLE

> We must play our role duly, but as the role of a borrowed character.
> Of the mask and appearance we must not make a real essence, nor of
> what is foreign what is our very own.
>
> *Michel de Montaigne, "Of Husbanding Your Will"*

IF PRACTICE positivism is correct, providing a good or exercising a skill does not by itself morally obligate the actor to comply with the obligations of a conventional role. Schmoctoring is possible. This implication of mediated moralization is troubling because it is a bad state of affairs that schmoctors are not morally obligated to comply with the role obligations of doctors. Roles can demand too little.

Roles also can demand too much. When the conditions for mediated moralization are met, a role claims to morally obligate occupants to defer to its authority and comply with its rules, even when the role demands acts that otherwise would be morally wrong. This claim, common in professional and political life, is especially well developed in the British civil service. "One may think a particular policy concept to be a square circle, and indeed within the confidence of Whitehall one may argue fervently to that effect," writes Sir Michael Quinlan, onetime permanent secretary of Britain's Ministry of Defense, "but once the decision is taken, it is a matter not just of duty but of professional pride to help make the very best square circle that effort and imagination can contrive."[1] On this view, unelected officials occupy roles that demand (with only rare exception) the loyal and unstinting devotion of energy and expertise to serve the ends of one's elected superior, no matter what the end or who the elected. An excavation of the view will help lay bare both the structure of and arguments for restricted moral reasoning within professional roles. I shall use Quinlan's thoughtful argument for a strict division of moral labor in public service as an example of the class, and show why an ethic of obedient service does not succeed.

Quinlan served in and speaks about the British government, where permanent civil servants fill all but the top post in a ministry. This

---

[1] Michael Quinlan, "Ethics in the Public Service," *Governance* 6 (1993): 538–44 (quotation from p. 542). See also his response to me on p. 558.

notably is different, of course, from the American practice, where the top few thousand positions in government are filled by the current president's political allies and supporters, whose tours of duty typically are short. So Quinlan's "Whitehall front line" between politician and bureaucrat is reproduced in the United States only at a lower level, and only imperfectly, where political appointees at the cabinet and subcabinet levels (who are not elected politicians) meet the senior executive service, career diplomats, and generals (who are not, typically, a department's highest-ranking advisers).

No matter: Quinlan stirs up a general question about obedience to political or professional authority in the face of substantive disagreement about policy, and his answer draws on general claims about the legitimacy of such authority. The problem of obedience and dissent recurs when cabinet secretaries disagree with presidents, assistant secretaries with cabinet secretaries, and congressional staffers with legislators. The fact that American political appointees almost always are of the same political party as their appointers does not insure against deep substantive disagreements that strain the loyalties of officials. The question is reproduced, though with important differences, in nonpublic professional settings: when an engineer disagrees with a business executive, a nurse with a physician, a junior lawyer with a senior partner, or a lawyer with a client. So, despite Quinlan's modest claim to speak only about the British civil service, his view has far-reaching implications for public officials and professionals in faraway institutional contexts. If he is right about political authority and administrative obedience in Britain, officials and professionals elsewhere had better attend.

But is he right? I think not. The role of public servant, as constructed by Quinlan, demands more than one morally ought to give. Either the role in fact does not require what Quinlan says it does, or the circumstances in which a public official morally ought to break out of such a role are less rare than Quinlan allows. To see why this is so, we will need to uncover some of the philosophical positions implicit in Quinlan's argument: what is the structure of his role-based ethic, how is this structure justified, why is it legitimate, and why does it obligate?

NEUTRALITY OF PERSONS AND RELATIVITY OF ROLES

Some moral prescriptions—requirements, permissions, or restrictions—are what have been termed *agent-relative*, in that they do not fall on everyone, but only on agents who possess particular attributes, face particular situations, or occupy particular positions. Agent-relative prescriptions are a common feature of the normative landscape, and there is nothing particularly mysterious about many of them. For example, you are ordinarily obligated to pay your *own* debts and keep your *own* promises, but you are not, ordinarily, obligated to pay *my* debts or keep *my* promises. But some agent-relative prescriptions are difficult to reconcile with some sorts of moral theories. Depending on whether one is more deeply convinced of the existence of the prescriptive relativity or of the correctness of the moral theory, either the prescription or the theory may puzzle. Arguments about agent relativity have a characteristic plot: the puzzle raised is that two moral agents who are the same in all morally important ways and face morally equivalent situations are claimed to be subject to different moral prescriptions. The resolution seeks either to show that there are morally important differences between the agents or that there is some previously overlooked difference in the moral situation that accounts for the different prescription.

Sometimes, it is not a claim of agent relativity that puzzles, but a claim of agent neutrality: why some important difference between moral agents does *not* lead to different prescriptions. Professional roles have the distinction of being puzzling in both ways: for claiming prescriptive relativity about an aspect of agents that does not appear to be morally important, and for claiming prescriptive neutrality in the face of differences between agents that do appear to be morally important. Why should the fact of occupying a role permit a person to violate another in ways that ordinarily are impermissible? And why should the fact of occupying a role require that a person ignore some of the most important ties and commitments that a person can have? The professional ethic of Quinlan's civil servant invokes this special sort of agent-relative prescription, and to get at it we need to distinguish two kinds of agent relativity.

First, moral prescriptions can be *relative to the role* of the agent, in that occupants of particular institutional or social roles face particular moral reasons for action that others, outside the role, do not face, and they are directed to ignore moral reasons for action that others, outside the role, may not ignore. A defense attorney has a role-relative reason to argue for the acquittal of a factually guilty client that the prosecutor does not share, and the defense attorney is not to count in her moral deliberations the social consequences of setting a dangerous criminal free. A business executive has a role-relative reason to maximize the profits of his company that competitors do not share, and he is not to count the miseries of unemployment as a reason not to close an unprofitable factory. The civil servant has a role-relative

reason to advance the settled policy directives of her superior, and
not to count as a reason against doing so the fact that such policies
are foolish or cruel.

Second, prescriptions can be _relative to the person_ of the agent, in
that particular persons, by virtue of their personal projects, commitments, and relationships, face particular moral reasons for action.
Family gives Antigone a person-relative reason to bury her brother in
defiance of the laws of the city; friendship gives Jonathan a person-
relative reason to help David in defiance of King (and father) Saul.
When Rilke writes to a young poet, "This most of all: ask yourself in
the most silent hour of your night: _must_ I write?" the prescription is
relative to a person with a commitment.[2]

The professions characteristically put forth _role-relative_ but _person-
neutral_ prescriptions: the lawyer faces the role-relative prescription of
zealous advocacy, and so is obligated to serve unsavory clients and
their unsavory ends with a zeal that, outside of the role, would be
wrong. But she is to exclude completely reasons for action that might
otherwise flow from the particularities of her person: her extrapro-
fessional projects, values, commitments, relationships. So, in his oft-
quoted dissent from a Supreme Court decision protecting public
school children who, for religious reasons, refused to salute the American flag, Justice Felix Frankfurter writes:

> One who belongs to the most vilified and persecuted minority in history
> is not likely to be insensible to the freedoms guaranteed by our Constitu-
> tion. Were my purely personal attitude relevant I should wholeheartedly
> associate myself with the general libertarian views in the Court's opinion,
> representing as they do the thought and action of a lifetime. But as judges
> we are neither Jew nor Gentile, neither Catholic nor agnostic. We owe equal
> attachment to the Constitution and are equally bound by our judicial obli-
> gations whether we derive our citizenship from the earliest or the latest
> immigrants to these shores.[3]

Quinlan's professional ethic requires both strong role relativity and
strict person neutrality. The person of the civil servant and so the
political commitments and the substantive judgments of that person
are to be completely submerged when the role demands deference to
the commitments and judgments of others. The epithet "faceless,
nameless bureaucrat" is in this sense a virtue: actions of an official
should not depend on her identity, attributes, or values. To varying

---

[2] Rainer Maria Rilke, _Letters to a Young Poet_ (1903; New York: Random House, 1984),
p. 6.

[3] _West Virginia State Board of Education v. Barnette_, 219 U.S. 625 (1943).

degrees, the professional roles of soldier, business manager, journalist, lawyer, and doctor also demand that actions taken within the role be faceless and nameless, in that the role occupant is required to ignore some set of personal reasons.

In return, the person-neutral role occupant is to be spared personal judgments that do not bear on performing the role well. Says the tolerant Montaigne,

> It cannot matter of what religion are my doctor and my lawyer. This consideration has nothing to do with the friendly services they do me; and, in the domestic relations between my servants and myself, I take the same attitude. I do not look too closely into a footman's chastity, but I do inquire if he does his duty. I am not so much afraid of a muleteer's gambling as of his being a fool, and I would rather have a cook swear than be incompetent.[4]

The starkest example of person neutrality I have seen is exhibited by the "professional" butler, Mr. Stevens, in Kazuo Ishiguro's novel, *The Remains of the Day*. Person neutrality to Stevens (he calls it "dignity") is the core virtue of a great butler.

Stevens recounts admiringly a story about his father, also a butler, who, thought the son, possessed this quality of greatness. The elder Stevens was called upon to serve as valet for a house guest, a retired general. This same general commanded an atrocious and incompetent battle in the Boer War, a battle that needlessly took the life of the butler's other son, Stevens's older brother. The father suffered "intimate proximity for four days with the man he detested," enduring the general's ugliness, coarseness, and self-congratulatory military anecdotes, but he never broke role, and won high praise from the unsuspecting guest.[5] Years later, the younger Stevens surpasses the elder in person neutrality: as the father lies dying in a small servant's garret, the son ignores calls to the deathbed and flawlessly attends to a gathering of demanding gentlemen below, the only sign of his unadmitted distress the silent tears that he cannot suppress.

Stevens is not merely a practitioner of a role-relative, person-neutral profession, but is its leading (and perhaps only) theorist:

> And now let me posit this: "dignity" has to do crucially with a butler's ability not to abandon the professional being he inhabits. Lesser butlers will abandon their professional being for the private one at the least provocation. For such persons, being a butler is like playing some pantomime role;

---

[4] Montaigne, "On Friendship," in *Essays*, 1:28 (1580), trans. J. M. Cohen (Harmondsworth: Penguin Books, 1958), p. 102.

[5] Kazuo Ishiguro, *The Remains of the Day* (New York: Vintage, 1989), p. 42.

a small push, a slight stumble, and the façade will drop off to reveal the actor underneath. The great butlers are great by virtue of their ability to inhabit their professional role and inhabit it to the utmost; they will not be shaken out by external events, however surprising, alarming, or vexing. They wear their professionalism as a decent gentleman will wear his suit: he will not let ruffians or circumstance tear it off him in the public gaze; he will discard it when, and only when, he wills to do so, and this will invariably be when he is entirely alone.[6]

Now, this person neutrality that Stevens took to be the essence of "dignity" we may take to be just the opposite: the one stripped of dignity is not the gentleman in shirtsleeves or the stumbling butler, but the person—gentleman or butler—alienated from the projects, commitments, and relationships that are worthy of self-respect and the respect of others. But even if Stevens is wrong about dignity, he may be right about greatness: deformation of character through person neutrality may be the price great servants, private or public, must pay.

Quinlan and other professionals deny that the person neutrality demanded of them must deform or impoverish character, of course. As a matter of psychological fit, they surely are right: some temperaments will fare better than others. But on the question of _moral deformation_, it may be that some socially useful roles require the development of vices and the suppression of virtues, so that good professionals become bad people, even when—or especially when—they are temperamentally well suited and psychologically well adjusted to the task.[7] Machiavelli thought that this was true of political leaders, and for civil servants, we have the example of the executioner Sanson, who served both old and new regimes with professional detachment. I am not sure that the role-relative, person-neutral demands of adversary roles or of an ethic of obedience in public service systematically put character in moral jeopardy in this way (though we no doubt can find particular horrors). But the more pressing question is the one of greatness: do the requirements of person neutrality and role relativity together make for great (or at least good) professionals and public servants?

The moral claims of Stevens the butler are undermined by his revelations of the ends to which he lent his loyalties and energies. We come to reject the conceptions of social class and citizenship that Stevens's profession generally professed to serve, and we gradually

[6] Ibid., pp. 42–43.
[7] Cf. Bernard Williams, "Persons, Character, and Morality," in his _Moral Luck_ (Cambridge: Cambridge University Press, 1981), pp. 1–19.

learn, with increasing distaste, of the particular purposes advanced by Stevens's particular loyalties: his Lord Darlington's diplomatic collaboration with Nazism. Clearly, the person neutrality he calls "dignity" is normatively entwined with the role-relative permission he thought he had to serve Darlington's nasty ends—as, for instance, when the butler fires the Jewish chambermaids without a murmur of dissent. This generally is the case: some adversary role permissions can succeed only if the reasons ordinary persons have to refuse such nastiness are successfully neutralized. And, as we shall see, some role-relative permissions fail their bid at moral justification precisely because they cannot make the case for person neutrality of a certain sort stick. Of course, Quinlan's ethic of obedience in public service will fare better than Stevens's anachronistic ethic of obedience in private service, for Quinlan's role aims at good ends. But what is a public servant to do when the rules of role miss their mark?

PERSONAL, PROFESSIONAL, AND POLITICAL MORALITY

Quinlan recognizes that a public official faces moral reasons that are external to the role—he calls them "the absolutes of personal morality" or "the basic moral requirements of any human behavior."[8] These moral requirements are understood to be more fundamental than the role, and when conflicts with professional ethics occur, one is to follow the absolutes of personal morality. But such conflicts are said to be extremely rare, and are to be settled by quietly withdrawing one's service through resignation or transfer—and not, one presumes, by refusal, disobedience, disclosure, public protest, the exercise of administrative discretion, or any other means of dissent that intends to effect a change in policy. Why is quiet withdrawal the only permitted course of action in the face of moral conflict, and why is such conflict rare? If we can unpack what Quinlan might mean by "absolute personal morality," the justification and authority of his professional ethic will become more clear.

The morality that challenges professional ethics may be "personal" in three ways, each of which attaches to the person of the moral actor with some particularity. A moral prescription may be personal in that it flows from particular relationships or ties of the actor; or it may be personal in that it flows from particular beliefs about the good life or religion that cannot reasonably be imposed on others in a pluralistic democracy; or it may be personal in the reductive sense in which all

[marginal handwritten note: Civil disobedience?]

---

[8] Quinlan, "Ethics," pp. 543, 538.

beliefs about moral prescriptions are personal, in that the belief is held in the mind of a person. Quinlan seems to hold that the requirement of person neutrality in professional ethics precludes the public servant from acting, in a public capacity, on each of these sorts of personal moral convictions. Let us call these three the *impartial* preclusion, the *liberal* preclusion, and the *skeptical* preclusion of the personal.

Though a moral prescription that conflicts with the role is personal in one or more of these ways, it may nonetheless have "absolute" moral force over the actor, in the sense that, as a matter of integrity or conscience, the actor must treat it as inviolable.[9] Should that be the case, we see why resignation is Quinlan's only solution to a conflict between absolute personal morality and professional ethics. The absolute may not be violated, but the personal has no place in public life. You may not impose on the public your personal, nonpublic promissory obligations (for impartial reasons), your personal, nonpublic morality (for liberal reasons), or your personal view of public morality (for skeptical reasons). You must preserve your integrity, but not on the public's tab, so off you go, gently, your integrity intact, our policies intact.

Is this the correct account of the conflict between the absolutes of personal morality and professional ethics, and its resolution? Something like the impartial preclusion is on the mark—to take ties in one's nonpublic life to be reasons for action in a public role smacks of corruption or bias, a conflict of interest as much as a conflict of value. The liberal preclusion works for moral reasons that cannot pass the test of what Rawls calls public reason, that cannot form part of a political, public morality in the face of reasonable pluralism in a democracy about the good life.[10] But this raises the possibility of another sort of moral conflict, not between personal morality and professional ethics, but between *political* morality and professional ethics.

Some moral values *are* the proper basis for law and public policy, because they *can* be justified to reasonable people holding different philosophical or religious views of the good life. I have in mind here some conception of ideas such as justice, liberty, equality, utility, legitimacy, and democracy. The resulting political morality is perfectly compatible with liberal premises, and so escapes the liberal preclusion. More important, a political morality specifies just those social ends that justify the institution of divided moral labor, and at which the role of public servant, in equilibrium, aims. The role of the public official is intimately connected to a political morality outside the role,

---

[9] This is not the only sense of "absolute."

[10] John Rawls, *Political Liberalism* (New York: Columbia University Press, 1993).

from where it draws its substantive justification, its legitimate authority to command, and its force of obligation.

Political morality clearly cannot be understood as a side constraint that contingently and infrequently conflicts with the exercise of one's professional duties—as one might understand personal morality in some of its senses. So, unless there is widespread agreement between elected politicians and civil servants about the correct specification of public morality, conflicts between a public official's political morality and the demands of the professional role will not be rare, and when they occur, are likely to involve the role's ends and roots. Whatever the demands of *person* neutrality, then, a civil servant cannot be neutral with respect to *political* morality, but must engage in its interpretation and fulfillment. Does this make a permanent civil service with an ethic of loyalty impossible? I do not think so, but it does create more moral conflicts than Quinlan supposes, and it does demand that policy-influencing dissent, rather than quiet withdrawal, be the response to at least some of these conflicts. The preservation of personal integrity and conscience is a poorly matched response when the principles of public, political morality hang in the balance.

What of the skeptical preclusion? Who is to say that one's judgments about political morality are correct? The skeptical preclusion is to be rejected as a basis for commanding loyal obedience for the usual reason that skepticism claims too much. If one is skeptical about the correctness of one's political moral judgments, why is one not equally skeptical about one's judgments about what the role demands? One has no choice but to judge all things from where one stands. Once one has employed methods of reflection and evidence that withstand the tests of publicity and universalizability, so that one reasonably believes that one's inferences would be reasonable for a reasonable person to make, skepticism has been answered as well as earthlings can answer it. If one is to be skeptical here, one is to be skeptical everywhere.

If the case is to be made for obedience to role in the face of conflict with one's judgments about political morality, it is not on grounds of skepticism, but on the grounds of legitimate authority: though the public official does not doubt her judgments, she may judge that she does not have the moral authority to act on such judgments. We need, then, an account of legitimate political authority.

Roles and Legitimate Authority

The role of the public servant, with its person neutrality and role relativity, is substantively justified because the values of political morality, such as justice, liberty, equality, and the common good, generally are advanced when public officials follow the rules of the role. But sometimes the direct, substantive consequences of a public servant's actions may set back these political values, because the role does not prescribe that the public servant aim directly at them, but at the aims of a political superior. When this is the case, the principles of political morality may still be better served by obedience to role, because the breaking of the role in this instance will cause sufficient damage to democratically legitimate and just institutions by undermining the settled expectations and trust of other actors. But this is in part a factual determination that will not always come out in favor of obedience. Not every act of loyalty is necessary to sustain the general institution of loyal service. And some forms of disobedience actually strengthen democratic institutions and increase trust in professional judgment. Widespread enforcement by municipal officials in the American South of voting registration regulations designed to thwart black voters did not strengthen the rule of law, and Martin Luther King's civil disobedience did not weaken it. Political morality's all-things-considered evaluation of a public servant's principled dissent is an open question, even after considering, among all things, possible harm to the institution of public service itself.

When all-things-considered substantive justification for obedience is lacking, a role must appeal to legitimate authority, and show why, nonetheless, the will of the political superior is morally authoritative. The argument, a familiar one, goes something like this: first among the principles of political morality is that a government and its actions must be morally legitimate. Legitimacy requires democratic consent, which elected representatives are presumed to have. Public servants who do not subordinate their own conceptions of the other principles of political morality—for example, conceptions of substantive justice or of equal opportunity—to the will of elected politicians violate the highest of political principles, the principle of legitimacy.

This argument turns on the supposition that elected politicians act with legitimacy by virtue of their connection to the will of the people. Is this connection a formal property of holding elected office, so that the actions of the elected are by definition legitimate, and an elected official cannot act without legitimacy even if he tries? Or is legitimacy a property with content, so that representatives act with more or less legitimacy, depending on the characteristics of their actions? Quinlan clearly understands legitimacy formally: the public is "personified" by ministers, so that informing the minister is informing the public;[11] and, although civil servants are accountable to the public, this accoun-

[11] Quinlan, "Ethics," p. 541.

tability is wholly satisfied by being accountable to the elected government.[12] But why should democratic legitimacy be understood formally? Elected officials sometimes act in ways that undermine the capacity of the public to understand and evaluate their actions, in ways that violate any contentful account of democratic consent. How can someone who works against the idea of a knowledgeable and competent citizenry be said to personify citizens? If politicians who do not in fact represent the will or the interests of citizens in a way that makes for a substantively valuable democracy are said to be acting with formal authority, why would such formal authority have moral weight?

Alternatively, by the logic of formal authority, why do senior civil servants, who have formal status and formal powers in the hierarchy, not also have formal authority to do what they will to dissent, and exercise discretion on behalf of their own views, so long as they break no law? If the formal authority of an elected official carries moral weight, no matter how badly the will or interests of the electorate are served, then the formal authority of the senior civil servant has moral weight, no matter how badly the will or interests of the elected official are served.

There is, then, at least one circumstance under which appeal to the legitimate authority of the elected politician is not sufficient to demand of a public servant obedience to role, and that is when the elected politician acts in ways that undermine the institutions of democratic legitimacy, and so acts without legitimate authority. But what about the skeptical premise? Who are you to say when an elected representative acts without legitimacy? Surely, one must treat one's own judgments, including one's own judgments about legitimacy, with some humility. But in the end, one cannot help but make judgments by one's own lights. Moreover, one cannot defer to the judgment of a formal authority when the moral legitimacy of such an authority is precisely what is in question.

ROLES AND POLITICAL OBLIGATION

What of the cases where the requirements of the role are not illegitimate, but violate other principles of political morality? Because properly constituted democratic majorities can properly authorize their elected representatives to do some pretty horrible things, public servants will on occasion confront possibly legitimate but substantially

---

[12] Ibid., p. 542.

unjust tasks. Northern antislavery judges such as Lemuel Shaw were called upon to enforce the Fugitive Slave Act.[13] Melville's Captain Verre was called upon to dispense summary justice to Billy Budd. When the requirements of the role are legitimate but unjust, are public servants obligated to comply?

To answer, we will need to say more about the nature of a public servant's moral obligation to act in role, for, as has been noted often, the legitimacy of a rule does not, by itself, create a moral obligation to comply with it.[14] For example, to find that a government may legitimately enact and enforce a law does not yet show that those subjected to the law are morally obligated to obey. There is a long history, of course, of trying to establish the foundations of the obligation of citizens to obey the law, and an equally long history of trying to establish the conditions of justified civil disobedience from the law. I cannot do justice to either topic here, and I will not try, except to point out some parallels to our question about the public servant's role, and to Quinlan's answer.

Quinlan suggests that public officials are obligated to perform in role by virtue of having accepted the benefits of high position and influence. This invokes the arguments from fair play offered by Hart and Rawls, which say, roughly, that if one voluntarily benefits from a scheme of social cooperation made possible by the adherence of others to rules, one is obligated out of fairness to obey those rules, and not to free-ride on the cooperative efforts of others.[15] Rawls no longer believes that the fair-play principle underwrites a general obligation for citizens to obey the law, because not all citizens benefit from the scheme of social cooperation and not all have freely ac-

---

[13] See Robert M. Cover, *Justice Accused: Antislavery and the Judicial Process* (New Haven: Yale University Press, 1975). I present the problem from the perspective of those judges, who mistakenly believed our slave constitution to be legitimate, though unjust. An account of political legitimacy that looks not only to the observance of formal procedure but to the legitimacy of reasons for government action would find the enforcement of slavery illegitimate as well as unjust. Such an account is embraced in Chapter 10, "Democratic Legitimacy and Official Discretion."

[14] See M.B.E. Smith, "Is There a Prima Facie Obligation to Obey the Law?" *Yale Law Journal* 82 (1973): 950–76; Jeremy Waldron, "Rights and Minorities: Rousseau Revisited," in *NOMOS XXXII: Majorities and Minorities*, ed. John W. Chapman and Alan Wertheimer (New York: New York University Press, 1990); and Frederick Schauer, *Playing by the Rules* (Oxford: Oxford University Press, 1991), pp. 128–34.

[15] H.L.A. Hart, "Are There Any Natural Rights?" *Philosophical Review* 64 (1955): 175–91; John Rawls, "Legal Obligation and the Duty of Fair Play," in *Law and Philosophy*, ed. Sidney Hook (New York: New York University Press, 1964); see also Chapter 6, "Rules of the Game."

cepted benefits. But, he says, the fair-play principle *does* obligate those who have assumed public office and its advantages.[16]

Now, the rules of the public servant's role normally are not *legal* requirements, and typically dissenting actions are available that do not involve lawbreaking. Still, should not the institution of divided roles in public service be considered a cooperative scheme, the rules of which public officials are morally obligated to obey under the fair-play principle? Indeed, but fair play here requires only that a public official not free-ride on the cooperation of others through self-serving violations of the rules of the game—an attorney general who violates immigration laws by hiring illegal aliens, for example. The fair-play argument fails to touch a conscientiously dissenting official, as opposed to a free rider. The conscientious official is not being unfairly advantaged by her role breaking—more likely, she will suffer for her dissent—nor does she harm the scheme of social cooperation. Just the opposite: by appealing to the public's sense of justice, and holding up for scrutiny the failure of the formal division of political and moral labor to attend properly to justice, she strengthens just and legitimate institutions of government. If we are to reach for analogies from political obligation, we should also reach for analogies from civil disobedience, which, on most accounts, is justified when it appeals publicly and persuasively to the majority's sense of justice and does not otherwise undermine just institutions. Civil disobedience has had a long and noble career. Would that official dissent—employed for similar purposes and justified on similar terms—had a similar career. The northern abolitionist judges who enforced the Fugitive Slave Act either gravely misunderstood their roles or gravely misunderstood the moral limitations of an unjust role requirement.

What, then, remains of Quinlan's role? Much. A role that generally aims at important social goods and political values, as does the British civil service, generally should be obeyed. The division of moral labor retains considerable bite in that, when their good counsel is ignored, public servants are to put loyalty above wisdom, and obedience before efficiency. Democratic majorities have the right to do foolish things to themselves, and the civil servant's job is to help in the exercise of that right. But democratic majorities may not inflict injustice on minorities, and politicians may not act without democratic legitimacy. Public servants who lend their moral energies to unjust ends and to the degradation of democratic deliberation serve neither the public

---

[16] John Rawls, *A Theory of Justice* (Cambridge, Mass.: Harvard University Press, 1971), secs. 18, 19, 51–59.

nor political principle, but an empty, destructive formalism—the service of a Stevens, not a Quinlan.

———

The task ahead is framed by Montaigne, who often vexes by being at once so right and so wrong. Here is the entire passage excerpted in this chapter's epigraph:

Most of our occupations are low comedy. *The whole world plays a role* [Petronius]. We must play our role duly, but as the role of a borrowed character.[17] Of the mask and appearance we must not make a real essence, nor of what is foreign what is our very own. We cannot distinguish the skin from the shirt. It is enough to make up our face, without making up our heart. I see some who transform and transubstantiate themselves into as many new shapes and new beings as they undertake jobs, who are prelates to their very liver and intestines, and drag their position with them even to the privy. I cannot teach them to distinguish the tips of the hat that are for them from those that are for their office, or their retinue, or their mule. *They give themselves up so much to their fortune that they even unlearn their natures* [Quintius Curtius]. They swell and inflate their soul and their natural speech to the height of the magisterial seat.

The mayor and Montaigne have always been two, with a very clear separation.[18] For all of being a lawyer or a financier, we must not ignore the deceitfulness there is in such callings.[19] An honest man is not accountable for the vice or stupidity of his trade, and should not therefore refuse to practice it: it is the custom of his country, and there is profit in it. We must live in the world and make the most of it such as we find it. But the judgment of an emperor should be above his imperial power, and see and consider it as an extraneous accident; and he should know how to find pleasure in himself apart, and to reveal himself like any Jack or Peter, at least to himself.[20]

———

[17] "'*Mundus universus exercet histrionium.*' Il faut jouer deuement nostre rolle, mais comme rolle d'un personnage emprunté." *Les Essais de Michel de Montaigne*, ed. Pierre Villey (1924; Paris: Quadrige/Presses Universitaires de France, 1992), p. 1011. Frame's translation, which I have taken the liberty to alter, has "part" for both *histrionium* and *rolle*.

[18] Montaigne was for a time mayor of Bordeaux.

[19] Frame translates *fourbe* as "knavery," which I have taken the liberty to change to "deceitfulness."

[20] Montaigne, "Of Husbanding Your Will," in *The Complete Essays of Montaigne*, 3:10 (1588), ed. Donald M. Frame (Stanford, Calif.: Stanford University Press, 1958), p. 773, except as indicated in notes 17 and 19.

We should accept Montaigne's precociously enlightened idea that the person, essential, and the role, accidental, are separate, and that this separation requires that a person's judgment not be subordinated to the role occupied. But we must reject Montaigne's faulty practical inference. Montaigne thinks that the moral upshot of judgment's independence is that the person is not accountable for the vice and stupidity of one's role. Quite the opposite: not only is the deceitful lawyer or financier also a dishonest man, but he has the critical distance from whence to judge this. The detachable person is more, not less accountable for actions taken within role, for the possibility of independent judgment blocks not only justification, but excuse. Montaigne is not alone in making this moral mistake, of course. We recognize the move from critical detachment to moral nonaccountability in today's lawyers and financiers, who argue that responsibility for an action taken within a role "falls on the role," not on the person.[21] I believe that the enduring appeal of this argument rests on a bit of sophisticated sophistry that we need to unroll. For it is, after all, with men and not with parchment that we quarrel.

[21] The phrase is from David Luban, *Lawyers and Justice* (Princeton, N.J.: Princeton University Press, 1988), p. 117, who argues against this shifting of responsibility.

just following orders

Chapter Five

ARE LAWYERS LIARS?

THE ARGUMENT OF REDESCRIPTION

The bladders print many unkind stories about Asleep when he is finally lumbered in 1931 and sent to college, and some of them call him a torpedo, and a trigger, and I do not know what all else, and these names hurt Asleep's feelings, especially as they seem to make him out no better than a ruffian. In fact, one bladder speaks of him as a killer, and this title causes Asleep to wince more than anything else.

He is in college at Dannemora from 1931 until the late spring of 1936, and although I hear he is back, this is the first time I see him in person, and I hasten to overtake him to express my sympathy with him on his treatment by the night manager of Mindy's and also by the jockey of the yellow short, and to deplore the lack of respect now shown on Broadway for a character such as Asleep. . . .

"Well, Sleeps," I say, "to tell you the truth, I am somewhat amazed that you do not out with that thing and resent these familiarities."

But Asleep seems somewhat horrified at this suggestion, and he sets his glass down, and gazes at me a while in pained silence, and finally he says:

"Why," he says, "I hope and trust that you do not think I will ever use that thing except for professional purposes, and when I am paid for same. Why," he says, "in all my practice, covering a matter of nearly ten years, I never lift a finger against as much as a flea unless it is a business proposition, and I am not going to begin now."

Well, I remember that this is indeed Asleep's reputation in the old days . . . and of course I am bound to respect his ethics, although I am sorry he cannot see his way clear to making an exception in the case of the night manager of Mindy's.

Damon Runyon, "Situation Wanted"

ICONCLUDED the chapter on the executioner of Paris with the cheap and some would say libelous suggestion that lawyers might accurately be described as serial liars, because they repeatedly try to induce others to believe in the truth of propositions or in the validity of arguments that they believe to be false. Good lawyers respond with some indignation that, in calling zealous advocacy "lying," I have misdescribed the practice of law.[1] But it is the practice of lawyering that engages in misdescription.

THE STRATEGY OF REDESCRIPTION

Professional roles are said to change the morally relevant description of actions. When our Sanson argues that only an executioner can perform an execution, he is claiming that the relevant description and so the moral meaning of his actions are altered by features of the institution in which he operates and by the institutional reasons on which he acts. Across the English Channel and several decades earlier, Lord Anglesea's lawyer makes the same claim. David Luban tells the twisted story of *Annesley v. Anglesea*: the earl of Anglesea has stolen the estate of his nephew, James Annesley, and contrives to prosecute the young man for murder after an accidental shooting. Anglesea tells his lawyer, James Giffard, that he would give £10,000 to have Annesley hanged. The murder prosecution fails, Annesley countersues to regain his inheritance, and Giffard is put on the stand. Asked, "Did you not apprehend it to be a bad purpose to lay out money to compass the death of another man?" Giffard replies, "I make a distinction between carrying on a prosecution and compassing the death of a man."[2] James Giffard, like Charles-Henri Sanson, seeks to preempt negative moral evaluation of what he does by redescribing his actions in institutional terms. Ever since Adam gained dominion over the animals by naming them, redescriptive strategies have been potent. Do they work here?

Telling the Right Story

Any philosophical account of agency has to grapple with the essential open-endedness of describing action.[3] Consider several descriptions of the same act: he is lowering his chin two inches while maintaining

---

[1] I am grateful to Robert Bennett, The Honorable Sandra Lynch, Bernard Nussbaum, and Professor David Wilkins for their spirited engagement with some of these arguments in a forum sponsored by the Harvard Law Review and the Harvard Program on the Legal Profession.

[2] *Annesley v. Anglesea*, 17 How. St. Trials 1139, 1248–49 (1743), cited in David Luban, *Lawyers and Justice* (Princeton, N.J.: Princeton University Press, 1988), p. 5.

[3] The indeterminacy of description has been widely noted in several contexts. For example, Joel Feinberg, *Doing and Deserving* (Princeton, N.J.: Princeton University Press, 1970), p. 134, notes the "accordion effect" in describing actions and causes; David Lyons, *Forms and Limits of Utilitarianism* (Oxford: Oxford University Press, 1965), ch. 2, discusses the problem it raises for utilitarian generalization.

a steady gaze; he is nodding; he is telling the bandleader to play the "Marseillaise"; he is helping the Resistance; he is wooing Ilsa; he is filming *Casablanca*; he is pursuing a career as an actor. All are correct answers to the question, What is Humphrey Bogart doing? Not all, however, are equally apt answers. Which is the most apt description depends on the point or purpose of asking the question. The best answer will vary, depending on whether the asker has stumbled onto the movie set, or is a student of acting technique, or is a researcher of nonverbal communication, or is Bogart's biographer, or is a film viewer who wants to know the story, or is a philosopher looking for fictional examples of ambiguity in moral character. Our purpose in describing the actions of the executioner Sanson or the lawyer Giffard is to render professional and moral evaluations of their actions, and so to render professional and moral prescriptions for future executioners and lawyers. So some of the many descriptions of what they do are more apt than others.

Alasdair MacIntyre, who has noted well the indeterminacy of description, writes that "We cannot . . . characterise behavior independently of intentions, and we cannot characterise intentions independently of the settings which make those intentions intelligible both to agents and to others."[4] He gives the example of a man who can be described as gardening, exercising, or pleasing his wife. The best description, according to MacIntyre, turns on what the man's primary intention is, and this is revealed by asking a series of counterfactual questions. Would he still perform this activity if it did not please his wife? If it did not give him exercise? On this view, the most apt description of what one does is what one thinks one is doing.

Intention, however, is not necessarily the clue to the best description of all actions. To capture exactly the expression he wanted, the director of *Casablanca* had Bogart meaninglessly nod at blank space, without telling him why—and the result is one of the more meaning-laden gestures in film. For the most interesting purposes, however, "nodding" is not the best description of what Bogart is doing in that sequence. Serendipity, negligence, and *lack* of intention are often essential to the proper description of an action, though such a description is unavailable to the actor at the time. The most relevant description of an event on the road to Thebes is that Oedipus killed his father, though he intended no such thing, and could not have described his action that way at the time. That James Giffard intended a prosecution, not the death of a man, and that Sanson intended to

---

[4] Alasdair MacIntyre, *After Virtue* (Notre Dame, Ind.: University of Notre Dame Press, 1981), p. 192.

perform executions, not massacres, does not rule out murder as the morally relevant description of what they do. For an event to be an action, the agent must intend to do *some* action, under some description, but need not intend to bring about the event described.[5]

On a closer read, intentionality is not necessary to MacIntyre's account. Rather, the "intelligibility" of an action is for him the central notion for its proper description. Since he rightly notes that actions intelligible to an observer need not be so to the actor, intelligible descriptions of action are available to the observer that the actor does not intend. For MacIntyre, the notion of "setting" appears to be more important than intention in rendering an action intelligible:

> I use the word "setting" here as a relatively inclusive term. A social setting may be an institution, it may be what I have called a practice, or it may be a milieu of some other human kind. But it is central to the notion of a setting as I am going to understand it that a setting has a history, a history within which the histories of individual agents not only are, but have to be, situated, just because without the setting and its changes through time the history of the individual agent and his changes through time will be unintelligible.[6]

This emphasis on the importance of setting in rendering an intelligible account of an action, and so in determining its proper description, seems right. But MacIntyre has a bigger point to make here, not about description, but about evaluation: the *good* of an actor is realized by acting in ways that fit into a unified narrative of the actor's life, a narrative that is, by implication, intelligible to *him*. Therefore, an actor *ought to* act in consonance with the demands of the social roles he inhabits, for a life lived in role is a life that tells an intelligible story.

> A central thesis then begins to emerge: man is in his actions and practice, as well as in his fictions, essentially a story-telling animal. He is not essentially, but becomes through his history, a teller of stories that aspire to truth. But the key question for men is not about their own authorship; I can only answer the question "What am I to do?" if I can answer the prior question "Of what story or stories do I find myself a part?" We enter human society, that is, with one or more imputed characters—roles into which we have been drafted—and we have to learn what they are in order to be able to understand how others respond to us and how our responses to them are apt to be construed.[7]

---

[5] Here I follow Donald Davidson, *Essays on Actions and Events* (Oxford: Oxford University Press, 1980), pp. 46–47.

[6] MacIntyre, *After Virtue*, p. 192.

[7] Ibid., p. 201.

Note the crucial introduction of the notion of a truth-aspiring narrative, opening the possibility that some narratives are false. For MacIntyre to be right about the moral force of received social roles, two steps must be surefooted: the set of intelligible descriptions of an action must be tightly, if not uniquely, limited by institutional and historical settings; and these intelligible narratives must "aspire to the truth."

If, instead, the necessity of intelligibility is not a tight constraint, so that there are a multiplicity of intelligible and plausibly apt descriptions, and if among the narratives intelligible to the actor are *false* narratives (and an account of their falsity is intelligible to *us*), then what I have called the redescriptive strategy will not succeed in preempting a negative evaluation of acting in role. We can agree with MacIntyre that one's good is closely tied up with living out an intelligible narrative that aspires to the truth, but leave open whether or not role actors who can tell an intelligible story of their lives are likely to tell true stories. Not every life that claims to be lived well *is* lived well. And perhaps there are hopeless souls for whom *only* falsely described roles are intelligible—King Lear, Don Quixote, Ivan Illich— though I doubt that such roles can be stable over time.

Using MacIntyre's terms, Sanson and Giffard claim that their actions are intelligible only when seen in their institutional settings. Sanson takes his place in an evolving social practice of criminalizing behaviors, trying and convicting criminals, and carrying out judicially imposed punishments. The scene at the scaffold, with its ceremonial choreography, its military guard, its cheering audience, makes sense only if understood to be a legitimate act of state carried out by its appointed agent. The scene is part of the narrative of the social practice of punishment and the role of state executioner within the practice, not the narrative of a serial killer. Lord Anglesea's lawyer is to be understood as taking his place in the emerging institution of the English adversary system of justice. The majestic authority projected by London's Old Bailey, the ritualized and regulated proceedings in its courtrooms, the references to learned traditions and precedents, all point to the aptness of the lawyer's description: he *is* carrying out a prosecution, and not compassing the death of a man.

But even granting, as we should, the importance of setting to intelligible description, these are not uniquely intelligible stories, and plausible, historically situated stories can be told that question not only their uniqueness but also their veracity. About Sanson, we tell of the need of an ignorant and superstitious population for a protective but punitive father-king, who periodically deflects the people's infantile aggression and rage toward some hapless sacrifice on the scaffold.

Come the revolution, the primitive bloodlust gets dressed up in a new ideology. About Giffard, we tell of the interests of both the emerging professionalized bar and its wealthy and powerful clients in denying to themselves and to each other any moral responsibility for the consequences of their division of labor, and their extraordinary success at such denial. There is no shortage of intelligible stories.

The redescriptive strategy attempts to characterize some descriptions as *mistakes*. Some descriptions indeed are mistakes, clearly and simply. When a determined gang, some bearing sharp objects, some with drugs on their persons, pounce on someone and pound him, one might think a mugging is taking place. But to describe a medical team administering cardiopulmonary resuscitation as muggers is to *misdescribe* the situation. When put in the proper setting, the motions that superficially resemble a mugging are seen to be something else entirely. CPR is not pretty, and the pain and indignity it can inflict may tell against its use in many cases, but it is never, except in rhetorical excess, a mugging. It therefore would be a conceptual contortion to proceed from such a description and then ponder whether or not CPR is an instance of *justified* mugging. But no simple mistake is made in describing Giffard as "compassing the death of a man," and Sanson as a cold-blooded killer. Rather, seeking another's death and killing in cold blood are not *complete* descriptions of what they do. Perhaps causing death by prosecuting or by executing are justified instances of causing death. But that is the conclusion of an argument about how to properly *evaluate* the richly described social practices of prosecution and execution. The redescriptive strategy seeks to preempt such an evaluation and bypass the hard work of moral argument by suppressing part of the true story. But this is itself a misdescription.

Constituted Description

Consider now a refinement of the redescriptive strategy that our Sanson invokes, which I will call *constituted description*. Heretofore, the claim has been that, among a set of possible descriptions for an action, the setting of a practice or role gives the most apt description, so that, if one engages in a social practice, then one's actions are to be described in terms defined by the practice. If Sanson is an executioner, then what he does is perform executions. The moral force of such a move is supposed to come in eliminating a description—serial murder—that invokes a negative prescription and evaluation.

The argument of constituted description begins by making the converse claim: if one's actions are aptly described using terms defined by a practice, then one must be engaged in that practice, because some descriptions are logically possible only within a practice or role. To use Clifford Geertz's examples, one cannot castle in dominoes, and one cannot mutiny in a bank.[8] Therefore, if one castles, one must be playing chess; if Sanson performs executions, he must be an executioner. The move gets started in those cases where a practice-defined description seems apt: whatever else Sanson is doing, he is performing an execution. The move gains moral force in subsequent steps that try to show that to engage in a practice is to follow its rules, so that one who does not follow the rules of a practice is not engaged in the practice, and so cannot logically be described as performing a practice-defined action. Therefore, if an action is aptly described using terms defined by a social practice, the only way to evaluate that particular action is with respect to the rules internal to the practice.

In an early article, "Two Concepts of Rules," John Rawls offers an account of descriptions that do not exist prior to the practices of which they are a part.[9] His larger purpose is to show how there can be a reason for acting in accordance with a rule that is logically prior to the reasons for taking particular actions. Right now, our concern is not with his conclusions but with his characterization of "rules of practices," which he contrasts with "summary rules," such as generalizations from similar particular cases or rules of thumb. His account is worth citing at some length:

> In contrast with the summary view, the rules of practices are logically prior to particular cases. This is so because there cannot be a particular case of an action falling under a rule of a practice unless there is the practice. This can be made clearer as follows: in a practice there are rules setting up offices, specifying certain forms of action appropriate to various offices, establishing penalties for the breach of rules, and so on. We may think of the rules of a practice as defining offices, moves, and offenses. Now what is meant by saying that the practice is logically prior to particular cases is this: given any rule which specifies a form of action (a move), a particular action which would be taken as falling under this rule given that there is the practice would not be *described as* that sort of action unless there was the practice. In the case of actions specified by practices it is logically impossible to perform them outside of the stage-setting provided by those practices, for unless there is the practice, and unless the requisite properties are fulfilled, whatever one does, whatever movements one makes, will fail to

---

[8] Clifford Geertz, *Local Knowledge: Further Essays in Interpretive Anthropology* (New York: Basic Books, 1983), p. 25.

[9] John Rawls, "Two Concepts of Rules," *Philosophical Review* 64 (1955): 3–22.

count as a form of action which the practice specifies. What one does will be described in some *other* way.[10]

Note the implication: if an action *does* count as a form of action which the practice specifies, then the practice exists and the action fulfills its requisite properties—that is to say, it follows the rules of the practice. Rawls's starting point differs from MacIntyre's. Rawls begins with a settled description of what the actor is doing, and proceeds from there to an inference about what practice the actor must be engaged in. Rawls continues:

> One may illustrate this point from the game of baseball. Many of the actions one performs in a game of baseball one can do by oneself or with others whether there is the game or not. For example, one can throw a ball, run, or swing a peculiarly shaped piece of wood. But one cannot steal a base, or strike out, or draw a walk, or make an error, or balk; although one can do certain things which appear to resemble these actions such as sliding into a bag, missing a grounder and so on. Striking out, stealing a base, balking, etc., are all actions which can only happen in a game. No matter what a person did, what he did would not be described as stealing a base or striking out or drawing a walk unless he could also be described as playing baseball, and for him to be doing this presupposes the rule-like practice which constitutes the game. The practice is logically prior to particular cases: unless there is the practice the terms referring to actions specified by it lack a sense.[11]

The tipoff to where Rawls is heading here is in the next-to-last sentence. One cannot draw a walk without playing baseball, and one cannot play baseball without following its rules. Someone who asks for a fourth strike, says Rawls, is charitably taken to be making a joke. If seriously proposed, midgame, on the grounds that the game would be improved, the questioner does not understand what it means to play baseball. If we follow this line, Anglesea's lawyer cannot prosecute without practicing law, and one cannot practice law without following the rules of the practice, which, let us say, include zealous advocacy without regard to the moral character or purposes of one's client. The lawyer who fails to advance the legal rights of clients who

[10] Ibid., p. 25 (Rawls's emphasis).
[11] Ibid., p. 25 (footnote omitted). I believe that this early account of rules of practices is important to understanding Rawls's later stance toward the general and the particular in political philosophy as shown in his development of the concepts of principles, the basic structure of society as subject, constitutionalism, and the rule of law.

have evil purposes does not understand what it means to practice law.

Rawls is no apologist for bad practices. He stresses that one can logically and, presumably, ought morally to engage in the activity of evaluating games and social practices, and to reform the ones in need of reform: "One can be as radical as one likes," he says clearly.[12] But the target of one's criticism can be only the practice and its rules, not particular practice-defined actions that comply with the rules of practice: "In the case of actions specified by practices the objects of one's radicalism must be the social practices and people's acceptance of them."[13] Evaluation of particular practice-defined actions that reaches outside of the rules of practice for justification is confused:

> To explain or defend one's own action, as a particular action, one fits it into the practice which defines it. If this is not accepted it's a sign that a different question is being raised as to whether one is justified in accepting the practice, or in tolerating it. When the challenge is to the practice, citing the rules (saying what the practice is) is naturally to no avail. But when the challenge is to the particular action defined by the practice, there is nothing one can do but refer to the rules.[14]

When one *does* engage in the evaluation of the entire practice, one no longer acts as a practitioner engaged in the practice, but as the occupant of a different office:

> If one holds an office defined by a practice then questions regarding one's actions in this office are settled by reference to the rules which define the practice. If one seeks to question these rules, then one's office undergoes a fundamental change: one then assumes the office of one empowered to change and criticize the rules, or the office of a reformer, and so on.[15]

The moral implications of Rawls's account of the logical status of rules of practice appear to be quite sweeping. Particular actions whose descriptions are defined by a social practice can be evaluated only by standards given by the rules of the practice itself—no moral evaluation of particular actions from outside of the practice is possible. Entire practices can be judged good or bad, and arguments can be offered in favor of their reform or against participating in an unreformed practice. But practitioners cannot engage in such evaluation and criticism or act by themselves on the ensuing judgments *as prac-*

---

[12] Ibid., p. 32.
[13] Ibid.
[14] Ibid., p. 27.
[15] Ibid., p. 28.

titioners. Someone who violates the defining rules of a practice no longer engages in the practice and performs an act that can no longer be described in terms of the practice (except as a practice-defined offense). A baseball batter in a particular turn at bat who demands a fourth strike on the grounds that it would be best on the whole no longer plays baseball, for until the rules of baseball are changed, fourth strikes do not exist. A lawyer advocating on behalf of a client who wishes to avoid paying an acknowledged debt cannot refuse to plead the statute of limitations and still call herself an advocate, for unless the defining rules of lawyering are changed, a lawyer who is not a diligent advocate for the legal interests of the client is not engaged in the proper practice of advocacy. An action that is defined by a practice can be evaluated only by standards internal to the practice. Moral criticism of the particular action from outside the practice is logically precluded.

It would be useful, before assessing Rawls's view and its implications, to consider a roughly compatible account introduced by John Searle in *Speech Acts* and developed at length recently in *The Construction of Social Reality.*[16] Searle distinguishes *regulative rules* from *constitutive rules.* "Regulative rules regulate a pre-existing activity, an activity whose existence is logically independent of the rules. Constitutive rules constitute (and also regulate) an activity the existence of which is logically dependent on the rules."[17] Searle explains:

> Where the rule is purely regulative, behavior which is in accordance with the rule could be given the same description or specification (the same answer to the question "What did he do?") whether or not the rule existed, provided the description or specification makes no explicit reference to the rule. But where the rule (or system of rules) is constitutive, behavior which is in accordance with the rule can receive specifications or descriptions which it could not receive if the rule or rules did not exist.[18]

Descriptions of actions that are defined by constitutive rules he calls *institutional facts,* in contrast with *brute facts,* which are descriptions of

---

[16] John R. Searle, *Speech Acts: An Essay in the Philosophy of Language* (Cambridge: Cambridge University Press, 1969), esp. pp. 33–42, 50–53, and *The Construction of Social Reality* (New York: Free Press, 1995).

[17] Searle, *Speech Acts,* p. 34. Searle is quite clear that his constitutive rules typically regulate as well; he means to distinguish those rules that *also* constitute from those that *only* regulate. A number of readers appear to have misread him: see G. J. Warnock, *The Object of Morality* (London: Methuen, 1971), pp. 37–38; Joseph Raz, *Practical Reason and Norms* (1975; Princeton, N.J.: Princeton University Press, 1990), pp. 108–11; and Frederick Schauer, *Playing by the Rules* (Oxford: Oxford University Press, 1991), pp. 6–7.

[18] Searle, *Speech Acts,* p. 35.

physical or mental states that do not depend on any social conventions or practices:

> Any newspaper records facts of the following sorts: Mr Smith married Miss Jones; the Dodgers beat the Giants three to two in eleven innings; Green was convicted of larceny; and Congress passed the Appropriations Bill. . . . There is no simple set of statements about physical or psychological properties of states of affairs to which the statements of facts such as these are reducible. A marriage ceremony, a baseball game, a trial, and a legislative action involve a variety of physical movements, states, and raw feels, but a specification of one of these events only in such terms is not so far a specification of it as a marriage ceremony, baseball game, a trial, or a legislative action. . . . Such facts as are recorded in my above group of statements I propose to call *institutional facts*. They are indeed facts; but their existence, unlike the existence of brute facts, presupposes the existence of certain human institutions.[19]

Institutional facts, says Searle, are created by constitutive rules that characteristically take the form "X counts as Y in context C." Constitutive rules assign to preinstitutional objects or behaviors institutional meanings. For example, there is a constitutive rule in the United States that certain scraps of paper with markings (X) count as (stand for, represent, symbolize) money (Y) if they are produced by the Bureau of Engraving and Printing (C).

Searle's well-known larger project, following J. L. Austin, is to show that "speaking a language is a matter of performing speech acts according to systems of constitutive rules."[20] I don't believe that we need to take a stand here about his larger claims about all of language. We need only attend to the implied claim about institutional practices, leaving open whether language is best understood as such a practice. To engage in an institutional practice is a matter of performing actions (some of which are speech acts) whose descriptions are constituted by systems of rules.

Searle's account of constitutive rules and institutional facts, if right, clarifies how Rawls's rules of practice might operate: how the reasons to follow a rule of practice can be logically prior to the reasons for applying the rule in particular cases, and why the reasons to apply a rule of practice to a particular case cannot invoke considerations that are not already specified within the practice. For the rules that make

---

[19] Ibid., pp. 51–52. Searle does not deny that a brute fact description of what happens in a ceremony, game, or trial can be given; he denies that such descriptions would be *adequate*. Raz's criticism of Searle here misses this.

[20] Searle, *Speech Acts*, p. 38; J. L. Austin, *How to Do Things with Words*, ed. J. O. Urmson and Marina Sbisà (1962; Cambridge, Mass.: Harvard University Press, 1975).

up a practice either are or rest upon constitutive rules of the form "X counts as a Y in context C," that is, rules that define and specify descriptions of states of affairs and actions. In defining states and actions, practices create the possibility of certain institutional facts, and they set out the conditions under which such institutional facts are realized: the fact that a couple has been married, a crime committed, a promise made, a touchdown scored.

"In our toughest metaphysical moods," says Searle, "we want to ask 'But is an X really a Y?' For example, are these bits of paper really *money*? Is this piece of land really somebody's *private property*? Is making certain noises in a ceremony really *getting married*?"[21] His answer is yes: as long as the rules that constitute them continue to exist, institutional facts are as real as brute facts—and Searle is a realist about brute facts. A constitutive rule exists as long as there is collective acceptance of it—collective thinking makes it so. "The secret of understanding the continued existence of institutional facts is simply that the individuals directly involved and a sufficient number of members of the relevant community must continue to recognize and accept the existence of such facts."[22] Searle is sketchy about the conditions for collective acceptance, though we can infer from his examples that what matters is the fact of collective acceptance, not how or why collective acceptance has come about. So, acceptance that rests on false belief is still acceptance: "The mechanism so described does not require that the participants be aware of what is actually happening. They may think that the man is King only because he is divinely anointed, but as long as they continue to recognize his authority, he has the status-function of king, regardless of whatever false beliefs they may hold."[23] Even acceptance brought about by willful manipulation or deception generates institutional facts. Searle offers a naughty example:

> One way to create institutional facts in situations where the institution does not exist is simply to act as if it did exist. The classic case is the Declaration of Independence in 1776. There was no institutional structure of the form X counts as Y in C, whereby a group of the King's subjects in a British Crown Colony could create their independence by a performative speech act. But the Founding Fathers acted as if their meeting in Philadelphia was a context C such that by performing a certain declarative speech act X they created an institutional fact of independence Y.[24]

[21] Searle, *Construction*, p. 45.
[22] Ibid., p. 117.
[23] Ibid., p. 96.
[24] Ibid., p. 118.

Armed with Rawls's account of rules of practice and Searle's account of institutional facts (though without attributing what follows to either Rawls or to Searle), we are prepared to restate and assess the argument of constituted description. The restatement:

1. If a description of an action is constituted by the rules of a practice, then that action, *so described*, can be evaluated only with respect to the criteria specified by that practice.

2. Whether an action is so described is itself a fact about the collective acceptance of constitutive rules of practices and the meanings they create.

3. The descriptions of actions performed by professionals in professional roles are constituted by such rules of practice so established by collective acceptance.

4. Therefore, actions performed by professionals in professional roles can be evaluated only with respect to criteria internal to the professional practice.

If this argument succeeds, then our Sanson succeeds in defeating external criticism of any particular act of killing. For, whatever else is said about him, it is an institutional fact of the matter that he is an executioner engaged in the practice of execution. This is so because there is collective agreement that certain brute facts X (slicing off heads) in context C (by a government appointee on the instructions of a tribunal) count as institutional fact Y (execution). This is not to say that there is collective *approval* of the practice. Of course there is not, and we can sensibly ask if the practice of execution is, all things considered, morally justified. But there is collective acceptance that execution exists as a social practice within which the fellow Sanson on the scaffold is the executioner and what he does is perform executions.

Therefore, goes the argument, it makes no sense to ask if a particular guillotining is, all things considered, morally justified, only whether a particular guillotining complies with the criteria of the practice of execution. Even if one thinks baseball is a boring waste of time, one shares in the collective understanding that there is a game of baseball in progress, that the fellow holding the stick is the batter, that balls hit over the fence are home runs, and that, in baseball, batters are supposed to score runs. It makes no sense to ask if a batter is, all things considered, justified in hitting a home run, only if he is justified in playing baseball. On the argument of constituted description, if we use institutional facts to describe actions, we can use only institutional criteria to evaluate those actions.

Similarly, the actions of other professionals that are described in institutional terms can be evaluated only by the criteria internal to the practices that create the terms. As executioners are to the death penalty, so are political consultants to smear campaigns, investment bankers to hostile takeovers, lawyers to nuisance suits, and generals to collateral damage. We can ask if the institutions and rules of electoral politics, capital markets, civil litigation, and warfare are justified, and can evaluate particular actions defined by those institutions by the criteria internal to the institutions. But we cannot evaluate particular actions created by practices by independent criteria. The central question of role morality in the professions is this: *How can an action that otherwise would be morally impermissible become permissible when performed within a role?* The argument of constituted description replies: *There is no "otherwise."* The action, so described, does not exist apart from the practice, and so cannot be performed outside of the role.

THE FAILURE OF REDESCRIPTION

The argument of constituted description fails. Some readers may think that its failure is so obvious that it does not deserve the attention it has already received here, much less a detailed refutation. But disposing of the argument will be a bit trickier than one might at first suppose, because the easy ways to defeat it require abandoning features of practices and roles that are worth retaining.

Judging the Practice

Because the possibility of external judgment of the entire practice is not denied by the argument of constituted description, the simplest reply is to show that, even if its conclusion is granted, the argument has no moral force and makes no moral difference. Rawls, as we have seen, insists that one can be as radical as one likes in evaluating whole practices. Searle also allows for outside criticism at the institutional level. He explains, using promising as an example:

> We need to make a distinction between what is internal and what is external to the institution of promising. It is internal to the concept of promising that in promising one undertakes an obligation to do something. But whether the entire institution of promising is good or evil, and whether obligations undertaken in promising are overridden by other outside considerations are questions which are external to the institution itself. . . . Nothing in my account commits one to the conservative view that institu-

tions are logically unassailable or to the view that one ought to approve or disapprove this or that institution.[25]

Why then does it matter that we cannot render an all-things-considered judgment of a particular execution, as long as we can render an all-things-considered judgment of both the institution of capital punishment (or of the *ancien régime*, or of the Terror) and of Sanson's decision to participate in it? Nothing turns on Sanson's antagonist, Louis-Sébastien Mercier, conceding that Sanson is a good executioner, as long as he can argue that the institution of capital punishment is not justified, and that being a good executioner is a great evil.

But what of institutions that, evaluated from the outside, *are* justified? The practice of execution may not be such an institution, but many social practices that create institutional facts arguably are. Suppose the practice of criminal prosecution in eighteenth-century Britain is justified. We still wish to pick out James Giffard's particular prosecution of James Annesley for moral criticism. But if we grant the argument of constituted description, we can fault Giffard only for failure to comply with the rules of a justified practice, for failing to "carry out a prosecution" properly. If we describe his action as a prosecution, we cannot fault him for "compassing the death of a man"— that is, we cannot apply preinstitutional evaluative criteria to a constituted description of an action. This, we recall, is Rawls's point: rules of practice are logically prior to the actions they define. They are not summary rules, statistical generalizations about which one can say the reasons that justify the rule do not hold in this case, so the rule ought not to be followed. The reasons that justify the rule apply only to the rule. In designing and evaluating the rules that constitute prosecution, we do consider an unrestricted set of reasons: whether charges brought by private parties should count as a valid prosecution; whether advancing the legal rights of a client with evil ends should count as proper legal representation; when, if ever, one may indeed compass the death of a man. But these considerations enter into the construction of the institutional fact of prosecution, not into the evaluation of particular prosecutions. So something does turn on the argument of constituted description: if a practice on the whole is justified, then actions constituted by that practice are immune from external moral criticism as long as they comply with the rules of the practice.

One might think that a practice cannot be justified if some valid application of its rules leads to actions that are wrong or conse-

---

[25] Searle, *Speech Acts*, p. 189.

quences that are bad on an all-things-considered evaluation, and that therefore one can always criticize a rule of a practice for not having made an exception for every such case. This, however, gives up too much. Although it is true that, to be morally justified, practices and rules within practices must attend to wrong action and bad consequences, to hold that a practice is not justified unless each and every action taken within the practice satisfies an all-things-considered evaluation is to reject the possibility of a practice in any meaningful sense. The rules of such a practice would act simply as rules of thumb, and the practice would not serve to shape and direct the activities of practitioners. If practices are to be taken seriously, then the argument of constituted description will need to be as well.

The Persistence of Description

The force of the argument of constituted description comes from the strength of our conviction that some activities are aptly described in practice-specific terms: we agree that the fellow swinging the stick has hit a home run, that the man wearing a wig is engaged in cross-examination, and that Sanson on the scaffold is carrying out a sentence, whatever else we want to say about them.

Whatever else we want to say about them. Constitutive description fails to preempt moral evaluation of specific actions because, even if Rawls is right about the proper use of practice-specific descriptions, there is no shortage of proper descriptions. We may grant the possibility of a meaningful and justified practice, and grant that practice-defined descriptions can be judged only by the terms set out by the practice, but deny that the practice-defined description is the only apt description. Our attachment is to the constituted description as a description, but not as *the* description. Recall the answer to MacIntyre: there is no shortage of intelligible stories.

Consider children throwing a small white leather sphere, swinging a wooden stick, and running about on a neighbor's freshly seeded lawn. When the neighbor scolds them, one child (are his parents lawyers?) replies, "You don't understand. We are not crushing the seedlings, we are playing baseball." What are we to make of this defense? Though it is true that baseball is a practice in which X, the brute facts of throwing a ball and running about on grass, count as institutional fact Y, playing the game of baseball, and though baseball is still baseball even when the neighbor is angry (since permission to use the field is not part of the specified context C), the description "playing baseball" does not supplant the description "crushing the seedlings." The children are doing both. Though there is collective agreement that brute facts count as institutional facts, the brute description does not disappear.

What if there is collective understanding that "X counts as Y and *not* as X"—that if one is playing baseball, one is not crushing seedlings? This strikes me as a collective mistake about how the world is. The seedlings are crushed and the children have done the crushing, whether or not the children, the neighbor, or the rest of us think it so, and however they or we choose to label the action and its consequence. Of course, there are important evaluative and prescriptive questions that may turn on what the children thought they were doing at the time or on what the neighbor and the rest of us think about the meaning of what was done. Did the children intend to crush the seedlings? Is it bad that the seedlings are crushed? Is it good that the children are playing baseball? Are the children morally responsible for crushing the seedlings? Have they done wrong? But these are all questions about the moral significance of the brute description, not about its correctness. Remember: the point of the strategy of redescription is to bypass certain evaluative and prescriptive questions, and our objective is to block this shortcut.

Now suppose another child, this one with philosopher-parents, says, "Yes, we are running all over your grass, but we cannot be *trespassing*, for we are playing baseball." What is the claim? There exists an institution, baseball, within which running about on a field in a certain way counts as institutional fact Y, "playing baseball." There exists another institution, private property, within which running about on the same field in the same way counts as institutional fact Z, "trespassing." Thus far, there is no reason why the action cannot count both as baseball and as trespassing: an action need not fall under one and only one practice. The child must be making a further claim, that the constitutive rules of baseball read: "X counts as Y, and not as Z."

What are we to make of this? It is not an obvious mistake, the way that the earlier attempt to erase the brute description was, for trespassing is an institutional description dependent on collective understandings, and it is not impossible for collective understandings of the rules of baseball and of law to read as the second child says. In fact, they do not—the game of baseball does not claim exclusivity of institutional description, and the institution of law would not recognize such claims if made. But suppose these children are playing a variation of baseball they call *acidball*, whose rules eat up the descriptions of other institutional practices. In particular, the constitutive rules of acidball explicitly read that using a ball field without permission does not count as trespassing, breaking a window during play does not count as a tort, and snatching bats and gloves from younger kids does not count as theft. All who play acidball understand that these are the rules of the game.

Clearly, the constitutive rules of acidball conflict with the constitutive rules of the institution of law that define property, trespassing, tort, and theft. Legal definitions typically take the form "X counts as Z (a legal description), even when X counts as Y (some nonlegal institutional description)." The institution of law claims for itself what we might call *descriptive persistence*. The law means its descriptions to stick, and does not recognize outside interference with its conceptualization of the social world. This is not to say that legal descriptions do not depend heavily on prelegal institutional descriptions in various ways: art precedes its censorship or legal protection, the social convention of money must exist before there is legal tender and the crime of counterfeiting, religious marriage may be recognized as legal marriage, and, as we will explore soon, some promises count as contracts. But once the constitutive rules of the law count a brute fact or a prelegal institutional fact as a legal fact, and once the context conditions are met (which may include various exclusions and exceptions that take nonlegal institutional facts into account), the legal description is meant to stand. If the necessary conditions for trespassing are met, then trespassing has occurred, and in our case these conditions have been met because playing acidball is not a legally recognized exception. The *prescriptive* persistence of legal descriptions is another matter: the institution of law may or may not claim for itself that it must always be obeyed, whatever extralegal considerations may arise in the games like acidball. Here, I am only claiming for the law *descriptive* persistence. Trespassing is trespassing, whatever acidball calls it.

If two institutions make jointly inconsistent constitutive claims, we need a way to reconcile them, but why must acidball lose? Why do we consider the claims to exclusivity of acidball silly, and not the claims to persistence of the legal system? A complete answer would require a careful exploration of the conditions for collective understanding, and that is a bigger task than can be tackled here. I will simply say that it appears to be the case that those conditions are met with respect to common legal concepts like trespassing, tort, and theft, but that the acidballers would have to make even stranger claims than they already do before the conditions are met for acidball concepts.

Legal concepts can be likened to money: once enough of the relevant people count certain pieces of paper as money, money is an epistemically objective description of those pieces of paper.[26] If one is ig-

---

[26] See Searle, *Construction*, pp. 7–13, for the distinction between epistemic objectivity

norant of this institutional fact, and fails to describe money as money, one has made a mistake about what is the case (though one does not make the same mistake if one holds that the institution of money is bad, refuses to use money, or counterfeits money). If you are handed an unfamiliar medallion in the marketplace of a foreign land, you are making a mistake if you do not recognize that it is a coin. It counts as a coin, and it counts as a coin *for you*, even before you recognize it as such. Similarly, enough of the relevant people count the crossing of land without the permission of the owner as trespassing (and count the neighbor as an owner, don't count the absence of a fence as permission, etc.) for trespassing to be an epistemically objective description of the action, and this is so even if the person doing the crossing is ignorant of the collective understandings of the legal concepts. Again, evaluative questions such as the justice of private property, the wrongness of trespassing, and the authority of the legal system remain unsettled.

The children respond that they are not ignorant of the collective understandings. They understand that the rest of us count certain behaviors as trespassing, but they reject our collective understandings and maintain distance from our legal concepts. Says a third child, whose parents are anthropologists, "It indeed is an objective fact that the rest of you count certain behaviors as 'trespassing,' but this is just a fact about the concepts that you in late twentieth-century Western societies use, not a fact about what I have done. Suppose a religion you do not believe in counts your walking on your own lawn as the desecration of its most holy site. Have you then desecrated a holy site? Of course not." The proper response, I think, is to show the children that they are not as distant from the concepts of the legal system as the neighbor presumably is from the concepts of an unfamiliar religion. One can use any concept with anthropological detachment, and deny that one is committed to using it with seriousness. But, as Searle argues, this comes at a cost: "The retreat from the committed use of words ultimately must involve a retreat from language itself."[27] If the children are truly uncommitted to using the terms theft and tort and trespassing in roughly the way that they are widely used in the legal system, then there is a great deal about modern social life that they cannot think or say. The rest of us, on the other hand, lose

---

and ontological objectivity. Pieces of paper are not intrinsically money, they are money because people count them as money, so the existence of money depends on the subjective judgments of people; hence, money is ontologically subjective. But with those subjective judgments in place, whether or not a certain piece of paper is money is true independent of any one person's thinking it so, and so is epistemically objective.

[27] Searle, *Speech Acts*, p. 198.

little in viewing the exclusive descriptive claims of acidball with anthropological detachment. This is so not merely because of the numerical insignificance of acidballers, but because of the peculiar exclusiveness of acidball's claims. We can remain committed to all of the descriptive concepts that acidball shares with baseball, and count an acidball hit over the fence as a home run, not a detached "so-called home run." But when the ball breaks a window, we count the home run as a tort as well, and note with appropriate detachment acidball's "self-styled" descriptive exclusivity.

Acidball and the legal system are instances of conflicting practices, and it seems that, in the face of conflict, there is a presumption in favor of descriptive persistence and, therefore, multiple apt act descriptions. Consider now the case of nested practices, where one practice builds upon the institutional facts created by another. A legal contract can be understood to be a kind of promise.[28] If this is so, the constitutive rules of contract law have the form: "X counts as Y, and Y counts as Z in context C," where X is a set of brute facts about statements, intentions, and expectations, Y is a promise, Z is a contract, and C is a set of conditions under which a promise counts as a binding legal contract (proper offer and acceptance, consideration, reliance, etc.). Now, if I make statements to you that count as a promise, and thereby make a promise that counts as a contract, my action is described both as promising and as contracting. The institutional fact of a promise is not destroyed by the creation of the institutional fact of a contract. Therefore, a party who has satisfied a contractual obligation may not have satisfied an underlying promissory obligation, though many a first-year law student taking a bracing bath in Oliver Wendell Holmes's cynical acid has thought otherwise.

Constance is looking for a roommate to share her apartment, and her best friend Fortuna—a first-year law student—promises that she will be Constance's roommate for at least a year. Fill out the story so that all the elements of a binding contract are in place: Constance acts in reliance by turning down other possible roommates, Fortuna gets tenancy in consideration, and so on. One month after moving in, Fortuna finds another apartment a few blocks closer to the law school. Now, the law usually does not require the specific performance of contracts: one may legally avoid fulfilling the terms of the contract as long as the other party can be compensated for benefits lost because of nonperformance. So Fortuna moves out. A hurt and betrayed Constance manages to find another roommate after a few weeks, and For-

---

[28] See, for example, Charles Fried, *Contract as Promise* (Cambridge, Mass.: Harvard University Press, 1981).

tuna sends Constance a check for the lost rent along with a cheery note: "I told you I was trustworthy, old friend." Fortuna apparently does not recognize that she has broken a promise to Constance because she thinks that there is no surviving promise to be broken. On her understanding of the practice of contract law, when a promise counts as a contract, it no longer counts as a promise, and so the rules of the institution of contract, rather than of the institution of promising, apply.

What is Fortuna's mistake? One way to look at her action is to split the promise into a part that is properly described as a contract (the monetary part) and a part that does not take a legal description (the commitment of friendship). On this view, Fortuna fails to acknowledge that the nonlegal part of the promise is not touched by the redescription of the legal part, and survives as a promise. I am making a stronger claim: even that part of the promise that counts as a contract continues to count as a promise. Why should we think otherwise? The rules of the institution of law do not in fact claim exclusive description the way that acidball does. Therefore, if an arm's-length business agreement in which friendship plays no part counts as a promise, the fact that it also counts as a contract does not destroy the original description, and so contract law does not replace the rules of the practice of promising—despite what is commonly believed in the business world.

Now, perhaps not every contract is also a prior promise, and so when economic actors arrange their affairs in the marketplace, their agreements count only as contracts, and not as promises. This certainly may be the case, but only if the agreement does not count as a promise according to the rules of the practice of promising. (One such plausible rule is that an agreement does not count as a promise if all parties to the agreement do not wish it to be counted as a promise.) But the rules of the practice of *business* do not determine whether or not an agreement is to be described as a promise. *Such a claim by business is no different from the descriptive claims of . . . acidball.*

Is Morality a Convention?

Before the persistence of morally relevant descriptions can be established, we need to make explicit a big question about morality that is lurking just below the surface. Does our discussion suppose that morality itself is an institution created by constitutive rules, so that moral terms are a kind of institutional fact defined by collective acceptance? Searle apparently holds this view, but nothing that we have said so far commits us to sharing it. Rawls clearly does not. Some morally relevant descriptions, of course, are institutional facts. For example, Rawls agrees with Searle that promising is an action defined by a set of constitutive conventions.[29] What counts as a valid promise, therefore, is a matter of institutional fact. But Rawls is careful to distinguish nonmoral obligations defined by constitutive conventions from moral obligations explained by moral principles. Moral principles are constructions of reason, not conventions of society. The principle of fair play, which I shall discuss at length in a later chapter, morally obligates one to play by the rules of cooperative ventures from which one voluntarily benefits. To the extent that the institution of promising is such a cooperative venture, the fair-play principle morally obligates one to keep promissory obligations, and what counts as a promise is constituted by the rules of the institution of promising.[30] But on Rawls's account, neither the institution of promising nor any other social practice, institution, or convention constitutes the principle of fair play or any other moral principle. So, though many morally relevant descriptions are institutional facts constituted by convention, this does not commit us to a form of moral conventionalism. Similarly, though many morally relevant descriptions are brute facts—"killing" and "lying," for example—this does not commit us to a form of moral realism.

To be clear, I am not claiming that the preinstitutional descriptions that persist are all natural or moral kinds that are independent of role, practice, or institution. The actions that practices redescribe may already be imbedded in or intersect with other constituted descriptions of other practices. The "otherwise" can itself be constituted, for professional roles are built upon prior social roles. The presumption: *all* act descriptions persist.

The Persistence of Actor Descriptions

What has been said about the nonuniqueness of act descriptions goes for the nonuniqueness of *actor* descriptions. Despite claims to the contrary, one cannot become lost in a role, so that the office acts, and not the person. It may be that the person does not act *alone*. One of the things that practices create is collective action, so that the act of one counts as or stands for the act of many, and the acts of many count as the act of one. Hobbes is correct in noting that an actor, in represent-

[29] John Rawls, *A Theory of Justice* (Cambridge, Mass.: Harvard University Press, 1971), p. 344, and note there citing Searle.

[30] But see Thomas Scanlon, "Promises and Practices," *Philosophy and Public Affairs* 19 (1990): 199–226, for the view that the moral wrong involved in breaking a promise does not depend on the existence of a social practice of promising.

ing another, *personates* the author of the action, and he is correct that, when doing so, the actor counts as an artificial person.[31] But how, by the creation of the institutional fact of artificial personhood, is it possible to do away with one's prior brute description as a natural person? Rather, when one acts for others or acts in role, one acts both as a natural person and as an artificial person. The lawyer Giffard who says, "I do not compass the death of a man, Lord Anglesea does," makes about as much sense as the acidballer who says, "I didn't break your window, sir, the batter did." The natural person may not always be *responsible* for actions taken as an artificial person—but that, again, is a matter to be considered at the levels of evaluation and prescription. The question of moral responsibility cannot be short-circuited by a constituted redescription of the actor. So, though Sanson may be correct in claiming that he acts on behalf of the people, he cannot claim that Sanson the man does not also act. As with descriptions of acts, the natural or preinstitutional descriptions of actors persist.

THE CHALLENGE OF PRACTICE POSITIVISM

If the argument that preconstitutive descriptions persist is correct, we can grant Rawls and Searle that actions described in terms of a practice cannot be evaluated apart from the standards set up by the practice and still evaluate the particular action under another description. Therefore, even if we cannot criticize Sanson or Giffard as executioners or lawyers, we can always evaluate them as persons. If this is so, whether to perform in the role of executioner or lawyer always is an open question. To answer it, one needs to offer arguments about why and when harmful acts permitted by a role are morally permissible. The mere invocation of constituted description does not preempt questions of moral prescription and evaluation. So we could declare victory over the redescriptive argument right now and be done.

Yet conceding that there are no grounds for saying that Giffard is a bad lawyer or Sanson is a bad executioner concedes too much. If we rely entirely on the nonuniqueness of description to defeat the redescriptive strategy, we preclude the critic from evaluating practice-defined actions *as* practice-defined actions. But the good lawyer wishes at times to dispute what constitutes good lawyering. She doesn't want to say merely that a certain action properly takes two descriptions, the good act of lawyering called "cross-examination" and the bad preinstitutional act called "humiliation." She wants to say that, in some

---

[31] Thomas Hobbes, *Leviathan* (1651), ch. 16.

cases, the humiliation of a truthful witness renders a cross-examination an act of bad lawyering. Similarly, she wants to say that some acts described by the practice as "zealous advocacy," because they take the preinstitutional description of "deception," are for that reason instances of bad lawyering. Can a particular practice-defined action, so described, ever be evaluated on grounds other than its conformity to the existing rules of the practice? The answer is a qualified yes. I will briefly sketch out the conditions under which such evaluation is possible, although a thorough answer would require far more discussion of some perennial topics in the philosophy of law than I can provide here.

Rules of a practice can specify criteria of evaluation that reach outside of the terms defined by the practice, but to show that is not enough. Of course rules can, in both their regulative and constitutive functions. No practice of lawyering permits counsel to bludgeon a hostile witness to death on the stand or counts the bludgeoning of a hostile witness as cross-examination, where "bludgeoning to death" is a brute, preinstitutional fact taken from outside the practice of law. What is clearly true for bludgeoning could be true for humiliating and deceiving: nothing prevents a practice of lawyering from adopting, as one of the conditions that define which actions count as cross-examination, the proviso that acts of humiliation do not count, and nothing prevents a practice of lawyering from importing criteria for what counts as humiliation from outside the practice. Similarly, nothing prevents a practice of lawyering from not counting deception as advocacy. But nothing requires such provisos, either.

So far, we have shown only that ordinary moral judgments can be brought to bear on particular practice-defined actions, so described, insofar as the positive rules of the practice invite such judgments. In Searle's formulation of a constitutive rule, "X counts as Y in context C," there do not appear to be any normative constraints on or requirements of C relevant to our question. The rules of a practice can internalize all of the judgments of morality under C or can be indifferent to them, and still be a practice. But the critical practitioner wants to reach *outside* the quotes, so to speak, for evaluative criteria, so that "X counts as Y" *in context* C. This, the redescriptive argument continues to maintain, cannot be done for particular practice-defined actions. Either an evaluative criterion is built into the rules of the practice or it can be applied to the entire practice only.

For example, in the *ancien régime*, confessions were extracted from the accused by interrogation under torture, an institution known as the *question extraordinaire*. In one technique, the *estrapade*, the victim's hands were tied behind the back with a rope by which he was hoisted and dropped from a height with a jerk. The *question extraordinaire* undeniably was a practice, defined and governed by rules, complete with established roles for the king's torturer and interrogator. There were ways to practice the *question extraordinaire* badly, no doubt: one wanted a confession, not a corpse. But the infliction of unimaginably extreme pain counted for, not against, a judgment that the interrogation was performed well. There simply were no criteria of moral evaluation recognized by the rules of the practice "inside the quotes" that would tell against torture. We must of course revile a practice of interrogation that makes an excellence out of nearly ripping a defendant's arms from their sockets, for it is evil to be an excellent interrogator in such a practice.[32] But the interrogators who employed the *estrapade* did not perform the *question extraordinaire* badly, and were not bad interrogators.

The line I have taken here implies a view that earlier I called practice positivism.[33] The concept of a practice does not impose any general content requirements or restrictions on the rules of all practices. Subject to certain consistency requirements, the rules of a practice simply are what they are, not what they ought to be. This is not to say that a particular practice cannot be rendered incoherent by rules that do not bear the right relationship to each other or to the aims of the practice. If all the members of the American Medical Association wake up Sunday morning committed to the rules of the National Football League, what they are practicing in the hospital parking lot cannot possibly be medicine. More controversially, it has been argued that if they begin to assist in the suicides of their terminally ill patients, what they are practicing cannot possibly be medicine. But they can be engaged in some other coherent social practice called something else. And if practice positivism is correct, the moral wrongness of the practice of euthanasia, if it be wrong, does not, by itself, render incoherent actions taken by "euthanasists" in accordance with its rules.

Practice positivism does not entail the view known as legal positivism. It may be that a legal system, to be a legal system, must have a minimal moral content that involves, among other things, not treating those subject to it arbitrarily. If this is so, it is because of some tight

---

[32] Nearly, but not completely out of their sockets—the procedure *was* governed by rules. Machiavelli, who was subjected to six applications of the Florentine *strappado*, implies in his prison sonnets that victims could protest if hoisted too high. See Sebastian de Grazia, *Machiavelli in Hell* (New York: Vintage, 1989), pp. 34–40, 392. I am grateful to an anonymous reader for the reference.

[33] See Chapter 3.

conceptual connection between the idea of law and the idea of morality. But if legal positivism is false, it is not because some minimal moral content is a conceptual necessity of *all* practices, institutions, and roles, but rather, of *legal* practices, institutions, and roles. The idea of a practice is much too general, and the aims and content of particular practices much too diverse, for minimal morality to be built into the very concept of a practice. Each role might have some particular necessary minimal content driven by the aims, goods, purposes, or external justifications of that role. But it would not have to be a minimal *moral* content. Is not organized crime a practice, and gangster a role? We can come up with minimal content: practitioners of organized crime do have to be organized and do have to commit crimes. But there is nothing moral about this minimal content.

So, I need not choose sides here in a debate between legal positivists and their opponents about whether lawful torture is a contradiction. Whether necessarily incompatible with the concept of legality or not, the *question extraordinaire* was a practice with roles and rules, just as organized crime, unlawful by definition, is a practice with roles and rules. Now, the existence of the practice of the *question extraordinaire* may have depended on the mistaken belief that it was a lawful practice. But institutions that rest on mistakes are still institutions. Though the monarchy depended on an illusion about the divine right of kings, the monarchy was no illusion. If practice positivism is correct, are there any grounds to criticize, under a practice-defined description, an action that conforms with the posited practice?

Requirements of Consistency

One way already has been mentioned. Though there are no general content requirements on all practices, there may be practice-specific consistency requirements that give a practitioner a place to stand within the role and evaluate posited practice-defined acts as practice-defined acts. Parts of the posited rules may be internally incoherent or may undermine the point of the practice. An example of incoherence, perhaps apocryphal, from the early days of the railroad: "When two trains approach on a single track, each shall come to a complete stop and neither shall proceed until the other has done so." Since one cannot practice train engineering at all with this rule in place, to be a good train engineer requires that one not follow this rule strictly.

For an example of a practice that undermines its point, consider a society whose practice of promising contains the following exception: "Promises may be broken when to do so would be for the best, on the whole."[34] Now, this exception misses the point of promising. Perhaps, despite its regular use of the formula "I promise," such a society simply lacks a practice of promising, so to ask about good or bad applications of promising in particular instances is senseless. But alternatively, each instance of promise breaking in accordance with this exception can be criticized as a mistakenly broken promise, because the exception cannot be squared with any plausible aim that a practice of promising can have. Practice positivism demands, however, that we invoke this ground for criticism quite sparingly. A rule does not undermine the point of its practice simply because it is not a perfect rule. Four outs a side each inning would make baseball more exciting to watch and more demanding to play, but there is nothing incoherent about the present three outs. Also recall that nothing constrains the point of a practice to be a moral point—organized crime is no contradiction.

Contested Constitution

So far, the account of roles and practices has supposed that practitioners largely agree about what the constitutive conventions of the practice are, even those practitioners who wish the rules were otherwise. But since constituted descriptions are created by shared meanings, genuine disagreements can arise about just what meanings are shared and who shares them. The assumption of widespread agreement about the positive rules accurately describes sports and parlor games, and comes close to describing practices that have formal rule-making and rule-applying organs, at least over the domain of easy cases. But most social and professional roles and practices are not formally constituted. When this is so, critical evaluation of a practice easily takes the form of a genuine disagreement among practitioners about what the practice is, rather than a reformist proposal about what the practice should be—recall the antiquated librarian in "Doctor, Schmoctor." When constituted descriptions are contested, criticism of particular practice-defined actions is possible in this special sense: critical practitioners can claim that others are making particular mistakes about what the constitutive conventions of the practice are. Challenges to orthodoxies in artistic practices often take this form. The originality of Joyce, Picasso, and Stravinsky can be understood as new claims about what their art forms already were and already meant, rather than as revolts against the existing meanings.

[34] Rawls considers the status of such an excuse when invoked by an individual promisor. See "Two Concepts," p. 17.

Contested constitution, however, does not escape the demands of practice positivism. To repeat, genuine contestation is a claim in good faith about what shared meanings actually are, not a proposal for what they should be. Some contestations can only be self-fulfillingly correct, in that they will not be shared, if at all, until they are put forth as shared: recall Searle's account of the Declaration of Independence. If the contester knows that this is the case, I think that it is more accurate to describe her actions as those of a subversive reformer, rather than a practitioner, unless the posited rules of the practice recognize such a gambit as a valid method of internal rule revision. The validity of the self-fulfilling gambit is itself a contingent fact about the actual practice (a fact that the self-fulfilling contester may wish to contest as well . . .).

Constituted Criticism

Consider one last way to mount criticism of practice-defined actions. A practice may recognize its practitioners as authoritative shapers and interpreters of the practice. Rawls distinguishes the office of practitioner from the office of reformer or rule maker.[35] But some practices may allow for their own revision by practitioners. Indeed, one might claim that a capacity for self-reflection and self-criticism is part of what distinguishes professions from games and other sorts of rule-governed practices. If the substantive criteria for reform and revision are themselves well specified by the rules of the practice, we have not found grounds for external evaluation of particular actions, for then engaging in criticism conforms to the internal rules of the practice. What I have in mind is a practice that, at least over some of its domain, is incompletely specified, and so incompletely governed by constitutive conventions. A self-reflective, self-revising practice may simply recognize who does and does not count as a practitioner, without constraining what is to count as valid criticism by practitioners. When this is the case, qualified practitioners are free to bring the evaluative criteria of their choosing to bear on actions taken within the practice.

In such a practice, a lawyer who opposes the humiliation of truthful witnesses on ordinary moral grounds makes the claim that, on the question of humiliation, the practice of lawyering is simply what qualified lawyers do, and the proper way to evaluate acts of lawyering is by using the criteria of evaluation that lawyers use. What results can continue to be called a practice only if the unspecified do-

[35] Ibid., p. 28.

main is small, or if the criteria of judgment that practitioners employ turn out to be close enough to each other. And, as before, practice positivism requires that this move be employed only where such open-endedness is a fact about the actual practice.

These attempts to find grounds for the evaluation of practice-defined actions so described in the end are less than satisfying. Each works only insofar as the positive rules of the practice make room for it to work, and whether that is the case is a contingent matter. For many practices, we may have to concede to the argument from redescription that there are no evaluative grounds, other than compliance with the rules, by which practice-defined actions can be judged. But the most potent claim of the redescribers has been defeated, for every particular action can be evaluated under some prepractice description.

Are They Liars?

We are now positioned to answer the dangling question about lawyers. Are they liars? Both in the courtroom and out, lawyers—good lawyers—intentionally attempt to convince judges, jurors, litigants, and contracting parties of the truth of propositions that the lawyer believes to be false. The act of intentionally inducing a belief in others that one believes to be false ordinarily counts as deception, whatever else it may count as. When deception is accomplished by making an untrue statement, the deception is a lie. If the argument against redescription is correct, then good lawyers certainly are serial *deceivers*—indeed, deception is one of the core tasks and skills of legal practice. And, because sometimes lawyerly deception is accomplished by making untrue statements, sometimes lawyers—again, good lawyers—deceive by lying. But my stake in showing that many lawyerly deceptions are also lies is poetic, not moral. "Are lawyers deceivers?" doesn't have quite the same ring, but a yes answer does have approximately the same moral force. Since deception also is a presumptive moral wrong, the burden is on the practice of law to justify lawyerly deception as well as lying.[36] The question of moral evaluation cannot be redescribed away.

Consider some examples of clear deception. Many lawyers spend

[36] More precisely, deception aimed at bending another's will is presumptively wrong. One may induce false beliefs in art, amusement, or play in ways that do not influence the will, and so that either do not count as deception or do not count as presumptively wrong deception. But lawyerly deception aims at the will.

much of their time in contract or settlement negotiations, and several common strategies for reaching agreement when the initial perceived zone of possible agreement is larger than a point involve inducing false beliefs about a number of matters: the alternatives of both parties to settlement, the proper assessment of probabilities when alternatives are uncertain, the proper valuation of those alternatives, the change in alternatives and their valuation over time, the proper assessment of probabilities when the outcome of a proposed agreement is uncertain, and the value of a proposed agreement to both parties. Some manipulation of belief in negotiation counts in the law as fraud, and some counts, both in the law and in positive legal ethics, merely as "puffing and bluffing." But no institutional redescription can do away with the prior description of "intentionally inducing a false belief," or can block counting intentionally inducing false belief as deception. Though the law and positive legal ethics may count certain representations as mere puffery or bluffery, legal rules and rules of professional practice cannot by themselves undo the prior description of deception. When puffing and bluffing is accomplished by making untrue statements, such as "My client will not accept anything less" when you have good reason to believe that this is not the case, or the disarming "That clause is standard boilerplate" when in fact it was specially drafted to cover a contingency that you have good reason to believe has a substantial chance of occurring, you are lying. That the law has some standard of what counts as a "material" misrepresentation of fact is of no consequence to the prelegal description. Because descriptions persist, the law does not determine what is or is not properly described as a lie.

Some astute readers have commented that, though the argument against redescription works well for many dubious lawyerly practices (humiliating a truthful witness, pursuing an unjust suit, or driving up the costs of litigation), lying and deception are bad examples of the general point because those practices are flatly prohibited by the constitutive rules of lawyering. ABA Model Rule 8.4(c) reads: "It is professional misconduct for a lawyer to engage in conduct involving dishonesty, fraud, deceit or misrepresentation," and there are numerous specific instances of prohibited deception. My response is that when the Model Rules get specific, they reveal that the "dishonesty," "fraud," "deceit," or "misrepresentation" that is prohibited has *already* been redescribed. False statements about only *material* fact and law are prohibited, so lies about most opinions, evaluations, and future intentions do not count. Indeed, the Comment to Model Rule 4.1 is explicit in its redescription of lying: "Under generally accepted conventions in negotiation, certain types of statements ordinarily are not taken as statements of material fact. Estimates of price or value placed on the subject of a transaction and a party's intentions as to an acceptable settlement of a claim are in this category." (Why then, we might ask, does anyone waste breath making such statements?) Lawyers are prohibited from offering evidence they *know* to be false, but may offer evidence they reasonably believe is false (3.3). ("Que sçay-je?" asks Montaigne. What do I know?) Lawyers have a duty to disclose material facts to third parties when necessary to avoid assisting a criminal or fraudulent act by a client (4.1(b)), but only when disclosure is not prohibited by the confidentiality rule (1.6). Since the relevant clause of the confidentiality rule permits disclosure only to prevent a crime that will cause imminent death or substantial bodily harm, a lawyer whose silence allows financial fraud apparently must keep silent. "Fraud" is prohibited by both positive legal ethics and tort law, but fraud is itself an institutionally defined concept in law that does not count all lies and deceptions. In the Model Rules, fraud is defined to *exclude* "failure to apprise another of relevant information." Thus, positive legal ethics does not prohibit what ordinary morality counts as dishonesty. Rather, it takes a more circumscribed set of actions and relabels it "dishonesty." So, though lawyers are not Liars®, they might still be liars.

Similarly, at trial, a good lawyer regularly intends to induce beliefs in juries that the lawyer believes to be false, and so deceives the jurors. In trying to evade this simple and obvious fact, much breath is wasted on clever equivocation or bad epistemology, such as "It is the job of the jury, not the lawyer, to render a verdict" (true but beside the point) or "The lawyer cannot know what is true or false until the jury decides" (false and beside the point). None of this speaks to the plain fact that, over the course of representing a client, a lawyer forms reasonable beliefs, at varying degrees of uncertainty, about the various factual propositions at issue in the trial, and that zealous advocacy often requires her to attempt to persuade the jury to believe the opposite, or to believe that a proposition is true with a degree of uncertainty that is much lower or much higher than the degree of uncertainty she holds.

It does no good to point out that cases ought to be decided, not on an all-things-considered belief about what is true, but on the admissible evidence subject to a specified standard of proof. For the lawyer cannot help but form beliefs about what inferences are correct to draw from the record at the appropriate standard of proof. She asks a hypothetical question: what would I reasonably infer, at what degree of uncertainty, if the only information I had about the case were from the record? Unless she takes only cases that she believes ought to win on those standards, she will devote much of her time to persuading juries to draw inferences that are incorrect by the rules and standards of inference juries are supposed to employ.

Perhaps a lawyer who believes that her client is factually liable on a preponderance of the admissible evidence could advocate her client's case without deception in the following way. She could announce to the jury that she believes the line of argument she is about to pursue is false, and explain why she believes it to be false. But under the rules of the court, it is her job to present to the jury the most favorable case for her client, even when that requires her to construct for the jury a story that she believes to be false. It is the jury's job to make up its own mind about what inferences are appropriate to draw from the evidence, subject to the rules of the court. And since members of the jury, not being experts at this sort of thing, might be inclined to forget what the task is, and lapse into making inappropriate commonsense inferences about and from the lawyer's own beliefs, she will remind them periodically that they are engaged in a highly structured and constrained exercise aimed at reaching a decision according to a set of rules. If she plants a suggestion that she believes is false, she will appropriately distance herself from it by saying, "I don't believe that witness told the truth, but you might. If you do, then you could reasonably infer . . . " Of course, this sort of distancing by a lawyer would count under the current rules of legal ethics as egregious malpractice. But nothing less is required if the lawyer is to be spared the description "deceptive."

It might be claimed that this sort of distancing is implicit in the design of legal institutions. All participants know, or ought to know, that the lawyer does not believe every inference that is suggested by the case she puts forward, and that these inferences are always offered in a subjunctive mood with a *sotto voce* disclaimer. Such an institution is not impossible, and perhaps the British system attempts to approximate it, but it is far from American legal practice. Good trial lawyers do everything within their power and within the rules of the court to establish personal authority, trustworthiness, and credibility, and to insert their own character into the trial for the benefit of their clients. If it helps their case, they do everything within their power and the rules to close the distance between presenting what could be believed and misrepresenting what they actually believe. If it suits their purposes, they try to hide from the jury a clear picture of the lawyer's job, steer the jury away from employing the constrained and structured rules of inference that the institution requires, and toward applying commonsense inference to a most uncommon task. In *voir dire*, lawyers seek out jurors who are especially susceptible to this sort of manipulation, least sophisticated about what lawyers are up to, and most likely to misunderstand the juror's task. When lawyers engage in these strategies, they intentionally misrepresent what they believe in order to induce what they believe are false beliefs in the jurors.

The good lawyer claims that, in the practice of lawyering, convincing others to believe the truth of what the lawyer believes to be false no longer counts as deception. Rather, it counts as zealous advocacy. Now, it could be that the rules of *morality* do not count certain untruthful behaviors as deceptions. Morality does not count fiction writing as deception, for instance. But the rules of the practice of *lawyering* cannot redescribe a lie as something else. *That is about as plausible as the claims of acidball*. Ordinary act descriptions persist.

The lawyer might concede that, for one side or another, most trials involve deception, but deny that it is the lawyer who is doing the deceiving. It is the client, not the lawyer, who deceives. The lawyer-in-role acts as an artificial person, personating or representing the will of the client, but the natural person who occupies the lawyer's role cannot be described as the author of the deception. This, I argued earlier, is untrue. *Pace* Hobbes, the argument of *actor* redescription also fails, and natural *actor* descriptions persist.

The lawyer is not lying only. She is also advancing the legal rights of her client, fulfilling her professional obligations, taking her part in a system that, in equilibrium, seeks truth and justice—the list goes on. The lies lawyers tell and the deceptions they stage may be justified. But that, to repeat the refrain, is an evaluative matter. We cannot evade the hard work of moral evaluation and justification by claiming for the action or actor a different description. Does "liar" misdescribe the lawyer?

The adversary's first line of defense against moral criticism, tracked in the three preceding chapters, appeals to the structure of roles. Roles claim to block critical evaluation in two ways: certain kinds of descriptions of harmful practices and certain kinds of reasons against engaging in harmful practices are filtered out of the role player's moral deliberations. If, as argued in "Doctor, Schmoctor," practice positivism is correct, the connection between role obligations and moral obligations is largely mediated by second-order moral reasons to follow the rules of a role. We might therefore think that moral reasoning about roles is restricted to judgments about whether we indeed have such second-order moral reasons. This is a mistake. Yes, as we saw in "The Remains of the Role," the characteristic person-neutral, role-relative standpoint of professions rightly views "personal" reasons through an impartial and liberal screen. But the public and political reasons that actors have by virtue of being simply persons or citizens penetrate this filter. As persons and citizens, we always have a place outside the role to stand and make judgments both particular and general about both substance and authority. On this, Montaigne is right. Similarly, because roles constitute new forms of action, we might think that actors engaged in those actions can be evaluated only on criteria internal to the role. "Are Lawyers Liars?" has argued that this too is a mistake. Roles cannot filter out morally pertinent preconventional descriptions of actions and actors. Descriptions, and so the grounds for moral evaluation, persist. Blocking strategies do not spare the adversary from criticism.

The two filtering strategies that roles deploy are unconvincing because, in focusing on the altered moral situation of the role-playing agent, they overlook the moral situation of the *patient*—that is, the target of adversary action. But the claims of the target not to be mistreated pierce the masks that role players wear. Role players cannot evade the reasons that apply to themselves as natural persons because the claims of victims are addressed to all; constituted descriptions cannot preempt natural descriptions because adding a description of an action does not ordinarily subtract from the bad that happens to the victim.

So, should roles be taken seriously? One family of claims that roles put forward should not. Roles do not overwrite moral prohibitions with moral permissions. Roles *can* overwrite moral permissions with moral obligations, and so, in that respect, are to be taken seriously, but that is another matter. If we are to defend nasty adversary practices such as deception and coercion, we will need to look elsewhere.

Part III of this book considers arguments that address the moral claims of the target head-on. In Chapter 6, "Rules of the Game," the dominant image shifts from *role* (a script assigned to an actor) to *game* (an interaction played out between actor and target). The idea is that the targets of adversary action are themselves players in a game whose rules permit their treatment as targets, and that moral permission to target them follows from something that they do—they play the game.

PART III

GAMES AND VIOLATIONS

The pure geometry of the white chessmen's fate burst upon Kelly's consciousness. Its simplicity had the effect of a refreshing, chilling wind. A sacrifice had to be offered to Pi Ying's knight. If Pi Ying accepted the sacrifice, the game would be Kelly's. The trap was perfect and deadly save for one detail—bait.

"One minute, Colonel," said Pi Ying.

Kelly looked quickly from face to face, unmoved by the hostility or distrust or fear that he saw in each pair of eyes. One by one he eliminated the candidates for death. These four were vital to the sudden, crushing offense, and these must guard the king. Necessity, like a child counting eeny, meeny, miney, moe around a circle, pointed its finger at the one chessman who could be sacrificed. There was only one.

Kelly didn't permit himself to think of the chessman as anything but a cipher in a rigid mathematical proposition: if x is dead, the rest shall live. . . .

. . . When human beings are attacked, x, multiplied by hundreds or thousands, must die—sent to death by those who love them most. Kelly's profession was the the choosing of x. . . .

"Jerry," said Kelly, his voice loud and sure, "move forward one square and two to your left." Trustingly, his son stepped out of the back rank and into the shadow of the black knight. Awareness seemed to be filtering back into Margaret's eyes. She turned her head when her husband spoke.

Pi Ying stared down at the board in bafflement. "Are you in your right mind, Colonel?" he asked at last. "Do realize what you've just done?" . . .

Kelly pretended to be mystified by Pi Ying's words. And then he buried his face in his hands and gave an agonized cry. "Oh, God, no!"

"An exquisite mistake, to be sure," said Pi Ying. . . .

"You've got to let me take him back," begged Kelly brokenly.

Pi Ying rapped on the balustrade with his knuckles. "Without rules, my friend, games become nonsense."

Kurt Vonnegut Jr., "All the King's Horses"

Chapter Six

RULES OF THE GAME AND FAIR PLAY

> However, I saw recently in my neighborhood at Mussidan that those who were forcibly driven out from there by our army, and others of their party, screamed as at treachery because during the discussion of terms, and while the treaty was still in effect, they had been surprised and cut to pieces: a complaint which might have had some plausibility in another century. But as I have just said, our ways are utterly remote from these rules; and parties should not trust one another until the last binding seal has been set. Even then there is plenty of room for wariness. . . .
>
> "To conquer always was a glorious thing / Whether achieved by fortune or by skill" [Ariosto], so they say. But the philosopher Chrysippus would not have been of that opinion, and I just as little. For he used to say that those who run a race should indeed employ their whole strength for speed but that, nevertheless, it was not in the least permissible for them to lay a hand on their adversary to stop him, or to stick out a leg to make him fall.
>
> *Michel de Montaigne, "Parley Time Is Dangerous"*

THE NOTION of a game has two complementary senses: a game as strategic interaction, and a game as rule-governed social practice. As a strategic interaction, a game invites players to engage in harmful tactics that are presumptively wrong, such as deception, coercion, or violence.[1] In defense of at least some use of such tactics, players commonly claim that they are engaged in a game as a rule-governed social practice as well, and that the rules of the game permit the use of tactics that would otherwise be morally impermissible. This chapter explores various arguments that might be offered in support of the claim that presumptively wrong actions, if permitted by the rules of a game, for that reason are not morally wrong.

The games I mainly have in mind are middle-level social institutions that order the activities of actors who have at least partly con-

---

[1] An action is presumptively wrong if there are sound reasons that count toward concluding that the action violates a moral duty. When these reasons are dispositive, the action is wrong, simply. There might be countervailing reasons—self-defense, for example—that fully justify the action, so that no duty is violated and no wrongness remains. But presumptively wrong actions always are in need of defense.

flicting interests, or who represent others who have such interests. The adversary professions of law, business, and politics are such games. On a smaller scale, so are parlor games and sports, and I will often analogize from deceptive parlor games and violent sports to larger and more complex social institutions such as lawsuits, political campaigns, and market competition.

The biggest game that will be considered is the game of law—not the practice of legal representation by lawyers, but the ordering of society by the rule of law. When asked about the game of law our question of whether game-permissible actions are, for that reason, morally permissible has a familiar ring and a familiar answer. The fact that an action is permitted by the laws of the state does not by itself render the action morally permissible. American law permits all sorts of horrible ways of treating others, and so the exercise of one's legal rights can be morally wrong. There are many perfectly legal ways to be vicious, cruel, hurtful, and deceitful—to wrong others through speech, or by causing psychological distress, or by hurting one's relations. It is often legal to dupe a retiree into investing his life's savings stupidly, to incite racial hatred for political gain, or to sell arms to murderous regimes abroad.

If these practices are wrong, the fact of their legality does not make them less wrong. This is so, not only for an imperfect set of existing laws, but for any ideal set of laws. As often noted, the regulation and coercive prevention of all morally wrong action would in itself cause grave restrictions of liberty, so that there are some morally wrong actions that would be morally wrong to outlaw. The optimal amount of legally permissible moral wrongdoing is not zero.

That legality does not, in itself, make presumptively wrong actions morally permissible is no surprise, and this conclusion is widely though not uniformly held. In the case of smaller social games, however, one is more likely to think that game permission *does* create moral permission. For example, deception and violence are presumptive moral wrongs, but the rules of the game of poker permit deception, and the rules of boxing, football, and hockey permit violence. It is widely believed that lying in poker and tackling in football are morally permissible, and widely believed that this is so because the rules of the games of poker and football permit such actions. Similarly, it is widely believed that the permissive rules of professional games such as lawyering, business management, and elective politics generate moral permissions to engage in deceptive and coercive tactics that, if not for their game permissibility, would be morally wrong.

Several arguments have been offered to back up the claim that the rules of games provide moral permission to use tactics that would otherwise be wrong, but they are weaker or more limited in scope than is often supposed. The next two sections briefly explore the arguments from consent and tacit consent, and show that they either fail to justify sharp practices or require stringent conditions that are unlikely to be met in practice. The second half of the chapter examines the argument from fair play—oddly enough, the most promising way to support at least some deceptive, coercive, and violent practices.

The fair-play principle was originally developed by H.L.A. Hart and John Rawls to establish a general obligation for citizens to obey the law even when they have not consented. Roughly, fair play obligates us to do our fair share in schemes of social cooperation from which we willingly benefit, and not to free-ride on the burdens shouldered by others. The fair-play argument ingeniously retains two important intuitions: that receiving benefits may lead to obligations, but that obligations must be connected to voluntary acts. Fair play thereby offers a grounding for political obligation that depends on voluntary action, but not on voluntary consent to be obligated. The fair-play argument is here employed in a novel way, to establish a moral *permission* that otherwise would not exist, rather than to establish a moral obligation that otherwise would not exist. I develop necessary and sufficient conditions for the fair-play argument to work in establishing a permission and, along the way, explore whether the games of business, legal practice, and elective politics meet these conditions.

THE ARGUMENT FROM CONSENT

One way that game permissions might generate moral permissions is by way of consent. For two well-known and complementary reasons, genuine consent is a very potent permitter of actions that, absent consent, would be wrong. First, some actions are presumptively wrong because they harm the welfare of others, but since we ordinarily presume that people know what is in their own welfare, their consent to a presumptively wrong action against them reverses the presumption that the action in fact harms them. Second, some actions are presumptively wrong because they override or undermine the will of others, and so fail to treat others as autonomous—that is, self-ruling—agents. But performed with consent, these actions properly respect the will of the target, and so become exercises in autonomy, rather than violations of it. Thus, players in a game consent to the rules of the game, and so consent to be subjected to the deception, coercion, or violence the rules of the game permit. So, for one or the other of the two reasons just offered, consent removes the presumptive wrong of actions taken in accordance with the rules of a game, rendering game-permissible deception, coercion, and violence morally permissible. Alternatively, consent changes the appropriate description of these actions, so that they are no longer instances of deception, coercion, or violence. (Unlike constitutive rules, which add to, but do not replace, prior natural descriptions, consent changes the nature of consent-sensitive actions. As we will see in the next chapter, consensual coercion is a contradiction.)

When players have actually consented to the rules of a game, the argument from consent is compelling. But the criteria of genuine consent are stringent, and may not hold for most players in social games with any complexity. Citizens, for example, rarely give genuine consent to obey the laws of the state. We must be careful in particular not to conflate the strong argument from consent with the much weaker claim about expectation, and assume that those who expect to be the targets of adversary tactics have consented to be such targets.

Deception in poker ordinarily is morally permitted because the conditions necessary for genuine consent are ordinarily satisfied: a player who sits down at the felt enters into an actual (not hypothetical), informed (not manipulated), and voluntary (not coerced) agreement to play by the rules. And since he may leave the table at virtually no cost, his acceptance of each deal of the cards signals continued acceptance of the terms of play. The argument from consent straightforwardly gives moral permission to actions permitted by the rules of poker because we presume that the player has chosen to participate and that the choice is both in his own interests and his to make. There are no doubt limits to the authority of self-rule, even when the stringent conditions of free and informed consent are met. Freedoms that destroy the worth of freedom—the classic and most extreme example being the conundrum of voluntary slavery—are deeply problematic. But choosing to play poker does not test the limits of the permission-generating property of consent.

Unlike poker, consent to the rules of larger social games played by business managers, lawyers, and politicians may be absent or defective. First, most public and professional games profoundly affect those who are not players. Campaign mudslingers take aim at opposing candidates, but also cloud public discourse and deceive citizens; defense attorneys aim to defeat the prosecution, but also malign the reputations of reluctant witnesses; a cigarette manufacturer's manipulative advertising aims to take market share away from a competitor, but also harms teenagers. Second, not all players are knowledgeable about the rules of the game. Marketers distract consumers from ca-veat emptor; real-estate brokers, who have a fiduciary responsibility to sellers, cultivate trust and dependency in buyers, and in the end work for themselves, depend on ambiguity about their loyalties. Third, even when players are knowledgeable, they may face exit bar-riers or their alternatives may be so poor that their continued partici-pation in an adversary game cannot be assumed fully voluntary.

When alternatives to participation are poor, expectation of an ad-versary game does not imply consent to its rules. In buying a used car, you may fully expect to be deceived about its defects. You may also "play the game" by reading *Consumer Reports* and by taking the car to a mechanic. Yet the inference to consent may be too quick. Here, precision about the moral significance of expectation is needed. Suppose you agree to buy a car "as is," with the expectation that the seller might have deceived you about its worth—say such deceptive practices are conventional in the used-car market—and it turns out that, indeed, you have been deceived. On a perfectly plausible under-standing of consent and its twin defects of coercion and ignorance, there was no defect in your consent to the exchange of money for car. Your agreement was uncoerced: the seller did not threaten to harm your interests if you did not buy his car, he did not cause you to want a car (say, by smashing your old one), and he is under no prior duty or obligation to compensate for your carlessness.[2] Your agreement was informed: you knowledgeably took into account the possibility of deception, and you reasonably believed that the deal was worth the risk. (We might suppose that, because of the widespread expectation, the market price of used cars is already discounted for deception, so that the expected value to a buyer, even with the chance of deception, is positive.)

Since your expectation of deception removed ignorance as a defect in your consent, you indeed have consented to the exchange, but you need not have consented to be deceived, let alone have consented to a regime permitting deception. Consent to one does not imply consent to the others. Therefore, if the rules of the game require consent for their legitimation, then consent to a transaction does not necessarily legitimate the rules under which the transaction has occurred. The deceptive seller can invoke your agreement, and your knowledge of and expectation of standard practices in the market, only to show that

---

[2] So, even on the view that finds coercion when moral expectations, rather than sta-tistical expectations, are violated, this transaction is not coercive. For the moralized view, see Robert Nozick, "Coercion," in *Philosophy, Science, and Method*, ed. Sidney Mor-genbesser, Patrick Suppes, and Morton White (New York: St. Martin's, 1969), and Alan Wertheimer, *Coercion* (Princeton, N.J.: Princeton University Press, 1987).

you voluntarily exchanged money for car, not that you volunteered to be deceived. So, though you may be morally obligated to perform your part in the exchange, even if tricked, the seller is not necessarily morally permitted to trick you. If the practice of deception here relies on your consent for its legitimation, the exchange by itself does not legitimate the deceptive practice. The argument from expectation therefore fails to justify adversary action against a target. At most, it denies the target certain remedies, such as canceling the transaction. Of course, consent need not be necessary or sufficient legitimating grounds: some adversary games do not need the consent of the target for their legitimation (for example, the prosecution of just claims in the legal system), while other games are not justified by consent of the target (such as Russian roulette).

The Argument from Tacit Consent

Consent is a potent way to establish a moral permission to engage in presumptively wrong actions permitted by the rules of a game, but its conditions—free and informed agreement—are stringent. So, not surprisingly, expansive claims are made to impute *tacit* consent to situations where explicit consent is absent. Locke famously makes this argument to establish an obligation to obey the law, claiming that anyone who possesses or enjoys the use of land in the territories of a government—even if only to travel freely on the highway—thereby gives tacit consent to obey the government's laws.[3] The argument from tacit consent is that a class of actions such as participation, compliance, or acceptance of benefit signals or constitutes tacit consent to the rules of an adversary institution, and that tacit consent is a species of genuine consent. Does participation or acceptance of benefit indeed imply tacit consent? If so, how? And does tacit consent have the moral force of explicit consent?

Consider two ways in which tacit consent can be understood to be a species of genuine consent. On the evidentiary view, a set of conditions such as participation, compliance, or acceptance of benefit is good evidence that the actor in fact has met the primary conditions of consent—free and informed agreement. Since the power of the evidentiary conditions depends on their contingent connection to the

[3] See John Locke, *Two Treatises of Government* (1690), *Second Treatise*, ed. Peter Laslett (Cambridge: Cambridge University Press, 1963), sec. 119. But Locke holds that tacit consent does not create a permanent obligation to submit to government, and does not confer membership in a society. Without explicit consent, obligation begins and ends with possession or enjoyment. See secs. 121–22.

primary conditions, the ascription of consent when the evidentiary conditions are met is merely a presumption, rebuttable by stronger evidence that one has not entered into a free and informed agreement. So, on the evidentiary standard, a citizen who pronounces, every time he walks on the sidewalk, that he refuses to be obligated by the laws of the state, and that his use of public streets should not be construed as tacit consent to the authority of the law, cannot be understood to have offered tacit consent by his use of the sidewalk. There may be *other* reasons that obligate him, and, as we will see, other reasons for which his use and benefit of sidewalks matter, but he is not obligated by way of tacit consent. Similarly for permissions: someone who buys a used car and signs a proclamation that explicitly denies that his participation in the used-car market implies his tacit consent to be treated as a target of deception has not, on the evidentiary view, consented to the rules of that market. (Again, there may be other reasons that permit actions against him on account of his participation.) If the evidentiary view of tacit consent is correct, then those activities that are presumed consensual must be grounded empirically in some statistical generalization about actual intentions. If, upon investigation, we find that most sidewalk users are philosophical anarchists, and that most used-car buyers expect to be deceived but do not intend to consent to be deceived, then an explicit denial of tacit consent is no longer needed to rebut the presumption of consent. Rather, the presumption runs the other way, absent further evidence that, for this particular actor, some action *does* signal tacit consent.

Against the evidentiary view of tacit consent, consider the constitutive view. Some actions constitute consent: to participate in or to benefit from a game *means* to consent to its rules. On this view, built into the meaning of "playing poker" or "bargaining with a used-car salesman" is the notion of consent to certain practices, which cannot be undone by contrary proclamations. What are we to make of the football halfback who, before the game, pins to his jersey a note that reads, in large letters, "I do not consent to be tackled," and then proceeds to take his place on the field, accepts a handoff, and runs with the football toward the goal line? One is tempted to say that he no longer plays football. If so, then he indeed has withdrawn his consent, he may not be tackled—and the referee should eject him from the game. But an equally plausible understanding is that he has not withdrawn his consent, that he cannot coherently deny consent so long as he takes the football in hand. Carrying a football under those circumstances means that one has consented to be tackled, no matter what he may signal or even intend to the contrary.

Consider an analogy. When Magritte adds to his drawing of a pipe the legend "Ceci n'est pas une pipe" (This is not a pipe), he does not undo the pipeness of the image. We don't say, "Oh. Before I read the disclaimer, I thought it was a pipe, but now I understand that it must be something else." Magritte's drawing tweaks at the notion that artists are authoritative interpreters of their art; tacit consent, understood constitutively, denies force to the explicit disclaimer "this is not consent" when one's behavior constitutes consent. The intention of the actor no more determines the meaning of an action than the intention of an artist determines the meaning of a work of art.[4]

Are we then to say that playing a game constitutes tacit consent to the game's rules, so that, if the rules allow deception, coercion, or violence, it is permissible to deceive, coerce, or do violence to the player? Not always. First, even if the possibility of constitutive tacit consent is granted, we must establish which actions do in fact constitute consent. Here the analogy to Magritte's pipe breaks down. Magritte's drawing is unproblematically pipish—hence the air of paradox; but participation in or benefit from adversary games does not unproblematically constitute consent, even if some acts—signing a check or running with a football, say—do so constitute. Even Locke understands that there are limits to what actions can be taken to mean. He holds that tacit consent does not create a permanent obligation to submit to government, and does not denote membership in a society. Without explicit consent, political obligation ceases when one's possession of land or enjoyment of residence in a country ceases.[5]

Alternatively, even if we agree that participation in adversary institutions *does* constitute consent despite the intentions of the actor, then the moral force of this sort of consent to obligate or permit may be questioned. We need then to distinguish between two types of consent, the consent that comes from intentional, free, and informed agreement, and the consent that does not. Consent of the second sort, which fails to satisfy the primary conditions of intention, freedom, and knowledge, quite plausibly does not do the moral work of consent of the first sort, and so is not a powerful presumptive source of permission or obligation.

---

[4] Some readers have objected that Magritte intended to make a point about representation, not artistic authority: the drawing is not a pipe, but an *image* of a pipe. But if the constitutive view of artistic meaning is correct, Magritte's intentions about the meaning of his drawing do not determine its meaning, and so do not undermine the use to which I put his pipe.

[5] Locke, *Second Treatise*, secs. 121–22.

The Argument from Fair Play

The most promising argument in support of the claim that game permissions generate moral permissions to deceive, threaten, or hurt another player is the argument from fair play. In the face of the failure of arguments from consent to establish a general obligation for citizens to obey the law, Hart and Rawls ingeniously offered the fair-play principle as a grounding for political obligation that depends on voluntary action, but not on voluntary consent to be obligated.[6] This section asks if the logic of fair play can be put to a new use: to permit actions that otherwise would not be permitted, rather than to require actions that otherwise would not be obligatory.

Roughly, the fair-play principle obligates us to do our fair share in schemes of social cooperation from which we willingly benefit, and not to free-ride on others. Rawls writes:

> This principle holds that a person is required to do his part as defined by the rules of an institution when two conditions are met: first, the institution is just (or fair), that is, it satisfies the two principles of justice; and second, one has voluntarily accepted the benefits of the arrangement or taken advantage of the opportunities it offers to further one's interests. The main idea is that when a number of persons engage in a mutually advantageous cooperative venture according to rules, and thus restrict their liberty in ways necessary to yield advantages for all, those who have submitted to these restrictions have a right to a similar acquiescence on the part of those who have benefitted from their submission. We are not to gain from the cooperative labors of others without doing our fair share.[7]

---

[6] H.L.A. Hart, "Are There Any Natural Rights?" *Philosophical Review* 64 (1955): 175–91; John Rawls, "Legal Obligation and the Duty of Fair Play," in *Law and Philosophy*, ed. Sidney Hook (New York: New York University Press, 1964), pp. 3–18; and John Rawls, *A Theory of Justice* (Cambridge, Mass.: Harvard University Press, 1971). In *A Theory of Justice*, Rawls refers to fair play as the fairness principle. Since the earlier rubric evokes the sorts of games under discussion here, I revert to it.

[7] Rawls, *A Theory of Justice*, pp. 111–12; note citing Hart omitted. The two principles refer to the content of Rawls's theory of justice for the basic institutions of society. In a recent restatement, they are as follows: "(a) Each person has an equal claim to a fully adequate scheme of equal basic rights and liberties, which scheme is compatible with the same scheme for all; and in this scheme, the equal political liberties, and only those liberties, are to be guaranteed their fair value; (b) Social and economic inequalities are to satisfy two conditions: first, they are to be attached to positions and offices open to all under conditions of fair equality of opportunity; and second, they are to be to the greatest benefit of the least advantaged members of society." See John Rawls, *Political Liberalism* (New York: Columbia University Press, 1993), pp. 5–6. But though the logic of fair play requires some conception of justice, it does not appear to require Rawls's conception.

If political society is such a cooperative venture, and citizens freely accept the benefits of social cooperation, then fairness obligates them to obey the laws of the state. The fair-play argument was thought to avoid the obvious difficulty with consent arguments, that citizens have not in fact consented to be obligated, while retaining two important intuitions: that receiving benefits may lead to obligations, but that some kinds of obligation must be connected to voluntary acts. Rather than relying on tortured accounts of consent to obligate anarchic pedestrians or demurring football players to play by the rules, we may simply say that fairness obligates these free riders, with or without their agreement.

Rawls no longer believes that the argument from fair play obligates all citizens to obey the law, because all citizens may not be advantaged by the scheme of social cooperation, or may not have freely accepted its benefits.[8] But his recantation should not deter our attempt to apply the fair-play argument to rules of strategic games. The argument for adversary permission from fair play may be stronger than the case for political obligation from fair play in two ways. First, many of the social institutions constituted by rule-governed games of strategy are more likely to be mutually advantageous cooperative ventures than is the whole of a modern society.[9] Second, establishing a permission to play by the rules of a game may be easier than establishing an obligation to play by them.

Does some version of the fair-play argument permit players in adversary games to lie, threaten, and inflict violence in accordance with the rules of the game, even if targets have not consented to play by the rules? To answer, I first lay out a very strong and restrictive formulation of the argument. These strong conditions appeal to our clearest intuitions about consent, benefit, fairness, and free riding, and anticipate some criticisms that have been leveled against the fair-play principle.[10] If any form of the fair-play argument establishes an adver-

---

[8] Rawls, *Theory of Justice*, pp. 113–14, 335–37, 344, 355. But see George Klosko, *The Political Principle of Fairness and Political Obligation* (Lanham, Md.: Rowman and Littlefield, 1992), for a recent attempt at reviving Rawls's earlier view.

[9] One might think "mutually advantageous *competitive* venture" is more apt. But there is no contradiction: here competitors cooperate, by their rule-abiding behavior, to create a mutually advantageous institution. Compare the distinction in game theory between cooperative and noncooperative games, where cooperation refers to the ability of competitive players to communicate and make binding agreements. See R. Duncan Luce and Howard Raiffa, *Games and Decisions* (New York: Wiley, 1957), p. 89.

[10] See M.B.E. Smith, "Is There a Prima Facie Obligation to Obey the Law?" *Yale Law Journal* 82 (1973): 951–76; Robert Nozick, *Anarchy, State, and Utopia* (New York: Basic Books, 1974), pp. 90–95; and A. John Simmons, *Moral Principles and Political Obligations* (Princeton, N.J.: Princeton University Press, 1979), pp. 101–42.

sary permission, it is this one. I then explore the force of the fair-play argument in generating adversary permissions by relaxing each of the conditions in turn.

Strong Conditions of Fair Play

A player in a game of strategy is morally permitted to take action against a target, so as to restrict the target's liberties or set back the target's interests, even if the target has not consented to be targeted, when five conditions are satisfied:

RULE PERMISSIBILITY: The rules of the game permit such adversary action.

NECESSITY: The rules permitting such action are necessary for the continued success or stability of the game as a mutually advantageous cooperative venture.

MUTUAL ADVANTAGE: The game is a mutually advantageous cooperative venture in that, considering all benefits and burdens, including the burden of becoming a target, and compared with the baseline alternative of there being no game, the game provides all its players positive expected net benefits. Players are those who voluntarily seek the venture's benefits.

JUSTICE: The venture is just in three ways: (a) on some reasonable conception of justice, this particular target is to receive a just share of the venture's benefits and burdens; (b) the venture generally distributes benefits and burdens justly to its players; and (c) the venture imposes no unjust externalities on those who are not players.

VOLUNTARY BENEFIT: Facing benefits and burdens that are of positive expected net benefit and justly distributed, and preferring the existence of the game with its benefits and burdens to there being no game, the target has voluntarily sought the game's benefits. The voluntary seeking of benefits is understood as an uncoerced and informed choice of action in circumstances where not to benefit is both possible and costless.

If fair play works at all to permit adversary action, it will work under these strong—probably excessively strong—conditions, where a player who claims immunity from targeting *does* seem to be asking for an unfair free ride that other players have no apparent moral reason to grant.

The case of the demurring football player satisfies these conditions. Other players have joined together in a mutually advantageous cooperative venture, football, whose rules permit violence against one another. Let us suppose that there is no injustice in the distribution of benefits and burdens (it is an amateur game, without salaries or shaving-cream endorsements to distribute; positions have been assigned fairly in accordance with skills and preferences; the neighbor's rose-bushes are not in danger). The demurring player seeks the advantages of running with the football—scoring—without the disadvantages of being tackled. This is unfair to the other players, who are all contributing to the venture and risking injury by playing by the rules. So long as he runs with the ball, fairness permits other players to tackle him. Similarly, fairness permits poker players to bluff those who seek the pleasures and rewards of the game. Others have joined together in a mutually advantageous venture, the game of poker, whose rules permit deception. One cannot voluntarily take the game's rewards and reasonably expect to be free from its burdens.

But are the conditions satisfied in the used-car negotiation case? Can we consider the used-car market to be a mutually advantageous cooperative venture, governed by the rule caveat emptor, so that the concealment of defects is permitted under the principle of fair play? Only if, among other things, benefits and burdens are justly distributed between buyers and sellers. Has a political candidate no reasonable complaint about a rival's appeal to racial bias and fear in campaign advertising? Complain he may, for the success and stability of the game of electoral politics does not depend on a campaign etiquette that admits deceptive and hateful advertising. Is a bar association that prevents its lawyers from advertising to be considered a mutually advantageous cooperative venture for the purpose of establishing and maintaining the monopoly pricing of legal services? If so, clients can hardly be understood to be cooperators, let alone advantaged cooperators, in such a venture. Professional institutions and adversary games are not self-contained systems. Some are designed to affect nonplayers, others inevitably do. What is seen as a mutually advantageous cooperative venture from the inside may be nothing of the sort. Adversary games more complex than poker and football that satisfy all of the strong conditions of fair play are rare indeed. If adversary action in the games of business, law, and politics is to be permitted under fair play, a formulation that is more relaxed but that still generates moral permission is needed. Can some of the specifications be loosened?

Necessity

Consider first the necessity condition, that the rules of the game allowing adversary action such as lies and threats are necessary for the continued success and stability of the mutually advantageous venture. At the core of the fair-play argument is the notion that to not play fair is to be unfair to *someone*. M.B.E. Smith argues that there can be no unfairness if there has not been either harm or loss of benefit, so the fair-play principle cannot obligate one to cooperate in a social venture if one's free riding does not cause some loss to at least one cooperator.[11] Smith's condition puts a serious limit on the likelihood of generating *obligations* to obey rules through fair play, because the marginal harms or losses of benefit of one incident of rule breaking attributable to the fact of rule breaking itself (apart from harms that would befall even if the act were not against the rules) is usually zero. If, at a sold-out Yo-Yo Ma concert, a couple sitting in the rear of Symphony Hall unobtrusively takes the seats of no-shows at seventh row center, and nobody notices, no one is worse off than if all complied with the rules and the best seats in the house went unfilled. If other concertgoers found out, they might cry unfair: "Why should they get better seats than they paid for, and not us?" or "Why should we have to pay for the best seats when they take them for less?" But on Smith's view, the cry is unwarranted: no harm, no unfairness, and since no one is worse off than had all complied, no harm has been done here (unless causing unwarranted feelings of resentment and unfairness is a harm). However, if known free riding encourages others to do the same, so that concert hall civility descends to the level of Filene's Basement, then the free ride does harm the cooperators in a cooperative venture, and is unfair to others. But whether or not one's rule breaking encourages others to do the same is a factual matter. Observing noncooperative behavior may instead reinforce the importance of cooperation (our typical reaction to litterbugs). On Smith's view, the morally decisive question is not the hypothetical generalization, "What if others did it?" but the empirical prediction, "Will others do it?" Indeed, many rules are robust against a fair amount of noncompliance. If Smith is right, the necessity condition is not strong *enough:* even when a general rule is necessary for the success and stability of a cooperative venture, if a particular act of noncompliance has no untoward effects on cooperators, either directly or by damaging the scheme of cooperation, then no unfairness has occurred.

Recall, however, that we seek to use the fair-play principle to permit players to act in accordance with the rules of a game, not to obligate playing by the rules. Smith's condition—that unfairness requires harm or loss of benefit—is more likely to be met when fair play is

---

[11] Smith, "Is There a Prima Facie Obligation?" pp. 954–58.

invoked to permit, rather than to obligate. A player who cannot take aim at a particular target usually *is* denied a benefit—winning the hand, making the tackle, closing the sale, convincing the jury, gaining the votes. If the would-be target has sought the benefits of the rules of a cooperative scheme, even on Smith's account the fair-play principle permits targeting in accordance with those rules.

In any case, Smith's condition does not *need* to be met, for moral permission to follow a rule does not depend on the rule's underlying reasons being satisfied in each particular case, even if a moral obligation to follow a rule does so depend. If a rule allowing sharp adversary tactics is necessary for the success of a cooperative scheme, and the general practice of regulation-by-rule is necessary, each adversary act under the rule need not be necessary for the act to be permitted. If permission to target many but not all is necessary, and there is no relevant distinction to be made among the all, or if requiring players to make such distinctions undermines the usefulness of regulating behavior by general rule, then the targeting of all is fair. Of course, rules can be overly broad, and for that reason be unfair. But rules can be overly narrow as well, as would be a rule that exempted a few named free riders for no other reason than that the inclusion of each and every player is not necessary. Though the game of poker would survive if players were permitted to bluff anyone but Ernest, Ernest is not treated unfairly if he is not granted immunity from bluffing. The game requires that most players be permissible targets, and Ernest can give no good reason why he should be treated specially. Generalization can make adversary rules fair, so that one has moral permission to follow them in specific cases. This is so, even if specific noncompliance with those same general rules is not unfair, so that one has no moral obligation to obey. Suppose that concertgoers have a general practice of throwing rotten tomatoes at those who move up to unoccupied seats, and the existence of the general practice, and common knowledge of its existence, is necessary to deter widespread free riding. Even if particular free riders have no obligation to stay in their assigned seats, because their particular acts of free riding cause no loss of benefit, they have no justified complaint if they are the targets of tomatoes. If some but no particular tomato tossing is necessary for the success and stability of concerts, then any particular tomato tossing is permitted.

But why must an adversary rule contribute to the "success and stability" of a game? An adversary rule may generate benefits and add value to an already mutually advantageous cooperative venture without the rule being necessary for the continued existence of the venture as a mutually advantageous scheme. The adversary legal system would successfully survive the repeal of most any single adversary permission, as it survived the introduction of discovery in civil proceedings, but many of its adversary permissions plausibly make the cooperative venture more advantageous to its players. Rawls appears to require a less stringent test—that rules be necessary to yield advantages for all. This follows from the underlying logic of fair play itself: if the prospect of justly distributed mutual advantage justifies the formation of a rule-governed cooperative venture, additional mutual advantage should justify additional rules.

Mutual Advantage

Consider now the mutual advantage condition. What constitutes, in games of strategy, a "mutually advantageous cooperative venture?" The strong formulation requires that all players be advantaged, and that the advantage of a player be assessed relative to the baseline of no venture (rather than to the baseline of nonparticipation). Leaving for later the question of who counts as a player, is this criterion of mutual advantage needed for the fair-play argument to permit players to harm targets in accordance with the rules of a game?

The requirement of universal advantage seems too strong as long as other conditions, such as justice and voluntary acceptance of benefit, are met. Certainly it is too strong if advantage is assessed ex post: to guarantee good outcomes to all would rule out any venture that involves irremediable risks such as physical harm, even if the ex ante expected advantage to all is great. No barns would be raised, no wells dug. Nor do we want to rule out games that add value over the no-game alternative but are zero sum within the game—for example, purely distributive bargains.

But even ex ante universal advantage is too tough. Why should the permissibility of an entire cooperative venture be called into question simply because one player is mistaken about his interests, preferences, or skills at playing the game? Perhaps the one who is not advantaged is under no obligation to comply with a game's rules, if fair play is invoked to obligate; and perhaps the one who is not advantaged is not a permissible target under an adversary rule. But it is not clear why the disadvantage of a few (if they are not unjustly or involuntarily disadvantaged) should block the fair-play principle from obligating others who are advantaged. Rawls's requirement of "yielding advantages for all" seems too strong. Surely, the disadvantage of a few should not block a permission to target the advantaged. A small, onetime litigant may be disadvantaged by rules of the court that permit an adversary to engage in costly delay tactics. But why should that render the tactic unfair if used against players who use the same tactics advantageously? The universal advantage requirement can be saved by considering only the advantaged to be participants or players in the cooperative venture, but such a move simply shifts the question to the voluntary-benefit condition: why are those who voluntarily seek the benefits of a just cooperative scheme not to be considered participants in that scheme, merely because they would be better off had they not sought such benefits? It appears that universal mutual advantage is too strong.

Next, consider the baseline condition. Is advantage to be reckoned from the alternative of not receiving the benefits or burdens of the existing cooperative venture, or the alternative of there being no such venture at all? The standard description of circumstances in which the fair-play principle is in play does not need to make this distinction. Consider four states: FREE RIDING, where the player receives the benefits but shirks the burdens of an existing cooperative venture; COOPERATION, where the player receives the benefits and shoulders the burdens; NONPARTICIPATION, where the player neither receives benefits nor shoulders burdens; and NO VENTURE, where the cooperative venture does not exist. The preferences or interests of players are assumed in the standard case to be ordered so that FREE RIDING is superior to COOPERATION, and COOPERATION is superior to both NONPARTICIPATION and NO VENTURE.

But suppose my neighbors have mowed a shortcut through a common meadow. I was more advantaged by the open meadow—I do not like the foot traffic, I did not want to disturb the flowers or rabbits. Now that there is a shortcut, I use it, rather than walk around the long way, because what I valued about the undisturbed meadow has already been ruined. The shortcut *is* convenient, and if I had to pay a small fee to continue using it, I would, though I would rather let the path grow over and have no one use it. The neighbors slip a note under my door asking for a modest annual contribution for the upkeep of the path.

Under this scheme, I prefer NO VENTURE to FREE RIDING, FREE RIDING to COOPERATION, and COOPERATION to NONPARTICIPATION. Am I advantaged by participation in the cooperative venture? Yes, relative to nonparticipation, but not compared with there being no venture at all. Do I violate the fair-play principle in refusing to pay my share? I think not. The venture was not organized for *my* advantage, and my preferences and interests are frustrated by its existence. Must I refrain from participation, and not use the path? Reasonable intuitions go both ways, but if we consider "free riding" as an attempt to compensate for the involuntary loss imposed by the cooperative venture, then the free ride (or walk) is not unfair to cooperators on the fair-play principle. My situation, after all, is different from theirs: they are made better off by the cooperative venture, and I am made worse off.

Many adversary games share this structure. The introduction of competitive markets for goods that previously were allocated through nonmarket mechanisms has not advantaged all players in the new markets. This is obvious when market forces challenge those who had access to resources through traditional means. Not all wives are advantaged by the opening of labor markets to women, though they may now seek employment; trade liberalization creates many losers who nonetheless compete to cut their losses. When Alexander Hamilton freely accepted Aaron Burr's challenge to duel, perhaps he wished that there were no such institution for settling affairs of honor—and perhaps Burr wished the same. If fairness obligates players in these games to abide by the rules, it must be a notion of fairness different from the one underlying the fair-play principle, because these players have been disadvantaged by the existence of the cooperative venture.

Is this strong condition of advantage relative to the no-venture alternative necessary to *permit* adversary action? If Hamilton is better off without the institution of dueling, is Burr forbidden to fire? The answer appears to depend on a richer description of the burdens imposed on participants in the cooperative scheme, the disadvantages that befall nonparticipants, and the connections of both to the benefits sought by the disadvantaged player. If the player participates to defend against the disadvantages that are imposed by the existence of the venture, and if the burdens that befall players restrict their liberties or set back their interests in ways that would be wrong in the absence of the venture, then there does not seem to be any moral justification to impose burdens on the disadvantaged participant.

If the correct specification of the mutual-advantage criterion is advantage in comparison with there being no venture, the scope of the adversary actions permitted by fair play is severely restricted. But it would be a mistake, I think, to interpret the criterion even more stringently, and require that players be advantaged in comparison with any possible cooperative venture. For any set of rules governing a game, there will almost certainly be a different set of rules or a different game more favorably tailored to a particular player. But one is not treated unfairly just because one does not get the most favorable treatment possible, and a free rider can be understood to take unfair advantage of cooperators, even when the rules upon which one free-rides are not one's first choice.

Voluntary Benefit

We turn now to the voluntary-benefit condition. The strong formulation defines players as those, and only those, who have voluntarily sought the benefits of the cooperative venture, where voluntarily seeking benefits is understood as an uncoerced and informed choice of action in circumstances where not to benefit is both possible and costless. But why are not all who benefit from the cooperative venture considered participants or players, whether or not such benefit is voluntary? If voluntary benefit is necessary, why must benefit be actively sought, rather than willingly but passively accepted? If benefit is voluntary, why must the possibility of not benefiting be necessary? Why must the possibility of not benefiting be costless?

In rejecting the fair-play principle as a source of obligation, Robert Nozick offers a series of engaging examples: neighbors who take turns playing musical entertainment over a local public address system that you enjoyably overhear; neighbors who mow their lawns more frequently than is your habit; people who throw valuable books into your house for exercise; neighbors who cooperate to sweep the streets. "Must you imagine dirt as you traverse the street, so as not to benefit as a free rider?" he asks rhetorically.[12] Must you take your turn at the neighborhood microphone or mow your lawn more frequently? No, because you have not volunteered for the benefits involved, though, in all, the benefits you receive outweigh the burdens requested of you. Nozick's examples point out the importance of some sort of voluntary action in our intuitions about fairness, and not merely the receipt of benefit, but do not tell against the fair-play principle as Rawls understands it.

No voluntary participation in receiving benefits, no obligation to assume burdens under fair play. But does this formulation extend to adversary permissions? Or is it sufficient, in order to permit burdening a target, that he has received greater benefit, willingly or not? Suppose you live downwind from a polluting steel mill. You benefit from the economic activity the mill has brought to your town, and the benefit outweighs the health risks of pollution, but this hardly robs you of reasonable complaint. Just as you are not obligated to pay for uninvited valuable books thrown in your house, the book thrower is not permitted to smash your windows, even if the books are more valuable to you than the glass.

---

[12] Nozick, *Anarchy, State, and Utopia,* pp. 90–95 (quotation from p. 94).

The remaining stipulations in the strong formulation of the voluntary-participation condition share an underlying logic: without each, voluntary participation in the cooperative venture is difficult to demonstrate. Passive acceptance of benefit may signal willingness, but may result from indifference, ignorance, or the difficulty of avoiding benefit. If refusing benefit is impossible, as with unavoidable public goods like national defense, voluntariness is hard to demonstrate. Again, if avoiding benefit is possible but in itself burdensome (imagining dirty streets and unkempt lawns, or not walking out of doors), not refusing benefit does not necessarily signal willing acceptance of benefit, even if one is better off with the benefits and its associated burdens than without.

As was seen in the earlier discussion of tacit consent, there is a constitutive and an evidentiary interpretation of the connection of these requirements to voluntary acceptance of benefit—and the evidentiary interpretation is the correct one. When a player passively receives a benefit, cannot refuse it, or can refuse it only at a cost, we may not presume, without further evidence, that acceptance of benefit is voluntary. Here, there is good reason to be *more* stringent in finding adversary permissions to impose burdens than in finding obligations to assume burdens. Since one ordinarily knows the state of one's own will better than others can know it, one may in fact be obligated because of voluntary acceptance of benefit in ways that others cannot detect, though others are not permitted to presume such voluntary acceptance. Given the presumptive wrong in restricting liberties and setting back interests, when it comes to adversary permissions there should be a (rebuttable) presumption against assuming the voluntary participation of others.

Once voluntary acceptance of benefit has been established, however, to require the further condition that exit from the game be costless as well is too stringent. Earlier, easy exit was offered as an evidentiary test of a player's continued consent to play by the rules. But recall that the point of the fair-play principle is to establish obligations and permissions when prior or ongoing consent to rules is lacking. Costly exit may block the inference that the acceptance of future benefits will be voluntary, but does not undo the voluntary acceptance of past benefits. As long as the conditions of ex ante mutual advantage and justice are satisfied, exit barriers do not preclude application of the fair-play principle to past benefits voluntarily accepted. So, if we are in the middle of a high-stakes round of poker, even though you cannot fold your hand and decline further pleasures of the game without a big loss, I may still bluff you. Hamilton and Burr cannot

both freely leave the dueling ground, but this exit barrier is not why
the duel is impermissible.[13]

Justice

Finally, consider the justice conditions. How do the justice conditions
limit the reach of the fair-play principle? Straightaway, we should
back off from Rawls's particular conception of justice and its two
principles. The fair-play argument requires *a* theory of justice, but not
A Theory of Justice. Our strong formulation requires, on some conception of justice, that the cooperative venture be just in three ways: *local
justice,* in that this particular target of adversary action receives a just
share of the venture's benefits and burdens; *internal justice,* in that the
venture generally distributes benefits and burdens justly to its players;
and *external justice,* in that the venture does not impose unjust externalities on those who are not players. How do these stipulations
work, and why are they needed?

The requirement of local justice for permitting adversary action is
straightforward enough: we may not treat others unfairly, and so we
may not target others if such targeting is unfair to them. Why one has
no *obligation* to obey rules that treat oneself unfairly is a bit more
complicated. The reasons given here have a bearing on whether or
not one has an obligation to obey rules that treat others unfairly, and
whether or not one is permitted to target another fairly under rules
that also permit unfair targeting.

Rawls reasons that one cannot acquire an obligation to an unjust
institution. He argues that extorted promises are void ab initio, and
unjust social arrangements are a kind of extortion, so even direct consent to obey an unjust institution is coerced consent.[14] Similarly, we
may draw the implication that no obligation of fair play arises when a
cooperative venture is unjust, because what appears to be voluntary
acceptance of benefit is coerced acceptance.

Rawls's conclusion that one cannot acquire an obligation to an unjust
institution claims too much, however, as John Simmons has pointed
out.[15] Even if injustice is a form of coercion, unjust institutions do not
coerce everyone with respect to everything. Suppose a bank is involved in coercive dealings with others. If the bank has not coerced
you, and you borrow money with the promise to repay, you have met
all the conditions of free and informed consent, and so you are obli-

[13] An observation I owe to Jim Sebenius.
[14] Rawls, *A Theory of Justice*, pp. 112, 343.
[15] Simmons, *Moral Principles*, pp. 77–79, 109–14.

gated not to default on the loan. One could perhaps argue that one *should* not freely consort with and acquire obligations to unjust institutions, and argue further that there sometimes are overriding reasons to break one's obligations to unjust institutions (if, say, keeping one's obligation will cause great further injustice). But those arguments are to be distinguished from the present claim, that one logically *cannot* freely consort with unjust institutions, and so cannot acquire an obligation to them, even if one tries.

Simmons is right that one can enter into obligations to unjust institutions, but Rawls's claim can be saved in a way that preserves its force for our purposes. Though one can acquire obligations to an unjust institution, one cannot become *generally* obligated to obey its rules. An unjust institution, or an institution that is unjust in certain extortionary ways, does not have the legitimacy to make morally authoritative rules, so the fact that such an institution has issued a rule is not by itself a good reason to obey the rule. (There may be other good moral reasons to act in ways that the rules of an unjust institution demand—the action may lead to good consequences, for instance.) And though I can enter into specific obligations to unjust institutions by way of a voluntary promise, I cannot, by my voluntary promise, grant or contribute to the granting of legitimate rule-making authority to an unjust institution.

The questions about the local and internal justice conditions can now be answered. By seeking the benefits of a cooperative scheme that treats one unjustly, one has not acquired a specific obligation to shoulder burdens, because actions taken in response to injustice are not fully voluntary.[16] By seeking the benefits of a cooperative scheme that treats others unjustly, one has not acquired a general obligation to submit to the scheme's rules, because the rules of unjust institutions lack moral authority. However, one may have acquired specific obligations to specific players (most likely, to those who are treated unjustly).

Similarly, with regard to adversary permissions, an unfair institution does not have the legitimating power to permit what would otherwise be forbidden, such as deception or threats in a business nego-

---

[16] This requires several qualifications. It is not meant that one is not responsible for actions taken in response to injustice, or that the slightest injustice calls into question the freedom of all action. The claim is limited to the application of the fair-play principle: free riding on a scheme that is substantially unjust to you is not unfair, because, under a moralized understanding of coercion, injustice introduces a defect in the voluntariness of your acceptance of benefit, and the fair-play principle requires voluntary acceptance. See Nozick, "Coercion," and Wertheimer, *Coercion,* for moralized conceptions of coercion.

tiation. If some business activity as a cooperative venture is unfair (say, workers are wrongfully exploited on some view of exploitation), then the fact that business rules permit adversary practices that further the success of the scheme of cooperation adds no further justification to engage in those practices. If such practices would be wrong without a cooperative scheme, the existence of an unfair cooperative scheme does not legitimate the practice. This is so even if the target of some specific adversary action is not being treated unfairly.

Consider now the external justice condition, that the venture imposes no unjust externalities on those who are not players. Under the rather stringent definition of a player that seems to be required, adversary institutions of any social importance that do not have substantial effects on nonplayers will be extremely rare. All legal and political institutions, by their very purposes, affect nonplayers. (However, some minor schemes of internal governance may have no external effects—rules of etiquette in the Senate's private dining room, or the allocation of corner offices in a law firm.) Despite the game-playing images we have encountered, the effects of business enterprise are neither restricted to an inner arena of competitors nor to a larger market of voluntary customers, suppliers, workers, and investors. Let me be clear: I have not provided a reason to suppose that these externalities will be systematically unjust. But when they *are* unjust, permission to inflict external injustice finds no support in the argument from fair play. That piracy is a mutually advantageous and internally just scheme of social cooperation for pirates does not begin to justify a practice devoted to robbery and kidnapping, Gilbert and Sullivan notwithstanding. Much may turn on whether and when various clients, patients, customers, workers, and voters are to be considered players or outsiders, because what counts as unjust treatment of someone who cannot be understood to have voluntarily sought the benefits of a game may be far more demanding than what counts as an injustice to a player.

———————

The widely held notion that one is morally permitted to harm another if the rules of a social game permit such harm is harder to justify than one might have thought. The notion is intuitively plausible because consent can generate moral permissions, but mere participation in a game does not imply that one has consented to be harmed in accordance with the game's rules. Just as consent-based arguments to obligate citizens to obey the laws of the state founder on stringent evidentiary requirements, consent-based arguments are likely to fail to permit presumptively wrong actions in adversary games. A more promising route is to appeal to the notion that free riding in a game is unfair to the players who are willing to risk harm in accordance with the game's rules. Though this argument from fair play may fail to obligate free riders to play by the rules, we do not need to establish as much. We need only to show that players are permitted to harm free riders in accordance with the rules, just as they are permitted to harm willing players.

Though the best case for an adversary permission that we have seen rests on the fair-play argument, even fair play has limited applicability. It takes its biggest normative bite when the harms of games are internalized among those who seek its benefits, but harms generated by most middle-level social institutions—notably, the practices of the competitive professions—are not so internalized. Even on a loose construction of the conditions for fair play, the targeting of nonplayers is not permissible if, game aside, such targeting would be an impermissible restriction of liberty or a setback of interest. This is so even for nonplayers who on balance benefit, and the specification of a player must remain fairly tight. To call all consumers players in the game of market competition, all voters players in the game of electoral politics, and all litigants players in the game of the adversary legal system is too quick, for many consumers, voters, and litigants neither are advantaged by the game nor voluntarily seek the game's benefits. But business managers, public officials, and lawyers may satisfy the conditions of fair play in their deceptive or coercive dealings with one another, and there may be market segments, political elites, and corporate legal clients who meet the criteria of player. If the burdens and benefits of these games are fairly distributed, a player who is deceived or forced may have no reasonable grounds for complaint.

Chapter Seven

ARE VIOLATIONS OF RIGHTS EVER RIGHT?

> What liberalism requires is the possibility of making the evil of cruelty and fear the basic norm of its political practices and prescriptions. The only exception to the rule of avoidance is the prevention of greater cruelties.
>
> *Judith N. Shklar, "The Liberalism of Fear"*

THE PRINCIPLE of fair play puts stringent conditions on the moral permissions an adversary game can mint. But the conditions might be stronger still. Perhaps some ways of treating others—killing, lying, coercing—are unjust no matter how we organize our collective life. Some ways of being treated might persist in their moral wrongness, despite the victim's voluntary participation in a mutually advantageous social institution whose rules permit such treatment. Rawls distinguishes an obligation, which is created by social interaction, from a natural duty, whose force does not depend on any actual practice, institution, convention, or agreement.[1] If there are such natural duties (and so, correlatively, natural rights), how could something like the fair-play principle morally permit us to act in ways that violate our natural duties to one another?

One easy way out is to claim that, in the context of a social practice or institution, certain actions no longer count as deception, coercion, or violence, and so are not violations of duty. Sometimes the easy way out works: surgery performed with informed consent does not count as battery. But as we saw in Chapter 5, sometimes the easy way out is pure pettifoggery: deceit still counts as deceit, even when it counts as zealous advocacy. This chapter explores a harder claim: that some ways of treating other persons are morally permitted, even though the actions retain the descriptions "deception," "coercion," and "violence" and remain violations of persons and their rights.

If this claim is successful, a larger worry arises. For if moral con-

---

[1] John Rawls, *A Theory of Justice* (Cambridge, Mass.: Harvard University Press, 1971), pp. 114–15. These duties are natural in the sense that they are preconventional, but they need not be natural in any metaphysical way. To use the concept of a natural duty we do not need to take a stand on where they get their force—whether from natural properties in the world, human nature, god's law, or, as Rawls holds, from a construction of reason.

straints against deception, coercion, and violence may sometimes be violated, perhaps these constraints and, correlatively, moral rights are not fundamental and serious elements of morality.[2] This, of course, is the claim of utilitarians. If utilitarianism is the correct moral theory, there are no serious objections to adversary practices and institutions that permit serious harm, as long as these institutions in the end succeed in delivering goods that outweigh the human wreckage left along the way. For the consequentialist who values a plurality of goods, not only utility, the calculation is a bit more complicated. But there again is no fundamental objection to an adversary practice that produces more of each valued good by inflicting along the way some of each corresponding bad.

This chapter explores a class of actions where the claim that the actor is morally permitted to violate moral constraints is thought by many to be most plausible, and therefore most challenging to those who want to take constraints seriously. These are cases of *violation minimization*, where the violation of a constraint against one will prevent more numerous or more severe violations of the same constraint against others: violence to the few that prevents bloodier violence to the many, the lie that leads to fewer lies, the coercion that frees others from coercion. Consequentialists argue that, if not violating a constraint is good, preventing many violations of the same constraint must be better. Their opponents reply that that misses the point of constraints, which is to govern how you should treat other persons, despite the consequences. Consequentialists answer, Why should how you treat another have more moral importance than the way many treat many others? And on it goes.[3]

The permissibility of violation-minimizing violations has been vigorously debated recently because many consequentialists and their opponents seem to agree that, if violating constraints for the sake of minimizing violations is morally permissible, then such constraints cannot be fundamental and serious elements of morality. They disagree, of course, about whether such action indeed is permissible. I hope to show that permitting violations under certain circumstances does *not* undermine the moral point of constraints, and that violating constraints to avoid greater violations is not a contradiction. Why this may be so for violation-minimizing violations of constraints becomes more clear once we look at reasons for permitting the violation of

[2] Roughly, constraints and rights are fundamental if they cannot be reduced to some other moral concept; they are serious to the extent that they have force in moral justification independent of the force of some other moral reason.

[3] The problem of violation minimization is first posed, and imaginatively treated, by Robert Nozick, *Anarchy, State and Utopia* (New York: Basic Books, 1974), ch. 3.

constraints in two related classes of cases: what I shall call *self-defeat-ing constraints*, where not violating a constraint against harming a person will lead to a more severe violation of that constraint against harming that *same* person, and *Pareto-inferior constraints*, where not violating a constraint against harming a person will not prevent the constraint against harming that person from being violated, and, in addition, will lead to more violations of constraints against harming others.

NONVIOLATION AND INVIOLABILITY

Frances Kamm and Thomas Nagel have argued, in somewhat differ-ent ways, that rights are independently valuable because they express the inviolable status of persons.[4] The fact that persons are, are viewed as, and view themselves as the sort of creatures that others must not violate is itself valuable, quite apart from whether persons are actu-ally violated, and quite apart from whether having the status of in-violability reduces the likelihood of being actually violated. Nagel presents the value of inviolability as a substantive reason why viola-tion-minimizing violations of constraints ordinarily are impermissible. In addition to the substantive reason Kamm offers a logical one: to violate a constraint against violation for the sake of inviolability in-volves a contradiction.

Although Kamm's is the earlier account, let us begin with Nagel's.[5] "Morality is possible," says Nagel, "only for beings capable of seeing themselves as one individual among others more or less similar in general respects—capable, in other words, of seeing themselves as others see them."[6] Our lives matter to us, but we realize that the lives of billions of others matter to them. Either we concede that, from an impersonal point of view, no one really matters, or we recognize that

[4] I am grateful to Elizabeth Kiss for introducing me to their arguments about in-violability. See her paper, "Rights and Inviolability: A Critique of Nagel and Kamm's Anti-Instrumentalism," which was presented at the eastern division meetings of the American Philosophical Association, Atlanta, 1993; Thomas Nagel, "La Valeur de l'invi-olabilité," *Revue de métaphysique et de morale* 99 (1994): 149–66, portions of which appear in Nagel, "Personal Rights and Public Space," *Philosophy and Public Affairs* 24 (1995): 86–93; F. M. Kamm, "Harming Some to Save Others," *Philosophical Studies* 57 (1989): 227–60, and "Non-consequentialism, the Person as an End-in-Itself, and the Signifi-cance of Status," *Philosophy and Public Affairs* 21 (1992): 354–89.

[5] Nagel acknowledges his reliance on Kamm in "La Valeur de l'inviolabilité," pp. 160–63.

[6] Ibid., p. 160.

the fact that each life matters to the one who is living it *does* matter, in some way, from an impersonal perspective. If one ought to matter to no one but oneself, then one cannot continue to think of oneself as a being that matters very much at all. Since we think of ourselves as beings that matter, consistency demands that we extend that status to others. Says Nagel, "I believe, as did Kant, that what drives us in the direction of universalizability is the difficulty each person has in regarding himself as having value only *for himself*, but not *in himself*. If people are not ends in themselves—i.e. impersonally valuable—then they have a much lower order of worth."[7] If one wishes to view and value oneself as a being that is an end in itself, and not as a means to be used for the ends of others, then the status of an end must be extended to others. The violation of other persons—using them as means—therefore is an impersonal bad, something we all have reason to avoid and prevent.

But if such violation is bad, why should we not seek to minimize violations, even if that sometimes requires a lesser violation? Because a violation-minimizing violation uses one as a means for the ends of others, and so fails to treat persons as ends in themselves. If persons are to matter in the highest possible way, then morality must value not only the absence of violations of persons, but the treatment of persons as beings who have the status of being inviolable—whose violation is not permissible. "What actually happens to us is not the only thing we care about: What *may* be done to us is also important, quite apart from whether or not it *is* done to us—and the same is true of what we *may do* as opposed to what we actually do."[8] Since having the status of inviolability is of great value, if morality permits violations so as to maximize the good of not being violated, all persons cease to have a high degree of inviolability, which is a great bad. We all may be better off in a world in which morality always treated us as ends, and so where it is always morally impermissible to violate us, even though we are thereby more likely to suffer violation at the hands of immoral actors.

We might think at this point that Nagel is simply adding another variable to the consequentialist calculation, weighing the value of having the status of inviolability against the value of actual nonviolation. If that were so, constraints and rights would not be serious and fundamental after all, but rather, rules of thumb summarizing the trade-off between two more fundamental values of similar conse-

---

[7] Ibid., p. 161.
[8] Ibid., p. 157; Nagel, "Personal Rights," p. 91.

quential structure. Nagel invites this interpretation, for he speaks of one value outweighing the other,[9] and he believes that there are thresholds beyond which the right of inviolability must give way to the consequence of reducing violations. To prevent a large enough number of killings, one is permitted to kill. "Even if rights are not instrumental, they are not absolute. Their extent depends in part on other values besides the noninstrumental value of inviolability."[10]

Let us set aside what Nagel means by "noninstrumental," and what he thinks has that attribute, the right not to be violated or the value of inviolability. Nagel holds that the status of high inviolability is the outcome of universalization, rather than a maximization: by asking what ways of being treated by others are reasonable to want, we arrive at how others should be treated by us.[11] Nonviolation and inviolability are not, in the first instance, possibly competing values to be weighed across persons from some impersonal perspective—that *would* entail a consequentialist maximization. Rather, nonviolation and inviolability are weighed in the first instance within the life of a person who values them because his life matters to *him*—and this result is universalized to others. This opens the possibility that a person can imagine circumstances under which his own violation ought to be permitted. Therein lies part of the solution to the puzzle of violation minimization . . . but we are getting ahead of ourselves.

Nagel borrows this distinction between inviolability as a status to be respected and nonviolation as a consequence to bring about from Kamm. Both acknowledge the substantive value of treating persons as creatures that have a high degree of inviolability by virtue of being ends in themselves.[12] But Kamm goes further, arguing that violating

---

[9] Nagel, "La Valeur de l'inviolabilité," p. 164.

[10] Ibid., p. 165.

[11] Ibid., p. 162. The substantive content of the outcome of some such process of universalization may be "maximize good consequences," but the justificatory force of such content comes from the fact that it is the result of universalization. See, for example, T. M. Scanlon, "Contractualism and Utilitarianism," in *Utilitarianism and Beyond*, ed. Amartya Sen and Bernard Williams (Cambridge: Cambridge University Press, 1982), pp. 103–28.

[12] In an important difference, which will not be explored here, Nagel believes that noninstrumental rights cannot be explained without invoking agent-relative reasons and values, while Kamm holds that an entirely agent-neutral, "victim-focused" account of rights is both sufficient and correct. See Thomas Nagel, *The View from Nowhere* (New York: Oxford University Press, 1986); Kamm, "Harming Some to Save Others," pp. 244, 249–51, 255, and "Non-consequentialism," pp. 382, 385–86. For another argument against Nagel, see Christine M. Korsgaard, "The Reasons We Can Share: An Attack on the Distinction between Agent-Relative and Agent-Neutral Values," *Social Philosophy and Policy* 10 (1993): 24–51.

constraints for the sake of minimizing violations of constraints involves confusion and contradiction. Kamm asks:

> Why is it not permissible, indeed obligatory, for us to do this—i.e., engage in what has been referred to as a utilitarianism of rights—as an expression of respect and concern for rights?
>
> I suggest, in answer to this question, that a moral system—where a moral system is our attempt to represent moral truth—that permits minimization of the violations of a certain right by transgression of that very right essentially eliminates that right from the system, hence it would be futile as a way of showing respect for rights: it would be a "futilitarianism" of rights. This is so, at least, if the right is what I shall call a *specified* right, and rights with at least some sort of specification, we shall see, are the serious rights.[13]

Kamm believes that it would be confused to violate a specified right— a constraint that is not vague about the extent of protection it accords—to minimize violations of that right. For example, suppose (as Nagel allows) there is some threshold beyond which the harms of violation do outweigh the value of inviolability, so that the correct specification of the right not to be killed is: "Do not kill one to prevent the killing of fewer than six others." Further suppose that others will violate this constraint five times, by killing five persons without justification, unless you violate the constraint once, by killing one to save the five. To violate the constraint for its own sake under such circumstances is confused, says Kamm, because it denies that "Do not kill one to prevent the killing of fewer than six others" is the correct specification of the constraint against killing. "Suppose people are covered by such constraints whose ground is the expression of personal inviolability of a certain sort. Then it would be simply self-contradictory for it to be morally permissible to minimize violations of the constraint itself for the sake of showing concern for *it*."[14]

VIOLATING PERSONS AND VIOLATING RIGHTS

At bottom, I believe, Kamm's and Nagel's arguments traffic in an ambiguity about the subject of nonviolation or inviolability. Are *persons* not to be violated and treated as inviolable, or are *rights* not to be violated and treated as inviolable? Kamm and Nagel distinguish, ap-

---

[13] Kamm, "Harming Some to Save Others," p. 252. "Utilitarianism of rights" is Nozick's coinage; see Nozick, *Anarchy*, p. 28.

[14] Kamm, "Non-consequentialism," p. 384.

propriately, nonviolation from inviolability, and see them as separate values. If we also distinguish persons from rights, we have four concepts and four possible values: the nonviolation of persons and the inviolability of persons, the nonviolation of rights and the inviolability of rights.

What do I mean by person violation? Semantically, rape is the clearest case: to rape a woman is to violate her, quite apart from violating her right not to be violated. The concept of person violation extends readily to other ways of damaging bodily integrity: stabbing, torturing, starving, chaining. But not all violations of bodily integrity are person violations, and not all person violations are violations of bodily integrity. Surgery involves penetration of the body, is painful, and can be disfiguring, but consensual surgery is not a person violation. Suppression of the freedom of thought and discussion is a person violation, though it involves no bodily harm. Let us say, provisionally, that a person is violated when her moral agency, and so her personhood, is either damaged or denied. One's moral agency is damaged when one's capacity to choose and pursue ends is impaired, as when one is killed, crippled, or severely deprived and degraded. One's moral agency is denied when one is treated merely as a tool for the ends of others, as when one is forced, coerced, or deceived. What distinguishes the scalpel from the stiletto, of course, is that the scalpel ordinarily is wielded for an agency-preserving end that the patient, exercising agency, has willed as her own. For now, we will have to make do with this suggestive but sketchy account of person violation. What is to count as damage to or denial of personhood, and so what is to count as person violation, will become more clear as we progress.

To violate a person usually is to do something terrible, which is why violations of persons usually are violations of the rights of those persons not to be violated. But the two notions of violating a person and violating a person's right not to be violated are separate, and some steps are needed to get from one to the other. Not all violations of persons are violations of rights: striking a willful attacker in self-defense is a person violation, but not a rights violation. Nor are all violations of rights violations of persons. I can wrongfully use your property without using you, and I can damage your property without damaging your capacity for moral agency.

Person inviolability, Kamm and Nagel argue, is a status persons have by virtue of being ends in themselves. This status is expressed and its value recognized through constraints against person violation, and correlative rights not to have one's person violated. The nonviolation of rights is of great moral importance because it realizes the value of not violating persons and expresses the value of the inviolability of persons. But the concept of nonviolation of rights and its value do not collapse into either the concept of nonviolation of persons and its value or the concept of the inviolability of persons and its value.

Because rights nonviolation is of great moral importance, it is a state of affairs to bring about, both through not violating rights oneself and by preventing others from violating rights. Posed this way, of course, we do not yet have an answer to the puzzle of rights maximization, for sometimes the way to prevent others from violating rights is to violate rights. For Kamm and Nagel to be correct about the impermissibility of violating rights to minimize their violation, *rights* must have the status of inviolability.

Rights inviolability is a claim about the status of rights, not, at least not directly, about the status of persons. Now, rights must claim *some* measure of inviolability if rights are to be reasons for action with any sort of prescriptive force. But why this is so, and why rights are to be taken seriously, cannot be because *rights* are ends in themselves. That is a fetishistic claim, both untrue and unnecessary for taking rights seriously. *Persons* are ends in themselves, and so have a high degree of inviolability, expressed by rights to nonviolation, and these rights have moral force—that is, *some* measure of inviolability. But it does not immediately follow from the recognition of a high degree of person inviolability that rights should have an equally high degree of inviolability—that is, that rights should be absolute, or nearly absolute, even when specified. Here, then, is a preliminary answer to Kamm: though indeed it may be a contradiction to violate a constraint in order to express the high inviolable status of constraints, constraints do not have the status of high inviolability. It is no contradiction (though it may be a mistake) to violate a constraint in order to express the inviolable status of *persons*. The primary objects of our respect and concern are persons, not rights; so there is neither futility nor contradiction in violating the rights of persons if that is what circumstances demand to treat them as ends in themselves. Let us see if there can be any circumstances where this is so.

The problem of rights maximization is one of a family of cases where more or less violation, either of persons or of rights, will occur, depending on what an actor chooses. Through action or inaction, actor A can bring about one of two courses of events. In one, call it the *lesser violation prong*, actor A violates target T. In the other, call it the *greater violation prong*, actor or actors A′ violate more severely or more frequently or in greater numbers target or targets T′. We have distinguished person violation from rights violation, so the violations that

TABLE 1
Violation Types

| | | LESSER VIOLATION PRONG (A violates the person or right of T) | |
		PERSON	RIGHT
GREATER VIOLATION PRONG	PERSON	I	II
(A' violates the person or right of T')	RIGHT	III	IV

are to occur in the lesser and greater violation prongs may be either violations of persons or of rights, yielding the four violation types illustrated in Table 1.

Next, we specify the identities of actors and targets in both prongs. Target T' in the greater violation prong may be identical to target T, may include target T among other targets, or may be different from target T. Similarly, actor A' in the greater violation prong may be identical to actor A, may include actor A among other actors, or may be different from actor A in the lesser violation prong, yielding the nine identity types illustrated in Table 2. For example, in Type 9, actor A faces the decision to violate target T in order to prevent some other actor or actors, A', from causing greater violation to some other target or targets T'. If the violations in both prongs are rights violations (Table 1, Type IV), then the case described is the standard problem of

TABLE 2
Identity Types in the Greater Violation Prong

| | TARGET(S) T' | | |
ACTOR(S) A'	T' is T	T' includes T	T' excludes T
A' is A	1	4	7
A' includes A	2	5	8
A' excludes A	3	6	9

rights-violation minimization, of violating a constraint against one in order to prevent worse constraint violations by others against others. This is the case in which the choice of the lesser violation prong is contradictory, according to Kamm.

Note, however, that this is but one of thirty-six possible combinations of the four violation types (Table 1) and the nine identity types (Table 2). The reader will be spared an elaboration of all thirty-six, since each is not uniquely interesting, but a few are, and shed light on our question.

SELF-DEFEATING CONSTRAINTS

Consider the cases of *self-defeating nonviolation*, where not violating a target will lead to a more severe violation of that *same* target—that is, where T and T' are identical. We begin with an obvious example, where A and A' are also identical, and the violations in both prongs are person violations, but not rights violations (Type I-1). Suppose that I am attacked by someone who wishes to kill me, and I can defend myself using either the lethal force of a gun or the nonlethal force of my fists. Either way, I do not violate the rights of the attacker but, either way, I violate the person of the attacker. Using lethal force is a greater violation of the person of the attacker. May I take the lesser violation prong and use nonlethal force? Of course I may, and perhaps I must, if I can defend myself just as well. Though striking a person is a violation, killing a person is a greater violation. I am the one who is harming another in either case. To use a gun in order to avoid using fists is bizarre; surely I may choose the lesser person violation.

Now, a less obvious example: the same attacker menaces me, I have no gun, but I see that an onlooker does, and if I do not defend myself with my fists, the onlooker will shoot the attacker in my defense (Type I-3).[15] Again, I certainly am permitted to punch the attacker. He has no right not to be punched. Though I violate his person, I spare him a graver violation, being shot. If I punch him, I do so for the sake of his personhood: to minimize the violation of *him*. Acting for the sake of another's personhood is not simply to act in another's interests. Rather, it is to respect and preserve, insofar as the circumstances allow, his moral agency. Here, of course I do not share the attacker's end to do me harm, and, in using violence to thwart his will, I violate

---

[15] I suppose here that the onlooker is permitted to defend me. If she is not, then this is a case of Type III-3.

him; but in sparing him a graver violation, I both respect an end I reasonably assume he does will, not to die, and in so doing I preserve his capacity for moral agency. If person violation is permitted in simple cases of self-defense, a fortiori it is permitted here, where to refrain from person violation is self-defeating.[16]

Another example of the same type: the horn of the rhinoceros fetches an astronomical price on the black market because in parts of Asia it is believed to be a powerful aphrodisiac. So conservationists in African game parks saw off rhino horns to prevent poachers from killing the endangered creatures. Now, a rhino is not the sort of creature that has rights, but is the sort of creature that can be harmed, so that the mutilation involved in having its horn sawn off is a "creature violation," a bad to avoid and prevent. But if the conservationists do not inflict this lesser violation, the poachers will commit a far greater violation of the same rhinos. If the reason one ordinarily should not saw off a rhino's horn is that rhino violation is bad for rhinos, not to saw off the horns in this case for *that* reason is *self-defeating*, for the outcome of not sawing off the horns will be much worse for the same rhinos.

A harder case: in imperial Russia, young boys were sometimes impressed into the tsar's army for many years of harsh, cruel, and dangerous service. Some parents, to spare their sons this fate, would cut off the boys' trigger fingers at a very young age. Unlike rhinos, boys do have rights, and to cut off a boy's finger under the circumstances described is to violate a right not to have one's person violated. Let us suppose that the conditions of conscription amounted to involuntary servitude to a tyrant, and so was a greater violation of these boys' rights. This is a case of Type IV-3, for the parents violate a lesser right of their child to prevent a greater violation by the tsar of the rights of

---

[16] I note in passing the type variations in which A' includes A, or where A' excludes but is more numerous than A. Cases of these types are useful for exploring our intuitions about various agent-centered reasons and about constraints as objects of concern in themselves. Suppose many actors are to violate the right of a target. Is it morally better that only one actor commit the same violation of the same target, and is that a reason for the one to do so? If so, is this because the number of constraint violators morally matters, or because the number of constraint violations morally matters? It is true that moral wrongness is a nonconservative, non-zero-sum property, so that if three lie to another, each of the three has told one full lie, not a third of a lie each, and the constraint against lying has been broken three times. Still, these are cases that point out the overriding moral importance of the wrong done to the patient, rather than of the wrong done by the agent, or the wrong done to constraints themselves, so to speak. It would be very strange to favor an action that involved more severe violation of the target in order to reduce the number of liars or the number of broken constraints against lying.

the same child. Such a desperate choice is ghastly to contemplate, and I cannot say with confidence that it is morally permissible. But if the act of mutilation is morally wrong, it is not because the parents fail to respect their child's personhood, insofar as circumstances allow. The child is too young to give genuine consent to either fate. The parents violate his rights for the sake of his personhood, to prevent the tsar both from denying his status as a moral agent by treating him like a tool and from damaging his capacity for agency through deprivation and degradation.

A still harder case: you are a military commander fighting a just war facing the problem of civilian casualties. Success in your campaign requires that you direct bombers to destroy enemy artillery batteries on a nearby hilltop that have been shelling your troops and causing heavy losses. The enemy guns are placed in between a number of civilian houses in a small village on the hill. Hoping to deter your attack, the enemy army has falsely assured the villagers that they are safe. They cling to their homes, some paralyzed by fear, some manipulated into wishful thinking by their army. Your pilots are equipped with smart bombs that can pick off with precision the artillery pieces wedged in between the houses without in themselves causing much other damage, but the bombing is certain to ignite enemy ammunition stores that will blow up and destroy the houses and their inhabitants.

On most accounts of justice in war, you do not violate a moral constraint against violating the civilian noncombatants by bombing the enemy artillery. Either the killing of the civilians is an unintended but foreseen side effect, or the killings are causally more distant than the direct effect, and so the civilians are not being treated as means; the goal of destroying the guns is itself justified, and the civilian losses are proportionate to the gains. Believing that you have no better options, you are about to order the bombing, when an aide who studied moral philosophy before the war proposes an alternative: first aim machine gun fire directly at the houses in the hope that the civilians will be terrorized into fleeing. There is some risk that you will wound or kill the residents, but the alternative is certain death.

This is a case of Type II-1: the actor's choice is between causing greater person violation without violating a moral constraint or causing the same target lesser person violation by violating a moral constraint. If you shoot directly at the civilians, you do so for the sake of their personhood, not as a means to some other's end. Under the circumstances, to violate the constraint against shooting at them is in the service of their status as inviolable creatures. Given that they are otherwise permissibly doomed, to violate their rights is to treat them, as much as possible, as ends in themselves. Again, the question of consent arises. Do we not treat them in the most respectful way by respecting their choice to perish with their homes? By assumption, they have not genuinely chosen to do so. Their will is already undermined by their army's false assurances. In all the cases we have examined so far, some defect in the moral agency of the target makes nonviolation as a form of respect self-defeating. The attacker has an evil will; the rhino, no rational will; the child, an immature will; the villagers, impaired wills.

Kamm appears to endorse a permission in cases like Type II-1. After proposing a new formulation of the moral constraint on harming some to save others,[17] she briefly introduces an exception called the "Principle of Secondary Permissibility."[18] If an actor is permitted (under Kamm's formulation of permissible harms) to cause harm to a victim, and is physically able to do so, then the actor is also permitted to substitute a lesser harm that would otherwise be prohibited. Kamm does not elaborate on the reason that permits such substitutions other than to say that it is in the best interests of the person who will be harmed. But why should one's interest in minimizing the violations of one's own person be a good enough reason to limit the scope of the constraints that express that person's inviolability? The reason, I believe, is that an unlimited constraint in this instance is self-defeating: its observance would not be for the person's sake, but for the constraint's sake, and so would fail to treat the person as an end in himself.

If this explanation accounts for our judgment in the bombing case, then the explanation extends beyond the exception specified in Kamm's Principle of Secondary Permissibility. What if actor A' who is to inflict the greater but permissible person violation is not the same as actor A, who can prevent the greater person violation by violating a constraint? Suppose the bombing case were a case of Type II-3: actor A commands the machine gun battery, but has no control over the decision to bomb, and so cannot physically cause the greater permissible harm. On the irrevocable orders of air force commander A', bombing will begin at a certain hour. If A violates the constraint against the intentional and direct targeting of civilian noncombatants by shooting at the houses before the bombing begins, he will prevent the greater but permissible person violation that A' will cause. Why should it morally matter that the preventable but permissible viola-

---

[17] Roughly, the harm produced may not be causally closer to the act that causes both harm and benefit than the benefit produced.

[18] Kamm, "Harming Some to Save Others," p. 248.

tion is not to be caused by A? An expansive constraint against person violation is self-defeating in both cases in the same way: observing the constraint fails to treat the victims as ends. Indeed, when A and A' are different, A treats T more as an end than in Kamm's case, where T is in harm's way because A is aiming in the first instance at the good of others. Here, sparing T the greater violation is the only reason A has for action.

If one follows the reasoning of self-defeating rights, once the greater person violation is to be caused by another (A and A' are different), why should it matter that the greater violation prong is not also a violation of rights? In the tsar's army case (Type IV-3), the parents have a *stronger* moral reason to mutilate their child, not a weaker one, because military service violates their child's rights, and is not merely a grave but permissible person violation.[19] When T and T' are the same, minimizing rights violations recognizes the inviolability of persons in the highest possible way. Minimizing violations within a life avoids the objections against minimizing violations across lives.

Let us take stock before continuing: by exploring cases of self-defeating nonviolation, we have driven a wedge between constraints and their point, and shown that, when the point of constraints is undermined, one morally may, and perhaps must, attend to the point, not the constraint. This is not, however, a victory for consequentialism, for the point of constraints is to treat the person as an end, not the good as an end.

One can, alternatively, hold that no constraint is broken when the lesser violation prong is permitted. Rather, we recognize a new, narrower specification of the constraint. Moral rights can either be understood to be broad in scope but overrideable in the face of countervailing moral reasons—that is, not inviolable—or they may be understood to be narrowly and perhaps elaborately specified in anticipation of all possible countervailing reasons, so that when the right so specified applies, it applies absolutely, without exception, and so is inviolable. Which is the right way to think about rights, and moral principles generally, is a question too large to tackle here, but one

---

[19] It is not generally the case, however, that the lesser harm is easier to justify when the greater harm is brought about by a rights violation, rather than by a permissible person violation or a natural misfortune, because one has a reason not to become a tool of evil. It may matter whether the lesser violation resists the greater violator, as in the tsar's army case, or collaborates with the greater violator, as in the Jim and the Indians case, presented later. For a discussion of these matters, see N. Ann Davis, "The Priority of Avoiding Harm," in *Killing and Letting Die* , ed. Bonnie Steinbock and Alastair Norcross, 2d ed. (New York: Fordham University Press, 1994), pp. 335–44.

comment is in order. For those who believe that the possibility of intrinsic, noninstrumental rights depends on their inviolability, it is an empty victory if the only way for constraints to hold absolutely is to specify their scope with excessive narrowness. Again, the point of moral constraints must be kept in full view: treating persons as ends by recognizing that they have the status of creatures with a high degree of inviolability. Moves to ensure that *rights* have a high degree of inviolability, by building into them inviolability as a formal condition, may not serve to treat *persons* as creatures with a high degree of inviolability. If the two ways of thinking about rights yield identical answers about when, *all things considered*, one is justified in violating a person, there is no reason to believe that the scheme that treats rights as inviolable treats persons as more inviolable, and there *is* a reason to believe that the opposite is true. One whose right has been justifiably violated may have a residual moral claim or complaint against the violator, and the violator may incur subsequent moral obligations to the violated.[20] One who rightly violates another's right has reason for reluctance and regret, and perhaps even remorse and resentment. Morality's recognition of these remainders reaffirms the moral importance of the victim even as it permits victimization.

PARETO-INFERIOR CONSTRAINTS

Consider now those cases, call them *Pareto-inferior constraints*, where not violating a constraint against violating a person will not prevent the constraint from being violated and, in addition, will lead to more violations of constraints against violating others. The much-studied, nightmarish story of Jim and the Indians offered by Bernard Williams is a case. Jim comes across twenty natives picked at random who are about to be executed to discourage political protest. The captain in charge offers Jim, as an honored foreign guest, the privilege of shooting one native, in which case the nineteen would be set free. The Indian who would be chosen by Jim has a right not to be killed, but will be killed in any case—will not merely die, but will be killed in violation of his right in any event. This is a case of Type IV-6: Jim, actor A, must choose between the lesser rights violation prong, in which he kills target T, or the greater rights violation prong, in which

---

[20] Compare the common law of necessity: I am permitted to use any port in a storm, but if I cause damage to your dock, I am liable. I find it implausible to say that in such situations one is merely excused, not fully justified, as if to drown and not trespass is a supererogatory action, rather than a neurotic one. But one still is responsible for the consequences.

the captain's henchman, actor A', kills the twenty targets T', including T among them.

Jim and the Indians is a case of Pareto-inferior rights because if Jim observes the right of one Indian, that Indian is no better off, and nineteen Indians are worse off. This is so, not only in the space of well-being, but also in the space of rights: the right of the one is violated just the same, and nineteen additional rights violations occur. Unlike in the cases of self-defeating rights, where A violates the rights of T for the sake of the personhood of T, here, A (Jim) violates the rights of T (one Indian) for the sake of nineteen others. But does that mean that Jim fails to treat the one that he kills as an end in himself, thereby denying that the one has a high degree of inviolability?

Suppose it is like this: the Indian to be shot by Jim is to be chosen at random, and Jim's decision to participate must be made before the lottery. Or suppose Jim is handed a rifle with nineteen blanks and one live round. If Jim can find the appropriate ex ante place to stand, he can understand what he does as subjecting each to a one-in-twenty risk of death in order to spare each certain death. More important, the Indians can understand Jim this way. Posed like so, this becomes a case of a self-defeating right: each, ex ante, faces the lesser violation at Jim's hand. He threatens each with the risk of death for the sake of each. Ex ante, all are violated less. Ex post, none is violated more. If Jim shoots, he does not obviously deny the point of rights.

Now, the next step: *all* cases of Pareto-inferior rights are cases of self-defeating rights from some suitably constructed ex ante perspective. In the face of unknown threats to one's moral agency over the course of a lifetime, a person generally is accorded more protection from those threats, and in no particular case is accorded less protection, by a morality that permits the violation of Pareto-inferior rights. If a general principle sometimes is to a person's advantage and never is to that person's disadvantage, then actors who are guided by that principle can be understood to act for the sake of that person. It would be self-defeating if, to respect and not deny that person's moral agency, an actor were guided by an alternative principle that *never* damaged that person's capacity for moral agency less and sometimes damaged it more.

But why should moral reasoning proceed from the ex ante perspective? There are many arguments for adopting many variations of the ex ante perspective, of course, and some version of the ex ante point of view has been offered to represent, model, or constitute a number of related but distinct moral ideas: impartiality, reciprocity, universality, generality, the rule of law, autonomy, and various forms of consent. Though this discussion will concentrate on the connection between the ex ante perspective and varieties of consent, I will not argue here for a favored formulation of the ex ante perspective, or for the primacy of any one of the moral ideas the ex ante perspective is said to explicate. Rather, I simply wish to point out one appealing feature of the generic ex ante strategy, which is that our imaginative ability to hold in our heads one version or another of the ex ante point of view while we deliberate about how to act ex post helps to explain why cases like Jim and the Indians perplex us. When we reason from both perspectives we see how a violation of a self-defeating or a Pareto-inferior constraint can both affirm the inviolable status of persons and still remain a genuine violation. This is so because there are some ways of being treated to which consent is impossible, ex post, but to which consent is both possible and reasonable, ex ante.[21]

Possible Consent and Reasonable Consent

Let us begin with the Kantian claim that some ways of being treated are impossible to consent to, so that when one is treated in those ways, one necessarily is used as a means. Christine Korsgaard explains:

> Kant's criterion most obviously rules out actions which depend on force, coercion, or deception for their nature, for it is of the essence of such actions that they make it impossible for their victims to consent. If I am forced, I have no chance to consent. If I am deceived, I don't know what I am consenting to. If I am coerced, my consent itself is forced by means I would reject. So if an action depends upon force or deception or coercion, it is impossible for me to consent to *it*. To treat someone as an end, by contrast, is to respect his right to use his own reason to determine whether and how he will contribute to what happens.[22]

If persons are violated when they are treated as mere means, and if persons are treated as mere means when they are treated in ways to

[21] By ex post here I mean the time of the particular violation, not some time after that. I do not here address what the moral force is, if any, of retrospective consent, except to say that one must distinguish between satisfaction after the fact with the outcome and endorsement after the fact of the violation that led to that outcome. One can keep the following two thoughts in one's head at the same time: I am glad that I have survived, but I do not forgive you for ignoring my wishes and forcing medical treatment upon me.

[22] Korsgaard, "The Reasons We Can Share," p. 46 (footnote omitted). See also Christine M. Korsgaard, "The Right to Lie: Kant on Dealing with Evil," *Philosophy and Public Affairs* 15 (1986): 332; Onora O'Neill, "Between Consenting Adults," in her *Constructions of Reason* (Cambridge: Cambridge University Press, 1989), p. 113.

which they cannot possibly consent, then, straightforwardly, persons are violated when they are treated in ways to which they cannot possibly consent. The argument runs in two directions. The forward claim: some ways of treatment, such as deception and coercion, by their nature undermine or overpower the will, and so cannot be the object of genuine consent. The backward claim: if, by hypothesis, one *has* given genuine consent to some way of being treated, then such treatment cannot have been deceptive or coercive.

The criterion of possible consent has been read by some very broadly, so that whenever I cannot veto an action that significantly affects me, either because I do not have the knowledge or do not have the power to refuse treatment, I am treated as a means.[23] Posed so, the criterion is extremely far-reaching. For instance, you apparently treat me as a means on this view if you seek to compete with my business in a way that would be economically harmful to me without giving me effective power to veto your plan. Without taking a stand on whether the broad reading is the best reading of Kant, I will construe the criterion more narrowly here in order to distinguish harmful actions that use the will of others as a tool (deception, coercion, and torture) from harmful actions that simply do not defer to the will of others (damaging property). Actions that fall under the narrow criterion most clearly involve treatment as means, and most straightforwardly fail the possible consent test, since the central aim of such actions is to subvert the will of the victim. With regard to actions of the second sort, there of course is a sense in which actions that affect another fall under two different act descriptions, depending on whether the person affected has the genuine opportunity and capacity to veto the treatment or does not. It indeed is impossible, in that sense, for you to consent to the act described as "damaging your property without giving you the opportunity to refuse," just as it is obviously impossible for you to consent to the act described as "damaging your property without your consent." Were you to give genuine consent to the property damage, you would be consenting to a differently described ac-

---

[23] The broad view is held by Onora O'Neill: "But those closely involved in or affected by a proposal have no genuine possibility of dissent unless they can avert or modify the action by withholding consent and collaboration. If those closely affected have the possibility of dissent, they will be able to require an initiator of action either to modify the action or to desist or to override the dissent. But an initiator who presses on in the face of actively expressed dissent undercuts any genuine possibility of refusing the proposal and chooses rather to enforce it on others." See O'Neill, "Between Consenting Adults," pp. 110–11; see also p. 139 n. 12, and p. 217. Korsgaard supposes that consent is possible as long as the target has "some power over the proceedings" (Korsgaard, "The Right to Lie," p. 333), but not necessarily a veto.

tion. But there is no redundancy in the description "damaging your property without your consent" as there is in the description "coercing you without your consent," and there is no internal contradiction in the description "damaging your property with your consent," as there appears to be in "coercing you with your consent." I will focus on the clear, core instances of impossible consent.

In instances where consent is impossible, it makes no sense to ask if consent is reasonable. Even if reasonable consent is the correct test of moral permissibility, it can be applied only to act descriptions to which consent is a possibility. Genuine consent to a particular act of coercion is a conceptual impossibility, for genuine consent renders the act something other than coercion. What, then, could be meant by asking if it is reasonable to consent to a particular act of coercion? How can one have reason to do what is conceptually impossible? Possible consent is a precondition for reasonable consent. So, even if the correct test of moral permissibility is reasonable consent, insofar as violations are actions to which consent is impossible, the notion of a permissible violation does not get off the ground.

One way to get the notion of a permissible violation going is to show that persons and their rights can be violated even when they can consent to their treatment. The forward claim, that some ways of treatment cannot be the object of genuine consent, does not hold for the sorts of violation that are not as intimately tied to the undermining or overpowering of the will as are deception and coercion. It is conceptually possible to consent to be maimed or killed. Therefore, for some sorts of violation, the backward claim also fails: having consented to have one's person violated by maiming or killing, such treatment ordinarily remains the person violation, and also the rights violation, of maiming or killing. There are exceptions, where consent changes not only the prescription but the description of the action: surgery certainly is not battery, voluntary euthanasia probably is not murder, and we need not describe either as a person violation. But the violation involved in most instances of wounding and killing survives consent. I am inclined to think that prizefights are morally impermissible because fighters aim at and inflict grave person violation on each other. But there is nothing about the concepts of consent and violence that renders consensual violence, and, therefore, a consensual prizefight, a conceptual contradiction.

Willing treatment that aims at the destruction of one's capacity for moral agency, such as killing, crippling, or extreme degradation, may involve a contradiction in the *will*, and so involve a kind of irrationality.[24] This is a reason not to accord such consent the moral force

---

[24] See Onora O'Neill, "Consistency in Action," in her *Constructions of Reason*, pp. 89–

consent usually has to render actions permissible. But it does not follow that irrational but nonetheless genuine consent by an otherwise competent, free, and informed person is *impossible*. So, consent to at least some violations is possible, without eliminating the violation. Sometimes such consent justifies the violation, though the violation remains a violation; and sometimes such consent does not justify the violation, though the violation remains consensual. Whether actual consent permits violation in these cases could turn on whether such consent is reasonable, for, where consent is possible, there is no conceptual block to the application of a test of reasonable consent. And if that is so, then there is no block to applying a test of reasonable consent to possibly consensual, but actually nonconsensual, violations. Though we should expect most of such violations to fail such a test, some could pass.

Ex Ante Consent That Is Impossible to Endorse Ex Post

Can the notion of a permissible violation get off the ground in the harder and more interesting case, where consent to the violation appears to be impossible? If reasonable consent is the test of moral permissibility, we seem to be in a bind, for the question of reasonableness does not arise where consent is an impossibility. The way out is to note that the reasonable consent test can be applied not to particular acts but to general practices and policies. Even for those treatments that are intimately tied to undermining the will, such as deception, there is no conceptual impossibility in actually consenting in advance to a policy of deception, even though it remains impossible to consent to each particular incidence of deception. For example, one can consent to a central bank's general practice of lying about interest rate hikes, or the police's general practice of undercover sting operations, and still be successfully deceived in the particular case.[25] It can be both possible to will the general practice, ex ante, and impossible to will the particular application, ex post. Whether or not such deception is justified by general consent, general consent is at least possible, though the treatment remains deceptive.[26]

94, for the notion of volitional inconsistency without universalizing. See also Barbara Herman, "Murder and Mayhem," in her *The Practice of Moral Judgment* (Cambridge, Mass.: Harvard University Press, 1993), pp. 113–131, who argues that—Kant's treatment of the suicide example notwithstanding—a universalized maxim of killing fails only the contradiction of will test, not the contradiction in conception test.

[25] See Dennis F. Thompson, *Political Ethics and Public Office* (Cambridge, Mass.: Harvard University Press, 1987), pp. 22–24, 26–29, for a discussion of general consent.

[26] Korsgaard seems to hold that, while one successfully can consent in advance to be

The claim that it is possible to will the general practice ex ante but impossible to will the particular application ex post is open to two obvious objections, and answering them will help to clarify the claim. The first objection is that the possibility of ex ante consent entails the possibility of ex post consent. Yes, it is possible to give consent to a general practice of deception, but, in so doing, one renders the particular instances of deception that fall under the practice consensual via some distributive property that consent possesses. To consent ex ante to the general practice simply is to consent to the particular acts ex post. Deception, it turns out, is not really different from violence: consensual deception is no contradiction. With deception, we need to interpose some uncertainty-creating distance to allow for deception's success, and this does not need to be done in the case of violence, but once this gap is opened, consensual deception is possible.

Alternatively, one may object that, for other ways of being treated, neither ex ante nor ex post consent is possible. Consider force. If consent to a general practice renders particular instances consensual, then one cannot give genuine consent to the practice without thereby giving genuine consent to the particular acts. But if one has given genuine consent to the particular acts, then what one has given consent to cannot be described as force, because consensual force is a contradiction. And if the particular instances cannot be described as force, then it would not be a general practice of *force* that one was consenting to, but a general practice of something else.

This objection can be posed another way. For consent to be genuine, it must be free and informed. For general consent to distribute genuine consent over particular instances, and so be genuine general consent, one must be free enough and informed enough with respect to particular treatments up front. But the standard of free enough and informed enough is quite stringent. Because filling out information about future deceptions in a way sufficient to satisfy the informed consent condition undermines the possibility of success of future deceptions, one cannot give genuine consent to a general practice of

---

left uninformed, examples of consent in advance to be deceived that succeed in deceiving are more difficult to describe. See Korsgaard, "The Right to Lie," p. 333 n. 6. While this may be so about advance consent to a one-shot lie, in the case of advance consent to a general practice of deception, successful deception is not at all difficult to describe, because of the increased complexity of inferring that you are in a situation where lying is to be suspected. Indeed, Korsgaard herself describes a case where a publicized general practice of deception *can* succeed: she supposes that Kant's murderer at the door mistakenly thinks that his intentions are hidden, and so does not suspect that he will be deceived, even though he knows about the general practice of lying to murderers. In any case, merely withholding information can itself be a person violation: recall *Spaulding v. Zimmerman* in Chapter 3.

deception. Similarly, one cannot give genuine general consent to be forced, for there is a defect in the voluntariness of consent when one agrees to unspecified future forcings. For the consent to be truly free, one would need to give consent freely to each of the future forcings. This requires that, in the future, one will have a morally acceptable alternative to each proposed treatment.[27] But if this is so, each particular treatment is genuinely voluntary, not forced. Informed consent to a general practice of deception cannot succeed, and free consent to a general practice of force lacks sense.

These objections call for refinements. Insofar as the first objection is on target, clarify the claim like so: it is possible to give general ex ante consent to some ways of being treated for which consent would be impossible to *initiate* or *endorse* ex post. In situations where consent cannot possibly be initiated, we recognize a danger of person violation, because one cannot at the time of treatment endorse one's prior willingness. This is so, not simply because one does not have the contingent opportunity to endorse, as the wide view of impossibility would have it. If I give you general permission to reveal my confidences to others and it turns out that I am not present when you do so in particular, the person violation of betrayal does not threaten. But this is because there is no conceptual difficulty with endorsing permission to tell my secrets at the time of the telling. Success in the act of revealing my confidences does not require that I be unable to endorse the act. In granting you permission in advance to reveal confidences, I run the risk that your future treatment of me will be contrary to my future will. But, ordinarily, I can exercise that will in some way, either by withdrawing the granted permission in situations where I have the authority to do so, or, where the permission is not unilaterally revocable, by petitioning you not to exercise it. You need not accept such a petition, but it would be indecent to reject it without offering reasons that appeal to my moral agency. And in offering reasons, even if only to say "Stop whining, we made a deal, I did my part, now do yours," you treat me as a person, not as a tool. In contrast, when you rely on prior general consent to deceive me, you aim to undermine my future willing in a way that prevents me from genuinely endorsing my prior willing, and prevents you from offering me reasons in the face of my reluctance. Similarly, if you rely on prior general consent to force me, you plan to overpower any future reluc-

---

[27] Or perhaps it is sufficient that at the time general consent is given one expects to have a morally acceptable alternative in each ex post instance. But this is quite different from a much weaker test, that at the time general consent is given one has a morally acceptable alternative to the expectation of all the ex post instances—that is to say, an acceptable alternative to the *risk* of harmful treatment.

tance in a way that utterly disregards the question of endorsement. The practical success of deception and the conceptual coherence of force depend upon the local denial of my moral agency.

Ex post unwillingness by itself does not render harmful treatment wrong, of course. You may have the moral right or even the obligation to act on the strength of the prior consent, and this may be so even when the victim looks you in the eye and pleads "Stop!" But our sensibilities in such a situation are clear: we are inflicting harm on an unwilling victim, and, in some cases, this sensibility gives rise to a sense: a person is violated, even if no right of the person is violated. I think this is why capital punishment is indecent whether or not it is unjust.[28] Some such sense of violation may be behind the common-law principle that specific performance of a contract is rarely compelled, though an unwilling contractor is liable for the losses caused by nonperformance.

As the distance increases between the point of view of one who grants prior general consent to be harmed and the point of view of one subjected to harmful treatment, subsequent endorsement cannot be taken for granted. Minds change over time, of course. But by distance between points of view, I do not mean the passage of time only. The greatest distance between the ex ante and ex post perspective is that between the risk of some harmful treatment and its certainty. The difference between the two kinds of distance is the difference between a Faustian bargain and a Shylockian one.

The response to the second objection, that both ex ante and ex post consent are impossible, makes use of this second kind of distance, the distance between consenting to risks of treatment and consenting to certain treatment. For the familiar reasons, one cannot initiate genuine consent to a certain and immediate instance of force without rendering the treatment unforced. The novice skydiver, frozen in place, who asks his instructor to push him out of the plane is not forced. But one can genuinely agree, in advance, to the risk of force without rendering the ex post treatment unforced. A borrower who agrees to indentured servitude in the event of default is, upon default, forced.

The position stated in the objection, that one cannot give free and informed consent to the risk of harm if one does not have both full knowledge of and an acceptable alternative to each certain harm, is false. If it were true, then much of the vast network of agreements we

---

[28] See Avishai Margalit, *The Decent Society* (Cambridge, Mass.: Harvard University Press, 1996), pp. 280–81 for the notion of a just but indecent society, and pp. 290–91 for the notion of sense and sensibility in moral concepts.

engage in to pursue our plans and projects over time in coordination with others would be defective. To give informed and free consent to a risk, one need only be informed and free with respect to the *risk*. To be informed about a risk one needs rough probabilities and magnitudes, but not prophecy, and to freely accept a risk one needs to have a morally acceptable alternative up front to entering into an agreement under uncertainty up front. One does not need an acceptable alternative ex post to each harmful eventuality.[29]

Now, there is a perfectly understandable sense in which consent to the risk of harm distributes over the realized instances. If I place a bet on the horses and lose my stake, at first look it seems bizarre for me to claim that I consented only to the risk of losing, but did not consent to actually losing. Someone who sincerely made such a claim would appear not to understand what a bet is. But it does not seem bizarre at all to say that one who consented to the risk of dying in the boxing ring did not consent to actually die in the boxing ring. It surely is not the case that the boxer *wills* to die. The boxer, knowing the risks (and rewards), wills to box.[30] Why can we not say that the bettor, knowing the risks and rewards, wills to bet? It would be bizarre to claim that ex ante consent to risk does not ordinarily distribute the relevant moral permissions, obligations, liabilities, or immunities over the ex post realizations. But it is not bizarre to maintain that one who wills an agreement does not will each contingency under it, Rousseau's well-known argument notwithstanding. Rousseau says about giving up one's life in defense of the state: "The purpose of the social treaty is the preservation of the contracting parties. He who wills an end wills the means to that end: and the means in this case necessarily involves some risk, and even some loss. He who wills that his life may be preserved at the expense of others must also, when necessary, give his life for their sake."[31] But he who wills a means does not necessarily will all of its consequences. If Rousseau counts the fatal outcome as a means to the end of self-preservation, he is mistaken. The

[29] I mean to leave open just how to evaluate the moral acceptability of an agreement under uncertainty and its alternatives. Expected-utility theory is but one of several ways.

[30] Compare Kant on punishment: "No one suffers punishment because he has willed *it* but because he has willed a *punishable action*; for it is no punishment if what is done to someone is what he wills, and it is impossible to *will* to be punished." Immanuel Kant, *The Metaphysics of Morals* (1797), trans. Mary Gregor (Cambridge: Cambridge University Press, 1991), pp. 143–44 (Prussian Academy edition, p. 335).

[31] Jean-Jacques Rousseau, *The Social Contract* (1762), trans. Christopher Betts (Oxford: Oxford University Press 1994), bk. 2, ch. 5, p. 71.

assumption of the risk of death is the necessary means; actual death is a stochastically foreseeable but unwilled consequence. Whether one nonetheless is obligated to give one's life is another matter.

It follows that one can willingly accept the risk of a harmful treatment that one *could not* willingly accept ex post without changing the description of the treatment. Therefore, one coherently can consent to the risk of force or coercion, and still describe the realized treatment as force or coercion. As long as the treatment cannot be genuinely endorsed when it happens, it remains without contradiction a forcing, and so a presumptive violation. Therefore, it is possible to give genuine ex ante consent to risks of violations that are impossible to endorse, ex post.

About what is possible, we can ask what is reasonable. If one can possibly consent to a violation at the level of ex ante general practice, we are not precluded from asking what moral principles governing violation are reasonable to consent to. The answer may indeed be that it is never reasonable to consent to certain sorts of violation, but need not be. A moral principle that permits violating persons when not to do so is Pareto-inferior, but that nonetheless preserves the sense that a person has been violated, cannot be ruled out on conceptual grounds alone, for it involves no contradiction.

Grounding principles by appeal to some version of reasonable agreement is a major enterprise in contemporary moral and political philosophy, of course, and it is not my purpose here to add yet another friendly amendment to the projects of Rawls or of Scanlon. I simply wish to point out that contractualist accounts in general can make the following two claims. First, they can admit the moral permissibility of intentional violation in some cases without undermining or contradicting their commitment to the inviolability of persons, and so without conceding that rights are merely instrumental. Second, they can do so without having to redescribe the violation as something else.

THE POSSIBILITY OF PERMISSIBLE VIOLATION

For concreteness, consider one such view. I believe that the argument I have made here is roughly compatible with Thomas Hill's Kantian account of when doing "the lesser evil" is justified, though he reaches somewhat different conclusions.[32] Hill argues that the appropriate

---

[32] See Thomas E. Hill Jr., "Moral Purity and the Lesser Evil," in his *Autonomy and Self-Respect* (Cambridge: Cambridge University Press, 1991), pp. 67–84, and "Making Ex-

point of view from which to formulate moral rules is that of rational, impartial legislators who share a full range of moral ends and values, but are not yet committed to specific rules of conduct, and who are aware that not all will comply with the rules that they enact.[33] From that point of view, says Hill, "one might argue, all would favor any policy that promised to prolong the survival of representative persons as rational autonomous persons, other things being equal and provided that the policy is otherwise consistent with the dignity principle. Each legislator would favor the policy when looking at it from his or her own perspective (abstractly conceived) and also when reviewing it from the perspective of each other person."[34]

Hill concludes that a policy of rescuing otherwise-doomed hostages that will foreseeably but unintentionally endanger some in attempting to save all is not inconsistent with the dignity principle, and therefore could be agreed upon from the general legislative point of view. Hill therefore permits actions that cause violation as an unintended side effect where not to cause violation is, in the terms we have been using, self-defeating to the violated. Hill does not explicitly address the unintentional Pareto-inferior case, where, though the prospects of those who are foreseeably endangered are neither improved nor worsened, others will benefit from the rescue attempt. But, a fortiori, we can infer his stand from his views on a tougher case. Even when the innocents who would foreseeably be endangered are not already endangered, Hill holds that a carefully circumscribed permission "could be defended from the general legislative point of view even to those who turn out to be the victims under the policy."[35] If the policy increases the chances of all to live full lives as rational agents, and if all have roughly the same chance of becoming victims, a permission to endanger some bystanders in order to rescue many hostages could conceivably be consistent with human dignity. And if unintentionally

---

ceptions without Abandoning the Principle: Or How a Kantian Might Think about Terrorism," in his *Dignity and Practical Reason* (Ithaca, N.Y.: Cornell University Press, 1992), pp. 196–225. "Moral Purity" is largely concerned with showing why principles that *require* doing the lesser evil in some cases would fail to be adopted by ideal legislators. "Making Exceptions" aims to show why principles that *permit* doing the lesser evil in some cases might succeed in being legislated.

[33] Hill, "Moral Purity," p. 79. In an older essay, Hill puts it like this: "To adopt our principles *as* ideal legislators seems a good idea; but to make them *for* ideal law followers does not" ("The Kingdom of Ends," in his *Dignity and Practical Reason*, p. 66). See Korsgaard, "The Right to Lie," for a different way of finding room for nonideal theory in Kantianism.

[34] Hill, "Making Exceptions," p. 215. The dignity principle refers to Kant's second formula, that humanity in each person be treated as an end, not only as a means.

[35] Ibid., p. 216.

causing the violation of one who would not otherwise be violated in order to minimize the violation of many others might be justified, surely unintentionally causing the violation of one already fated to be violated—the Pareto-inferior case—might be justified.

Hill draws a clear line between merely foreseeable and intentional harming, however, and holds that the *deliberate* killing of someone already doomed could not be justified from the legislative point of view:

> Thus, to be justified in a deliberate killing, a person would need to be able to face the victim and say, sincerely and truthfully, "I choose to kill you (when I have an option not to); but still I regard you as more than a *mere* means, in fact, as a person with a worth that is incalculable." Now, it is hard to imagine that a human being could maintain this attitude while deliberately killing another, even though apparently Kant thought that public executioners could and many think that doctors administering euthanasia can.[36]

But this judgment about the moral importance of deliberateness does not follow inexorably from Hill's own argument. Though the thrust of his work is to show that Kantianism is not as rigoristic as is often thought, I think that here he retains more rigorism than his account requires. For impartial legislators reasoning about what principles to follow in the face of evil do not obviously devalue or disrespect each other if they agree to save each other from violation at the hands of evildoers by subjecting each other to lesser or less likely deliberate violation at the hands of fellow moral citizens. To repeat an earlier proposition: if a general principle sometimes is to a person's advantage and never is to that person's disadvantage, then actors who are guided by that principle can be understood to act for the sake of that person. It would be self-defeating if, to respect and not deny that person's moral agency, an actor were guided by an alternative principle that never damaged that person's capacity for moral agency less and sometimes damaged it more. It is not unreasonable for impartial moral legislators to permit the deliberate violation of constraints when the constraints are self-defeating, and such permission need not be interpreted as maximizing nonviolation across persons or putting a price on human dignity, for the permission is for the sake of each person, ex ante. Ex post, one could say to the particular victim for whom the constraint is no longer self-defeating, but simply Pareto-inferior, "A general policy of permitting deliberate violation in this situation would have been adopted for your sake, precisely because

---

[36] Ibid., p. 220 (qualifying footnotes omitted).

you are a person of incalculable worth. It would not have been unreasonable for you to have agreed to it, ex ante, and for you to withhold agreement now, ex post, is futile." Something like this, I have claimed, is how Jim can understand what he does if he shoots one Indian to save nineteen, and how both the one and the nineteen can understand that what is done to them by Jim is done *for* them.

Something like this, but not quite this—for though we can imagine the Indians understanding what Jim does, genuinely agreeing or withholding agreement to their treatment is not a possibility for them. Against the background threat of murder at the hands of the captain, there is no plan that Jim can propose to which the Indians can give uncoerced consent. It's not that Jim coerces them, of course—the captain does. But the Indians cannot freely consent to Jim's actions. This is in part why, if Jim shoots, he commits a grave violation, however the Indians understand what he does. In a suitably constructed ex ante choice situation, it is not unreasonable for persons who put the highest value on each other's humanity to agree to the violation of self-defeating and Pareto-inferior constraints—that is what might make such violations permissible. But we must not lose the sense that what is permitted is still, ex post, a genuine grave violation. Part of what makes the killing of the one Indian a genuine violation is that, against a coercive background, no one can possibly give genuine consent to such treatment.

This is not to say that what the Indians want Jim to do is morally irrelevant. On Williams's telling, the Indians not only *can* understand what Jim does, but *do* understand: they are begging Jim to accept the captain's offer. Korsgaard, in an illuminating discussion of this example, points out the importance of what the Indians in fact want Jim to do. It matters, she says, whether the Indians are pacifists who plead with Jim not to participate in the captain's violence, or whether the oldest Indian steps forward and volunteers his life:

> *Very* roughly speaking, you are not treating him as a mere means if he consents to what you are doing. Of course, the Indian does not in general consent to be shot, and his gesture does not mean that after all he has not been wronged. In the larger moral world he has. But if you and the Indians are forced to regard Pedro and the captain as mere forces of nature, as you are in this case, then there is a smaller moral world within which the issue is between you and them, and in that world this Indian consents.[37]

[37] Korsgaard, "The Reasons We Can Share," p. 46 (qualifying footnote omitted). In Williams's story, Pedro is the captain's gunman.

Korsgaard qualifies this by warning of the spuriousness of simply saying yes, and cites with approval O'Neill's test of having an authentic opportunity to say no. So Korsgaard apparently believes that, within this "smaller moral world," it is conceivable that the Indians can be given an authentic opportunity to refuse.

Now, the main point seems right—the way for Jim to treat the humanity of the Indians with as much respect as the horribly unjust situation allows is to let them decide their own fate, insofar as they are able. But one might be tempted to draw three mistaken inferences from this: that consent by itself is generally sufficient to permit violation, that consent always is necessary, and that the consent of Indians in the smaller moral world renders Jim's shooting something other than a violation. Consent is not always sufficient: if Jim ought to defer to the wishes of the Indians, it is because a policy of letting the victims decide insofar as they are able in such situations satisfies a test of reasonable agreement, and the futility of their refusing to be violated makes a decision favoring violation reasonable. If some weird but sane thrill seeker under no threat of death genuinely requested Jim to shoot him, Jim must refuse, because permission to aid in such self-degradation would not pass Hill's or any other test of reasonable agreement among person-valuing persons. Consent is not always necessary: if Jim cannot ask the Indians how they wish to be treated, he is not obviously required to let them all die. And, even though the Indians consent in the smaller moral world to risk being shot by Jim, Jim still violates the one he shoots. This is obscured by the example of the elder who volunteers to be sacrificed, for from his extraordinarily courageous standpoint the captain's threat does not crush all meaningful choice. He has a salient and reasonable alternative, a lottery that gives him a nineteen in twenty chance of surviving, and he chooses not to propose it. But suppose instead that none of the twenty Indians is as brave and selfless as the elder. The lottery is proposed, and all agree—after, let us say, each has been given by Jim the opportunity to opt out and be shot for sure by the captain. The choice looks a lot less free now, even in the "smaller moral world," for the only alternative each has is certain death. Straws are drawn. If the loser loses his nerve and pleads with Jim to be spared, I am not sure that the best response is, "In the smaller moral world you genuinely consented." The doomed man quite rightly replies, "But what choice did I have?" A better response appeals to what is reasonable for all ex ante and fair to the others ex post, rather than to an agreement forced by necessity. If the loser sees a way to escape both Jim and the captain, I am not sure that he is obligated to stick around. If he is, fairness, not consent, is the source of the obligation. If Jim is permitted to shoot him in the back as he runs for safety, the justification is not *volenti non fit injuria*: the Indian has not, in any meaningful sense, willed away the constraint against his own violation. And if this is so for the unlucky coward, it is also so for the unlucky stoic who accepts the results of the lottery and faces Jim's bullet with equanimity. Ex post endorsement of a coerced ex ante agreement is still unfree. The point still stands: when constraints against person violation are self-defeating or Pareto-inferior, what might render breaking these constraints permissible is that such treatment passes a test of reasonable ex ante consent. What might keep such treatment a violation is that it fails the test of possible ex post endorsement.

Kamm ends her discussion of harming some to save others with the suggestion that one might permissibly bargain away the status of inviolability for the outcome of fewer violations, but she sees such agreements as belonging to a different moral topic, that of permissible bargains.[38] If, instead, we try to represent what reasonable contractors might find reasonable to agree to in the face of unreasonable circumstances, we may find that the topic is the same.

Is one ever justified in violating the rights of some to prevent the greater violation of the rights of others? We can now see that one need not embrace a "utilitarianism of rights" to answer yes. A moral theory that views persons as intrinsically valuable does not require that *constraints* be treated as ends in themselves, or that they have a high degree of inviolability. Rather, *persons* ideally are to be treated as ends in themselves and understood to have a high degree of inviolability, which is expressed by constraints on how they may be treated. If constraints *are* understood to have a high degree of inviolability, nothing follows about the treatment of persons, for constraints that have the formal property of inviolability might be extremely limited in scope.

How can sacrificing the rights of one for another be compatible with highly valuing each person as an end in itself with a life to lead? The answer has both a formal and substantive part. Formally, anything that a person reasonably would accept in a suitably constructed position of choice is compatible with highly valuing persons. As a substantive matter, what sorts of sacrifices are reasonable to accept? In the face of injustice, sacrifices for the sake of establishing the principle that persons are of high intrinsic value strike me as plausible candidates for reasonable acceptance—more plausible than sacrifices for the sake of maximizing good consequences simply. Rawls distinguishes ideal from nonideal theory—the principles of justice that hold

---

[38] Kamm, "Harming Some to Save Others," p. 256.

in a well-ordered society, when all are in compliance with them, from the principles that hold in the face of injustice and unfavorable social and economic conditions that stand in the way of a well-ordered society.[39] The principles of nonideal theory adjust to the realities of injustice and misfortune, so that the ideal of treating others as ends sometimes gives way to the goal of a world in which others are treated as ends. Because the goal is justified by a test of reasonable acceptance in the face of unreasonable circumstances, not by its good consequences, nonideal theory does not, I believe, collapse into consequentialism. We may disagree about whether any cases of violating the rights of some to prevent the greater violation of the rights of others meet such a test of reasonable acceptance. We may disagree, as well, about whether any social practices and institutions that permit such violation in response to the nonideal conditions of injustice and misfortune meet such a test. But there is no conceptual difficulty in entertaining that some do.

THE REASONABLENESS OF PERMISSIBLE VIOLATION

The preceding argument opens up the possibility that under some conditions it would be reasonable for persons to consent to be violated by adversary institutions and professions. The possibility of reasonable consent, of course, is only the first step toward justification. The next steps are to specify criteria of reasonable consent, and then to test various professional practices of person violation against these criteria. In advancing the argument that morally permissible person violation is not impossible, I have thrown about a number of criteria. Though I make no claims to be comprehensive, gathering and sorting them suggests the sorts of reasons that need to be invoked to justify the violation of a person. A quick inspection of a few person violations permitted by the rules of adversary practices shows that, at least on the criteria picked out here, moral permission is elusive.

Genuine Ex Post Consent

Genuine consent is not simply actual consent. To be genuine, agreement must be free and informed, and those conditions might well be stringent. For instance, certain sorts of background injustices can make an agreement unfree. Sometimes genuine consent aptly changes morally pertinent descriptions, so that the act is no longer a person

---

[39] Rawls, *A Theory of Justice*, secs. 2, 11, 26, 39, 46, 53–59. See Korsgaard, "The Right to Lie," for a sketch of a Kantian nonideal theory.

violation. Genuinely consensual sex is not morally permissible rape—it isn't rape at all. But other kinds of person violation do not vanish under consent—dueling, for example. In cases where person violation survives consent, what is the connection between genuine and reasonable consent? When does genuine consent make the violation morally permissible?

I cannot here be more helpful than to say that we probably can find instances for all the combinations of necessity and sufficiency. For some violations, genuine consent is both a necessary and sufficient condition for reasonable consent, by which I mean that it would be reasonable to accept a proposed moral principle that permitted person violation of some sort in some case if and only if the person had genuinely consented to be violated. Perhaps charitable organ donation from live donors is such a case. For other violations, genuine consent is necessary, but not sufficient: another criterion, such as self-defeat, must be satisfied (recall Korsgaard's account of the Indian elder in the "smaller moral world"). For yet other violations, consent might be sufficient, but not necessary. So, recalling the free-riding football player in the preceding chapter, either the conditions of genuine consent or the conditions of fair play must be satisfied, but both need not be. For still other violations, genuine consent is neither necessary nor sufficient for reasonable consent: consent to some violations is never reasonable (slavery); for other violations, other conditions, but not genuine consent, are needed (punishment). The conceptual conclusion is rather weak: genuine consent may or may not render a person violation reasonable and so morally permissible.

As a factual matter, victims of professional and political person violation do not ordinarily give genuine ex post consent. Sanson's victims did not consent to die; Spaulding did not consent to the concealment of lifesaving information; runaway slaves did not agree to be returned under the Fugitive Slave Act, and blacks under Jim Crow did not agree to be disenfranchised by state and local officials. Consumers do not consent to be endangered by manufacturers or deceived by advertisers; innocent civil defendants do not volunteer to be subject to false and unjust claims, and truthful witnesses do not volunteer to be humiliated and smeared.

Genuine Ex Ante Consent

As we have seen, when genuine consent is given to a general policy or at some remove in time, it is more plausible to hold that the adversary treatment, when realized, remains a person violation. Genuine ex ante consent to be coerced is not a conceptual contradiction, and genuine ex ante consent to be deceived is not a practical contradiction.

The connections between actual advance consent and reasonable consent cover the same combinations of necessity and sufficiency as before. Are there grounds to hold that reasonable acceptance of a principle permitting person violation is either more or less likely in the case of ex ante rather than ex post consent of the victim? One might think that since actual ex ante consent is closer to the point of view one is to adopt in considering the reasonableness of a principle, reasonable consent follows directly from actual ex ante consent. Not so: the similarity between the two points of view is superficial. For the perspective of reasonable acceptance to have the moral force that it does, it needs to have the property of, to borrow a notion from economics, *dynamic consistency*: we should be able to adopt it wherever we are located in time and arrive at the same answer. If we do not, that is a sign that we have not properly specified the perspective, or the persons who occupy it, or the reasons that move them, or the scope of the principles under consideration.[40] Actual ex ante consent, in contrast, is simply what some person with some interests and purposes happens to accept at one of a number of perhaps importantly different prior moments. For actual consent to be genuine the agreement must be free and informed, but it need not be reasonable in the sense required by the reasonable consent test. Once this merely apparent advantage of ex ante consent is set aside, ex post consent is seen to be the stronger contributor to moral permission because it typically involves no local denial of moral agency by the violator: the current will of the target is respected by the violator, or respected as much as the circumstances allow.

As we saw in the preceding chapter, genuine ex ante consent to be violated by adversary practices and institutions faces the same factual difficulties as ex post consent. Targets typically do not give explicit general consent to be violated; when they do, there are good reasons to doubt that the consent is genuine—that is, free and informed; there are good reasons not to infer agreement to be violated from agreement to transact (recall the used-car case); and there are serious evidentiary problems with inferring genuine tacit consent from mere participation in an adversary game. There are no better grounds for supposing that victims of political violence, slavery, or oppression

---

[40] I am well aware that I have not myself specified this perspective. Doing so is a more foundational project than I have attempted in this book. For such projects, see John Rawls, *A Theory of Justice*, and *Political Liberalism* (New York: Columbia University Press, 1993); Thomas Nagel, *The View from Nowhere*, and *Equality and Partiality* (New York: Oxford University Press, 1991); Brian Barry, *Theories of Justice* (Berkeley: University of California Press, 1989), and *Justice as Impartiality* (Oxford: Oxford University Press, 1995); and T. M. Scanlon, *What We Owe to Each Other* (Cambridge, Mass.: Harvard University Press, 1998).

have genuinely agreed in general to their treatment than there are for supposing they have genuinely agreed in the specific. Participation in pervasive large-scale institutions such as managed medical care, auto insurance, the adversary legal system, and competitive markets does not imply genuine consent to be violated by the institution's adversary professionals any more than participation in politics implies genuine consent to be violated by public officials. Only rarely does one have a morally acceptable alternative to transacting with these institutions, and there is nothing to the view that existing forms of social organization, simply because they are, are reasonable.

Fair Play

Why person violation that satisfies the fair-play conditions remains a person violation generally is uncomplicated. Consenting to coercion is a contradiction, but risking or causing one's coercion is not. The fair-play condition of voluntary acceptance of benefit substitutes for actual consent: where consent to follow the rules of a cooperative venture is to no avail, voluntary acceptance of that venture's benefits doesn't work either. If a moral constraint against some sort of person violation is inalienable, then the acceptance of benefits will not relax the constraint. There are parallels between the additional conditions of fair play and the conditions of *genuine* consent. For consent to be genuine, it must be informed and free. For the voluntary acceptance of benefit to trigger the fair-play principle, there must be a cooperative scheme that is both mutually advantageous and just. And since genuine consent sometimes is not sufficient to generate a moral permission to violate persons (even where it would be sufficient to generate a moral obligation to do something otherwise morally permissible), fair play sometimes is not sufficient.

About fair play we have two familiar questions: when is it reasonable to consent to person violation permitted by an adversary institution that satisfies the fair-play conditions? Which adversary institutions in fact meet this two-step test of reasonable consent, given fair play? Much here turns on how to interpret the condition that mutually advantageous cooperative ventures be just. The justice condition clearly requires a just distribution of the benefits of social cooperation on some adequate account of distributive justice exogenous to the fair-play criteria themselves. But how do basic rights and liberties enter into the account of fair play? If certain sorts of person violation are always unjust because they violate natural duties, then an adversary game whose rules permit such violation never satisfies the conditions of fair play. This was a question asked at the start of this chapter. Recall, however, that on the view taken here, the moral wrongness of a person violation does not follow directly from the nature of the act itself, but from the absence of good enough justificatory reasons. Natural duties are natural only in the sense that their content is not defined by the rules of social practices or institutions.[41] Even the person violation of killing, when done for a good enough reason such as self-defense, is not morally wrong. We take it to be an open question whether the voluntary acceptance of benefit from a mutually advantageous cooperative venture is a good enough reason to morally permit certain sorts of person violation, just as it is an open question whether genuine consent is a good enough reason. So the justice of a person violation is not exogenously given—it is the conclusion we seek in asking if it is reasonable to accept violations that meet the fair-play test.

I have, all along, maintained that consent and its substitute, voluntary acceptance, are not always sufficient to justify person violation, even in the context of a mutually advantageous cooperative scheme. Though free and informed players might consider it mutually advantageous, Russian roulette played for a fortune is an abomination. Why would practices that meet the conditions of fair play still fail the test of reasonable consent? Because neither objective well-being nor subjective preference determine reasonable acceptance. To justify damage to or the local denial of moral personhood, one must appeal to the idea of respect for the moral personhood of others and of oneself, and show how a person violation, though still a violation, is the best way to respect persons under the circumstances. Practitioners of Russian roulette, prizefighting, and dueling lack self-respect, because they accept very high risk of very grave damage to their moral agency for reasons that do not appeal to the preservation or affirmation of moral agency. Their participation in those practices amounts to a *renunciation* of their humanity, and so when others take such renunciation as permission to inflict person violation, they not only damage, but participate in the denial of moral agency. That is why consent (even when free and informed) and voluntary acceptance of benefit (even when mutually advantageous) do not always create moral permission.

The factual question is easier to answer. Whether or not it is reasonable to consent to person violation that meets the fair-play criteria, these criteria typically are not met by professional and political adver-

---

[41] See Rawls, *A Theory of Justice*, p. 114. But the correct scope and application of a natural duty might very well depend on circumstances brought about by social institutions. I have a preinstitutional natural duty of mutual aid toward a drowning swimmer, but if a lifeguard is present, I needn't be the first to jump in.

sary institutions. The success and stability of the institutions of insurance, lawyering, and doctoring do not depend on denying young Spaulding lifesaving information. Citizens are not advantaged by a political game in which they are disenfranchised by corrupt campaign financing and deceived by advertising, and they have not volunteered for whatever benefits come their way. A justice system that withholds the fair value of legal rights from those who cannot afford a lawyer does not meet the most minimal demands of distributive justice.

Self-Defense and Rescue

There is a large literature on the moral permissibility of defending oneself and others against threats of unjustified person violation. The permission is not unbounded, and aspects are contested—most important, the question of what may be done to innocent threats who are the proximate cause of harm but do not intend it. But only pacifists deny the core: that one may use proportionate force and violence if necessary to thwart a willful, unjustified attacker. Kant's notorious example of the murderer at the door notwithstanding, one may also employ deception to thwart wrongful person violation. The justification for defensive person violation is straightforward: defending oneself or others not only prevents damage to personhood, but stops an attempt to deny personhood, so the violation of the attacker aims at realizing the ideal of inviolable persons.

Self-defense is easily conflated with an argument from contingent obligation (that a general obligation not to violate persons is contingent on the widespread compliance of others) or with an argument from reciprocity (that a specific obligation not to violate a target is contingent on the target's compliance with the general obligation to not engage in person violation). But arguments from contingent obligation or reciprocity fail if the wrong of the person violation is not contingent on the actions of others. Some obligations, such as the obligation to pay taxes, may not bind unless others pay.[42] But murder remains a grave wrong even in Medellín, Colombia, where it is widely practiced, for murder is not a contingent wrong. Similarly, individuals are not ordinarily permitted to murder murderers who pose no present threat. The violator does not become a moral outlaw because of past violations. Actual justice need not show the same symmetry as poetic justice. Punishment has its own reasons and justifications, but it should not be conflated with self-defense.

In adversary games, rarely is person violation directed at a wrong-

[42] See Thompson, *Political Ethics and Public Office*, pp. 109–10.

ful threat, even when the adversary is threatened. Self-defense does not countenance aiming at nonthreatening bystanders who can be used to mitigate the threat. The economic threat that business competitors pose to one another is not typically a person violation, but even if it were, self-defense does not permit tactics such as deceptive advertising aimed at consumers, who pose no threat. Perhaps a truthful hostile witness can be described as a threat to the interests or liberty of a defendant, but she is not an unjustified threat, so the principle of self-defense does not justify discrediting her through humiliation and smear. Self-defense is a good argument that fits adversary practices and institutions badly.

Self-Defeat

Earlier in this chapter we explored violations for the sake of moral agency of the person violated, and noted that a constraint against violation in such cases is self-defeating. Like self-defense, the self-defeat criterion is conceptually powerful but rarely met in fact by adversaries. With one important exception, professional and political adversaries do not ordinarily violate their targets for the targets' sake. This is not to say that the argument is not disingenuously invoked: perhaps the most sickening example is the often lampooned claim by a military spokesman that a Vietnamese village had to be destroyed in order to save it.

The notable exception is justified professional paternalism. Professionals and their clients are not ordinarily seen as adversaries of each other—the adversary is supposed to be the other side. But when serious disagreement arises between lawyer and client, doctor and patient, official and citizen about how to proceed, the wills of professional and client are pitted against one another even if their interests are in harmony. There of course is a considerable literature on paternalism, and I will not attempt to rehearse it here, except to show the connection between paternalism and the argument from self-defeat. The strongest case for paternalism is when A restricts B's autonomy for the sake of B's autonomy, rather than merely for B's own good, at a time when B's autonomy already is impaired. Such paternalism is a person violation because the target is forced, coerced, or deceived—a local denial of moral agency. But to respect the target's moral agency under the circumstances is self-defeating, because the target, by assumption, is employing an already damaged capacity for moral agency to inflict further damage on his future capacity for moral agency. Local denial of the target's personhood is in the service of its global protection and affirmation.

Pareto Inferiority

The logic of self-defeat, extended from the ex post to the ex ante point of view, gives rise to the Pareto-inferiority criterion: the claim that it is reasonable for a target to agree to a principle that permits violation when others would be spared, and when the target would be violated in any case. One might at first think that the Pareto-inferiority criterion slides into a kind of utilitarianism that fails to recognize the distinctiveness of persons, and so ends up allowing too much. But when we distinguish the criterion from another claim with which it can be confused, we see that it is compatible with contractualism and not excessively permissive.

The criterion of Pareto inferiority is not the same as what might be called the argument of any hands: if I don't do it, someone else will. Players in marketlike adversary practices with many, interchangeable actors often can claim that the bad consequences will occur anyway. Some other lawyer will represent the slumlord, some other cigarette manufacturer will profit from the teen market, some other journalist will scoop the salacious story—so why not me? On certain versions of utilitarianism, you have no reason not to, but this often is taken to be a telling criticism of utilitarianism, because the moral theory fails to recognize that how you treat people, and not merely how people are treated, morally matters. If I violate someone who will be violated anyway in order to prevent others from violation, I do so for reasons that arguably do not disrespect the violated. Ex ante, all are afforded more protection from violation from such a policy, and, ex post, none is afforded less. But if I violate someone who will be violated anyway merely because I or my clients will benefit, from no point of view do I act for the sake of protecting the victim's or any one else's moral agency. So a person can reasonably object that the any-hands argument does not express respect for persons.[43]

I have tried to make the best conceptual case for morally permissible violations of persons. With work, it can be done. But the effort pro-

[43] If we set aside benefits denied competitors, the any-hands argument does satisfy the Pareto criterion in the space of well-being, for someone is better off and no one is worse off. But the Pareto criterion as I am using it here has two additional requirements: that the preservation and affirmation of moral agency, not merely well-being, be the result; and that such preservation and affirmation be the aim. In so doing, we seek to treat the person as an end, not well-being as an end, and so satisfy the requirement that we treat persons with respect.

vides little shelter for adversary practices and institutions. Yes, there are conditions under which the exercise of force, coercion, and deception is consistent with respecting the moral agency of persons as much as possible. But these conditions do not ordinarily hold in the ordinary practice of law, business, and government. We have seen, instead, a conflation of weaker arguments with stronger. This should not surprise: the best intuitive support for the truth of contractualism is that we indeed are moved to give reasons and justify ourselves to those whom we treat badly. Alas, not all reasons given are good reasons.

Chapter Eight

ETHICS IN EQUILIBRIUM

Pangloss still maintained that everything was for the best, but Jacques didn't agree with him.

—It must be, said he, that men have corrupted Nature, for they are not born wolves, yet that is what they become. God gave them neither twenty-four-pound cannon nor bayonets, yet they have manufactured both in order to destroy themselves. Bankruptcies have the same effect, and so does the justice which seizes the goods of bankrupts in order to prevent creditors from getting them.

—It was all indispensable, replied the one-eyed doctor, since private misfortunes make for public welfare, and therefore the more private misfortunes there are, the better everything is.

While he was reasoning, the air grew dark, the winds blew from all directions, and the vessel was attacked by a horrible tempest within sight of Lisbon harbor. . . .

. . . The Anabaptist was lending a hand in the after part of the ship when a frantic sailor struck him and knocked him to the deck; but just at that moment, the sailor lurched so violently that he fell head first over the side, where he hung, clutching a fragment of the broken mast. The good Jacques ran to his aid, and helped him to climb back on board, but in the process was himself thrown into the sea under the very eyes of the sailor, who allowed him to drown without even glancing at him. Candide rushed to the rail, and saw his benefactor rise for a moment to the surface, then sink forever. He wanted to dive to his rescue; but the philosopher Pangloss prevented him by proving that the bay of Lisbon had been formed expressly for this Anabaptist to drown in.

Voltaire, Candide

PART OF what adversaries in public and professional life do for a living is violate persons by deceiving and coercing them. This is so because the constituted redescription that the role player wishes to invoke fails on conceptual grounds (natural descriptions persist) and the consensual redescription that the game player wishes to invoke fails on factual grounds (targets resist). Always a presumptive moral wrong, person violation is in need of justification: the violator must have reasons that reasonable targets would accept. But the justifications at hand—varieties of actual consent, fair play, self-defense, and varieties of self-defeat—for the most part do not work because they do not fit the circumstances of adversary institutions.

The adversary has yet another set of arguments that she can employ. Adversary practices are equilibrating mechanisms that, by design, anticipate and counteract much of the deception and coercion that adversaries attempt; and without these attempts, the important social goods that the institutions aim at—prosperity, justice, legitimate government, affordable medical care—would not come about. Earlier, we noted the power and limitations of likening the practices of adversary institutions to rules in a game.[1] Equilibrium arguments evoke a different and perhaps more potent sense of the game metaphor: the image, not so much of rule-governed action, but of strategic interaction, of calculating players acting in anticipation of the anticipatory actions of others. The metaphor is pleasing. To view, explain, and justify social institutions by appeal to the notion of strategic equilibria is to be associated with appealing intellectual traits—tough-mindedness, sophistication, analytical rigor, and recursive reflection—and to connect with fields of study that practice some of these appealing traits. The image of strategic equilibrium is associated with a discipline, economics, and a language of inquiry, mathematics. I mention the power of the metaphor to guard against too-quick, wholesale endorsements. Careful attention to concepts and claims is needed to unpack and moderate the broad programmatic pronouncements that sometimes surround equilibrium defenses of adversary practices. If these defenses are to be shown to work, they must stand up to close, detailed scrutiny of the factual and moral claims they make.

To many readers, an appeal to the good consequences in equilibrium of adversary institutions is both the strongest and most straightforward argument that a lawyer, businessperson, or politician can make, so you might be wondering why I did not begin the book here. I did not because it is not my purpose to argue directly for the priority of the right over the good or for the superiority of contractualist moral theories to varieties of consequentialism. Those are different, more foundational projects than mine, and I leave them to others. My strategy of persuasion has been indirect: I have argued *from* a contractualist point of view, hoping that you will feel enough of its tug by this point to question that morality is, at bottom, simply about the summing up of good consequences. But if consequentialism is the correct moral theory, there is no serious moral objection to an adver-

---

[1] See Chapter 6.

sary institution that produces enough social good to outweigh, on the theory's metric, the bad of the violence, coercion, deception, and injustice committed along the way. One can disagree about the outcomes of an adversary institution, and one can disagree about what weights to put on these outcomes, but once the sums come in, no deep puzzles about permissible violation remain.

If, however, moral justification is not at bottom about weighing benefits and burdens across persons, but about giving reasons to each person burdened that she, if reasonable, would accept, an appeal to good consequences alone is not likely to succeed. Reasonable agreement is not simply a matter of what serves the individual's own interests, for it is reasonable for me to accept some sacrifices to prevent much greater harms to others. But it is not reasonable to accept any burden that maximizes good consequences: it is not unreasonable for me to reject great sacrifices to provide small benefits to many, many others. The reasonable burden is not zero, but it will be lower, perhaps far lower, than the burden that maximizes net benefits.[2] So, if reasonable acceptance is the correct test of moral justification, the adversary will have to do more than simply invoke the balance of consequences. Rather, the adversary must show that there is something about institutions designed to channel presumptively wrong action into the production of socially beneficial consequences that either makes the actions morally permissible or that shields the actors from moral responsibility.

REDESCRIBING AIMS

Consider what we might call the argument of *aim redescription*. In the moral assessment of an action that results in harm to others, two factors, among others, come into play: the aims of the actor and the likelihood that the action will result in harm. In the pursuit of morally good aims, the imposition of some level of risk upon others can meet the test of reasonable acceptance. It is not morally wrong to operate a motor vehicle with due care or to operate a fairly clean manufacturing plant, though there is, and one knows that there is, a small probability of hitting a pedestrian or of making someone ill from pollution. In tort law, sometimes there are good reasons to hold an actor strictly liable for a harm, even though no negligence occurred, and a person

---

[2] See, for example, Arthur Isak Applbaum, "Racial Generalization, Police Discretion, and Bayesian Contractualism," in *Handled with Discretion: Ethical Issues in Police Decision Making*, ed. John Kleinig (Lanham, Md.: Rowman and Littlefield, 1996), pp. 145–57.

might appropriately feel remorse for having caused a harm, even though he took the morally appropriate level of precaution. But we say of such harms that they are accidental, and that the actor did no moral wrong.[3] The imposition of small risks, if fairly distributed, passes the test of reasonable acceptance because in a moderately complex society, all, including those who might be injured, wish to pursue valuable activities that impose small risks on others. The alternative would require a virtual halt of productive activity. Since the aim is not to injure and the risks are small, actors express respect for one another as long as they meet standards of care (which themselves are subject to a test of reasonable acceptance). An injurer who has met such a standard has damaged the moral agency of the injured, but has not denied it. In contrast, if an actor aims at harming another, even when the risks are comparably small, he has committed a presumptive wrong. If, wishing to kill, I aim a rifle at a distant target and shoot, knowing that there is a small chance of success, then I have murdered if successful, and have attempted murder if not—and this is so, even if some important social good results from the death. It could be reasonable to accept a principle permitting actions that accidentally harm and reasonable to reject a principle permitting actions that aim at harm, holding good results, probability and severity of harms, and beliefs about it all constant. As the saying goes, even a dog knows the difference between being stepped on and kicked. A fortiori, when the chances of success are certain, when I aim to do harm and succeed, I have committed a presumptive wrong. The fourth combination of aim and likelihood, aiming at a morally good end, though one foresees a harmful, certain side effect, has been extensively treated in the literature on the doctrine of double effect. I do not need to take a stand on whether there is a moral difference between aiming at certain harm and merely foreseeing certain harm, because I can illustrate my point with the uncertain cases, and most agree that, for small probabilities, there is a moral difference between unlucky accidents and lucky attempts.[4]

---

[3] Harm can be accidental even when the actor holds true beliefs about the chances that harm will result from his action.

[4] For the doctrine of double effect, see, for a start, H.L.A. Hart, *Punishment and Responsibility* (Oxford: Oxford University Press, 1968), ch. 5; Warren S. Quinn, "Actions, Intentions, and Consequences: The Doctrine of Double Effect," *Philosophy and Public Affairs* 18 (1989): 334–51; and Jonathan Bennett, *The Act Itself* (Oxford: Oxford University Press, 1995), ch. 11. The locus classicus in the Babylonian Talmud is *Shabbat* 75a. The distinction double effect attempts to capture is notoriously slippery. I don't think I need to take a stand on what the correct formulation is, because the adversary's attempt to help herself to the easier-to-justify side fails under any of the formulations: adversaries intend their target's harm, use their targets as means, the adversary's ends flow causally from the harm, and so on.

The argument of aim redescription claims that the violation adversaries inflict on each other should be considered unlucky accidents, not lucky attempts. Because adversary institutions in the aggregate aim at good ends, and because the institution is designed to anticipate and counteract individual adversaries' efforts to deceive or coerce, each adversary can be described as aiming at the overall social good that the institution generates, not at the particular violation that a particular adversary tactic inflicts. The institution's aim distributes over its practitioners, so that every lawyer can appropriately be described as aiming at justice, even though her local efforts are directed at advocating an unjust cause.

Consider this analogy: fencers wear gear designed to protect them from injury.[5] If they didn't, they would need to be so careful not to hurt one another that much of the enjoyment and beauty of the sport would be lost. With the gear, they can attack without fear. Indeed, to excel they must learn to thrust in a way that would seriously injure or kill if not for the protection. Now, on rare occasions, and despite the protection, fencers draw blood. Such injury is properly described as accidental, for surely fencers do not aim to stab each other, and take reasonable precautions to avoid that result. This is so, even though the physical motions of a fencer who accidentally injures are indistinguishable from the actions of a military swordsman who aims to kill, and even though fencers know that they pose some risk to one another. Fencing, professional adversaries might claim, is an apt analogy to well-designed adversary institutions that anticipate and counteract the harms that could result from adversary action. The lawyer who advocates an unjust cause or the company that deceptively advertises a worthless product are like the fencer who thrusts, trusting that the opponent is well protected. In equilibrium, the good results of justice, efficient markets, and safe sport usually result, and when protections fail, it is an accident. But now suppose that fencing has a sister sport, called *offencing*. Offencing is played with the same protective gear, but the rules of the sport reward players who knock off or tear through their opponent's defenses. Accomplished offencers are skillful at landing strokes that bare skin and draw blood. When an offencer injures, is it an accident? Do adversary professionals in business, law, and politics engage in the sport of fencing or of offencing? We will return to these questions shortly.

The assessment of particular arguments from ends in equilibrium has both an analytical and a factual side. Analytically, the justification of adversary practices by appeal to good ends must be shown to work under various equilibrium conditions. Just as reasons needed to

---

[5] The analogy and its shortcomings come from David Luban, *Lawyers and Justice* (Princeton, N.J.: Princeton University Press, 1988), p. 79.

be given why consent, if present in particular circumstances, is a presumptive permitter of adversary action, so too, reasons need to be
given why good ends, if present in particular circumstances, permit
what would otherwise be impermissible. The claim of aim redescription is one such reason, which may or may not succeed. There are
others.

On the factual side, arguments from ends obviously rely on predictions about good consequences that will come about. But some care
must be exercised to spell out just what sorts of assumptions about
outcomes these arguments require. Just as an argument from consent
requires that certain factual conditions of consent be met—that the
consenter not be under duress, or not be deceived—so too, arguments from good ends require that ends in fact be predictably good in
the right sort of ways. This is not an empirical study, and no evidence
will be brought in from the field to show that the legal system actually produces just or unjust outcomes, newspapers actually print
truths or falsehoods, or the best man or woman actually wins or loses
elections. What can be done from the armchair, however, is to specify,
with greater care than is usually done when these arguments are invoked, the sorts of facts that must hold if the arguments are to work
on their own terms.[6]

The appeal to the good ends of adversary institutions in equilibrium is notoriously underdemonstrated for most of the institutions
about which it is invoked. Appeals to equilibrium arguments assume
a *mechanism*, and *conditions* under which the mechanism will lead to a
favorable equilibrium. The mechanism must be described and the
conditions under which good results obtain must be specified. For
example, general equilibrium theory in economics describes a pricing
mechanism in which producers and consumers bid, and states the
conditions of perfect competition that must hold for the price system
to yield efficient allocations in the production and consumption of
goods: a large number of firms free to enter and exit, frictionless market transactions, costlessly enforceable contracts, markets for capital,
risk and information, and the like. This obvious idealization will
never be met by an actual economy, and economic theory goes on to
describe the equilibria that can be expected when these conditions are
only partly satisfied. Similarly, if factual claims for the good effects on
the democratic process of unregulated commercial journalism or for
the truth-generating qualities of the jury system are to be taken seri-

---

[6] For care in specification, see Thomas C. Schelling, *Choice and Consequence* (Cambridge, Mass.: Harvard University Press, 1984), pp. 195–212, and "Game Theory and
the Study of Ethical Systems," *Journal of Conflict Resolution* 12 (1968): 34–44.

ously, the conditions that must hold for the good results to occur must be specified, along with an account of how robust good results are to the relaxation of some of these conditions. The one area, outside of economics, where the description of mechanisms and the specification of equilibrium conditions is beginning to be done with any sort of precision is in theories of democratic deliberation, where the conditions necessary for a just and legitimate consensus appear to be extremely stringent and delicate. With these somewhat deflationary cautions in mind, let us take a look at some arguments from ends and illustrative cases in some detail.

False Prophets and Profits

In the passage from *Candide* that begins this chapter, Voltaire takes a cryptic swipe at the bankruptcy practices of his day. But Pangloss offers an equilibrium argument for the harsh treatment of parties to a bankruptcy, reasoning that since the private misfortune of debtors and creditors makes for the public welfare, the more their misfortune, the better everything must be. Current bankruptcy practice, in allowing corporations to seek protection of assets from creditors in order to reorganize the business and restructure its debt, is far more generous to troubled businesses. The Panglossian logic has not been abandoned, however, merely recast: today the misfortune of creditors is taken to be for the best of all. Consider the case of Braniff International.

In May 1982, the airline that once boasted "If you've got it, flaunt it" teetered on the edge of bankruptcy.[7] Braniff had taken on debt in a rapid expansion just before a major recession and a doubling of fuel prices. Its chief executive officer, Howard Putnam, had been brought on the previous September to restore confidence and to turn the airline around. But competition for a declining ridership was fierce, and despite bargain fares, asset sales, layoffs, and substantial labor concessions, cash to meet the next payroll was in doubt. In February, Putnam thought it prudent to engage bankruptcy counsel, who warned the CEO that secrecy and surprise were essential for three reasons. First, too much talk of bankruptcy could become a self-fulfilling prophecy: travelers would not buy advance tickets on an airline they thought might go under. Second, if word got out that Braniff was on

---

[7] This account is adapted, with the help of Harold Pollack, from Kenneth Goodpaster and David Whiteside, *Braniff International: The Ethics of Bankruptcy* (A) & (B), Harvard Business School Case 9–985–001.

the verge of filing for protection under Chapter 11 of the Bankruptcy Reform Act of 1978, secured creditors might seize pledged assets needed for the reorganization, such as planes. Third, a creditor, by filing first, could put Braniff in involuntary bankruptcy under Chapter 7, forcing liquidation of assets, rather than reorganization.

Putnam therefore faced strong economic incentives and clear legal advice to conceal from customers and creditors the true financial standing of the company. He did not do so consistently. At times he was frank about the company's future, at one point telling an interviewer, "I can't just name a date and say I know we have enough cash to operate until then. It's not that easy. We certainly have no current plans to cease operations, but I can't guarantee we won't."[8] But that same week he told his employees the airline had "more than a 50% chance,"[9] projecting more optimism than a man who spoke with his bankruptcy lawyer nearly every day could have reasonably believed.

At a May 6 meeting with stockholders, whose investment could be wiped out in the event of bankruptcy, Putnam's message was guarded but hopeful:

> We have proven to ourselves, to the industry, and to our lenders that on the operating cost side, we have a viable entity. We now have to generate revenue to make this airline successful for the long term. The shadow of doubt that hangs over our future creates a "chicken-and-egg" dilemma as we approach financial restructuring. We need to remove the cloud to get results. The lenders want to see results before they remove the cloud.
>
> The company continues to evaluate all possible alternatives including, but not limited to, continuing new market innovations, pricing promotions, new infusions of capital from outside investors, potential combinations with other entities, operating agreements with other airlines and, as a last resort, seeking protection under the federal bankruptcy statutes. This last alternative is obviously a last resort after all other alternatives have been exhausted.[10]

But in a private board meeting minutes later, he presented a more dire picture: unless that week's receipts were higher than he had reason to expect, the airline would not be able to pay that week's payroll or fuel bill, and would have to shut down. On May 12, Putnam quietly began ordering airplanes back to their guarded hangers in Dallas, citing mechanical difficulties as the reason for canceling flights. Chap-

---

[8] *Dallas Morning News*, March 4, 1982, in Goodpaster and Whiteside, (A), p. 6.
[9] Ibid.
[10] Ibid., pp. 8–9.

ter 11 bankruptcy papers were filed at 12:01 A.M. on May 13, beating out any creditors in New York who might have planned a Chapter 7 filing at the start of the business day.

Putnam's strategy of secrecy and surprise was not only perfectly legal, but widely accepted business practice. Indeed, CEOs in his situation would think it irresponsible to do any less to avoid bankruptcy, and to protect a firm's capacity to reorganize under Chapter 11 should bankruptcy prove necessary. Yet Putnam at times engaged in tactics designed to create in the minds of creditors, customers, workers, and stockholders beliefs about the viability of the firm and his intentions that he knew to be false. Whether or not he ever lied outright, he concealed information and made misleading or incomplete statements to maintain secrecy. Now, the keeping of all secrets is not presumptively wrong. Some secrets, the ones that create a private, personal sphere that is a person's own, are perhaps as important for the integrity of persons as the freedom to make plans and commitments.[11] But Putnam's secrets are what have been called strategic secrets: the concealment of information that will shape the actions of others so as to advance the purposes of the concealer.[12] Because strategic secrets may restrict the autonomy of others and may harm their interests, strategic secrets invite closer moral scrutiny.

Putnam's strategic concealment is perfectly legal, but legality is neither sufficient nor, in some cases, necessary for moral justification. Putnam's strategic concealment is also a conventional practice in the adversary game of bankruptcy, but we have noted the limits to arguments from convention, expectation, and rules of the game. Here, we focus on appeals to the good ends of concealing and manipulating information on behalf of companies in the bankruptcy game.

Consider the argument from *Pareto superiority*. The claim is that if Braniff is made better off, and no one, including the targets of strategic deception or concealment, is made worse off by the adversary tactic, then such deception or concealment is morally justified. The hope of a Pareto-superior outcome is the rationale behind Chapter 11 reorganizations. A petition for reorganization can be approved only if a company reasonably claims that its value as a going concern exceeds the liquidation value of its assets, and reorganization plans are approved by the courts only if each creditor consents or if each can be shown to receive more under reorganization than under liquidation.

---

[11] For the moral importance of such secrets, see Sissela Bok, *Secrets* (New York: Pantheon Books, 1982).

[12] For the distinction, see Kim Lane Scheppele, *Legal Secrets* (Chicago: University of Chicago Press, 1988).

On the assumption that a Chapter 11 bankruptcy is better for all than Chapter 7 bankruptcy, adversary tactics that aid a company in achieving the Pareto-superior outcome are morally justified, or so the argument goes. The good end of returning to creditors more than they would otherwise receive justifies the practices of concealment and deception that help Braniff outwit creditors who seek liquidation.

Of course, posing the justification this way immediately raises the question why any creditor would oppose Chapter 11 reorganization, if the interests of each are best served by allowing the firm to continue as a going concern. Are the creditors that Putnam seeks to outwit by pulling back planes under pretext and by midnight filings simply mistaken about their interests? In the absence of evidence to rebut the presumption, parties are ordinarily taken to know and be capable of willing what is in their interests. Knowledge-based tactics aim to subvert that will. Therefore, appeals to Pareto superiority as a justification for strategic concealment and deception must be treated with some healthy suspicion. Indeed, some creditors may reasonably believe that they will fare better by seizing collateral or forcing liquidation. They may get their shares many months sooner, at far lower cost in legal fees; or they may have differences in attitudes toward risk, discount rates, and beliefs about a reorganized Braniff's performance that lead them to put a lower subjective valuation on their share under reorganization, though by the standards of valuation used by the bankruptcy court, they have no complaint. Similarly, concealing Braniff's desperate condition does not serve the interests of employees who pass up alternative career possibilities, new creditors duped into bearing uncompensated risks, and new ticket holders whose travel plans are ruined.

Pareto-improving deception might occur in the context of a serious coordination problem: if the U.S. banking system were in jeopardy, we might want the president to mislead everyone (ourselves included) into thinking that there is no problem. If the president were to reveal the true risk, the banking system might well unravel as each of us rushed to withdraw his money before our jittery neighbors. But the game of strategy with creditors and customers that Putnam describes as a "chicken and egg dilemma" is not a pure coordination game like the banking problem, but a game with a different structure. In arguments from ends, details of specification matter.

Putnam's concealment cannot appeal to the argument from Pareto superiority. At best, Putnam can make a far weaker claim with which Pareto superiority is often conflated, the argument from *increased net benefit*. The claim from net benefit is simply that, on the whole, more good than harm is caused by an act of strategic concealment or deception. Like with the conflations we encountered before, expectation with consent and contingent obligation with self-defense, the factual circumstances in which the claim of increased net benefit can be made are far more common than are the circumstances in which the claim of Pareto superiority can properly be invoked, but increased net benefit proves much less.

Pareto superiority is a stronger justification because it appeals to reasons for deception that the deceived might share. The deception is in the interests of the deceived, and that suggests that the targets of deception would actually consent, or at least would have a reason to consent to the deception if all the facts known to the deceiver became or could become known to all. Much that we discussed in the preceding chapter is glossed over here: because deception undermines autonomy and so involves at least a local denial of moral agency, the deceiver needs to demonstrate more than that the deception is for the good of the deceived. Not all paternalism is justified. Rather, it must be shown why it would be reasonable for the deceived to consent to beneficial deception here. But increased net benefit is a still weaker claim, for it does not appeal at all to reasons that the deceived shares, unless the deceived already views himself as a resource to be exploited for the greater good. Therefore, on moral theories that take persons as morally important ends apart from their capacity to generate good consequences for all, increased net benefit by itself does not justify actions that might otherwise be wrong.

One might think that a self-fulfilling false prophecy is no deception at all, because the statement that would have been false if not said is made true by the reactions of others to its being uttered. So, if Braniff will survive with certainty if it can sell a thousand tickets in May, and if a thousand tickets will be sold with certainty as a consequence of Putnam announcing "Braniff certainly will survive," and Putnam knows this, then he does not lie in making the announcement: the saying makes it so. His statement, however, is still in a way deceptive, because in hiding the causal mechanism that makes it true, he induces his listeners to act for mistaken reasons, and so substitutes his judgment for theirs without their knowledge or consent. Note that this case, call it certain self-fulfillment, is an instance of a small equilibrium mechanism with good ends resulting from the collective reactions of others to a tactic, and note that it is a mechanism with a particular specification: the statement is self-fulfilling in its entirety. But suppose it were a case of partial self-fulfillment: given current ticket sales, the odds of Braniff pulling through are zero. If Putnam says "Braniff will survive with 100 percent certainty," consumer confidence and ticket sales will go up enough to give the airline a 50 percent chance.[13] Here, the statement is not entirely self-fulfilling, and is straightforwardly a lie: the belief it induces in the minds of others is not believed by the speaker. There may be reasons to justify such a lie, but it cannot be justified on the grounds that it is not a lie at all.

Consider now the case of contingent self-fulfillment, where the statement is completely self-fulfilling if believed, but the chances of it being believed are less than certain. Putnam must convince the jet fuel supplier to restore Braniff's line of credit, so the airline does not have to pay cash in advance. If the supplier extends such credit, the airline will survive; the supplier will do so only if it believes that the airline will survive; and it does not believe everything that is said. Putnam says "The airline certainly will survive," not knowing if he will be believed. The statement is a clear lie when made, because the belief Putnam attempts to induce in the minds of others is not believed by Putnam. But one might still think that no wrong has occurred in either the case of belief or disbelief. If believed, the lie becomes true—demonstrating that truthfulness and the truth are two different things. If disbelieved, the harms of deception do not come about, because the target did not in fact come to hold and act on a false belief. Ordinarily, a failed attempt at wrongdoing is still wrong—indeed, it is something of a puzzle why moral luck should ever play a part in moral evaluation.[14] But this is so either because to subject another to the risk of being wrongfully harmed is itself wrong or to intend to wrongfully harm is itself wrong. Here, by construction, the harm of fraud cannot occur, and fraud isn't intended—Putnam does not deceive in order to gain at the supplier's expense. But Putnam—or, our hypothetical Putnam—does attempt to undermine autonomy by imposing his judgment of the situation on others without their knowledge, and so he still commits a presumptive wrong.

Does the argument of aim redescription work for Braniff? Can Putnam plausibly claim that he aims at good social ends because the practice of voluntary bankruptcy aims at good social ends—protecting the assets of creditors, saving jobs, and maximizing the economic

[13] This hypothetical is based on material developed together with J. Gregory Dees. See Arthur I. Applbaum and Harold A. Pollack, *The Ethics of Truthfulness in Management: Notes, Cases, and Readings*, Harvard University Program in Ethics and the Professions Working Papers (Cambridge, Mass., 1990).

[14] See David Lewis, "The Punishment That Leaves Something to Chance," *Philosophy and Public Affairs* 18 (1989): 53–67, for an elegant argument for why punishing attempted murder less severely than successful murder might make sense; see also Hart, *Punishment and Responsibility*, pp. 126–31; Bernard Williams, "Moral Luck," in his *Moral Luck* (Cambridge: Cambridge University Press, 1981), pp. 20–39; Thomas Nagel, "Moral Luck," in his *Mortal Questions* (Cambridge: Cambridge University Press, 1979), pp. 24–38; and Martha C. Nussbaum, *The Fragility of Goodness* (Cambridge: Cambridge University Press, 1985).

value of the company? Can he plausibly claim that any deception of his that succeeds is accidental, because the bankruptcy game is structured to render deception harmless? That is, can Putnam claim that his deceptions are like the fencer's thrusts? Perhaps, if Putnam's predictions really were instances of certain self-fulfillment. But what he actually did was make partially fulfilling predictions, and that looks not like fencing, but like offencing. The offencer cannot plead accident, cannot even plead negligence, for he aims to subvert protections against injury, and this is true about his aims even if he believes that the odds of success are low. One cannot coherently claim that one aims at the good ends of a competitive system if one seeks to undermine features of the system that make it good. Perhaps the claims that adversaries make about their aims and the actions that they take cannot be made to cohere. Or perhaps the good ends of the system are for its practitioners a sort of idle hope that is unconnected to what their actions aim at. But there is no plausible way to redescribe the violation that adversaries aim at as accidental, a foreseen but unintended side effect. If, to pass a test of reasonable acceptance, actions cannot aim at violation, then much of the violation that results from adversary institutions does not pass the test.

The Invisible Hand

Consider the most famous invocation of an equilibrium justification, Adam Smith's invisible hand:

> In spite of their natural selfishness and rapacity, though they mean only their own conveniency, though the sole end which they propose from the labours of all the thousands whom they employ be the gratification of their own vain and insatiable desires, they divide with the poor the produce of all their improvements. They are led by an invisible hand to make nearly the same distributions of the necessities of life which would have been made had the earth been divided into equal portions among all of its inhabitants; and thus, without intending it, without making it, advance the interest of the society, and afford means to the multiplication of the species.[15]

In one way, the invisible-hand image is unfortunate, for it smacks of the designed and determined universe of Leibniz that Voltaire lampoons and Smith neither intends here nor needs. The idea, however,

---

[15] Adam Smith, *The Theory of the Moral Sentiments* (1759), 4:1, where he speaks of landlords; see also *Wealth of Nations* (1776), 4:2; and John Eatwell, Murray Milgate and Peter Newman, eds., *The New Palgrave: The Invisible Hand* (New York: W. W. Norton, 1989), pp. 168–72.

is simple and powerful enough: under certain forms of economic organization, the unintended consequence of many actors seeking their own advantage is to the advantage of others. But to avoid the absurdities that lead Pangloss to seek to multiply misfortune, the claim must be sharpened and delimited.

Such sharpening and delimiting has been one of the central tasks and great successes of several branches of modern economics, from general equilibrium theory to game theory to public finance to industrial organization, and I cannot begin to review those achievements here. Rather, my purpose is to learn how to evaluate the basic form of the invisible-hand argument, whether invoked in economics or exported to other adversary institutions and practices. To do that, we will need to unpack some of the various claims that have been made for the invisible hand in the marketplace.

Invisible-hand arguments typically involve some combination of the following claims: (1) that an adversary action leads to good consequences in equilibrium; (2) that an adversary action is necessary to produce such good consequences in equilibrium; (3) that the bad consequences of an adversary action have been anticipated and counteracted by self-correcting equilibrium mechanisms; and (4) that an adversary action is necessary to a self-correcting mechanism that anticipates and counteracts the bad consequences of the adversary actions of others. All of these claims should be understood to be *when-if-then* propositions: when institutions are structured in some specified way, if an adversary action or practice meets some specified conditions, then the proposition holds.

Consider the notion that markets are self-correcting mechanisms, in that the market itself provides strong disincentives to engage in some adversary actions that have bad consequences, all things considered, and the market properly anticipates and counteracts the bad effects of other adversary actions. For example, if it is common knowledge that market players will deceive or conceal when they can gain an advantage by doing so, the likely targets, forewarned, will take steps to protect themselves from manipulation. If customers are worried that merchants will provide shoddy products, they can subscribe to quality rating services, and the demand for such reports assures that many providers will emerge, competing to provide better information at lower cost. Firms that do not heed the market reactions that moderate deception undermine their own interests. In equilibrium, one would expect the market to generate an "optimal amount of fraud,"[16]

---

[16] The phrase is from Michael K. Darby and Edi Karni, "The Optimal Amount of Fraud," *Journal of Law and Economics* 16 (1973): 67–88.

with false and manipulative advertising flourishing mainly where the gains to sellers exceed the losses to buyers, and with buyers expending resources to protect themselves up to, but not past, the point of maximum net benefit.

By now, however, whenever good outcomes of a process of strategic interaction are alleged, we should be prepared to ask more specific questions about the equilibrating mechanism and the conditions that must be satisfied to produce those good outcomes. Asymmetries of information are actually notoriously difficult to counteract by market forces alone. Verification of a market player's representations is sometimes impossible or extremely costly. When concealment and deception are possible, the market may still work its way to a stable equilibrium, but there should be no presumption that such an outcome is either truth-revealing or economically efficient. Consider, for example, one well-known equilibrium process described by George Akerlof, the "lemons" phenomenon.[17]

In a market plagued by the lemons problem, the seller—say of a used car, to use Akerlof's illustration—knows the quality of the car he sells, but the buyer knows only the distribution of the quality of cars offered for sale in the market, and cannot verify the quality of any particular car. The buyer therefore will not pay more than what cars in the market are worth to her on average. So to attract buyers, the prevailing price must drop to reflect this average market quality. But as the price drops, owners of higher-quality cars will take their cars off the market. Average quality falls. The market price drops even further, and even more high-quality cars are withdrawn. The market may collapse entirely if quality falls so far that the only people willing to sell at the market price are those who own lemons that no buyer wants. The very fact that a seller is willing to accept the going price tells buyers that the car is a lemon.[18] A stable equilibrium is reached, but one that is neither efficient nor truth-revealing.

When lying and concealment have their rewards, can the ignorant induce truthful disclosure and can the knowledgeable make himself

[17] George A. Akerlof, "The Market for 'Lemons': Quality Uncertainty and the Market Mechanism," *Quarterly Journal of Economics* 84 (1970): 488–500, reprinted in his *An Economic Theorist's Book of Tales* (Cambridge: Cambridge University Press, 1984), pp. 7–22; see also Thomas C. Schelling, *Micromotives and Macrobehavior* (New York: Norton, 1978), pp. 99–100.

[18] More precisely, if S is the value of the car to the seller, distributed uniformly over some interval beginning at 0, B is the value of the car to the buyer, and $B = kS$, then for k less than 2, no offer that the seller will accept returns a positive expected value to the buyer. When the relationship between value to seller and value to buyer takes the functional form $B = a + kS$, offers with positive expected value to the buyer are possible, but joint gains to trade are lower than if quality were known to the buyer.

trustworthy through market means alone? Information economists and game theorists have developed three general market remedies, each of which attempts, in its own way, to give the informed player a good reason to tell the truth by exacting a sufficiently high price for lying. The contingent-contracts remedy, which emerges from the literature on the principal-agent problem, shifts variability in payoffs to the knowledgeable player. The randomization remedy, which comes from game-theoretic treatments of bargains under uncertainty, works by reducing the chances of agreement when the information conveyed could be a lie. The screening remedy, which emerges from the literature on market signaling, sorts liars from truth tellers by some test that is expensive to fake. But in each, the cost of inducing truthfulness is economic inefficiency, and each may fall short on truth revelation as well.

First, consider the contingent-contracts remedy. Merchants, knowing that consumers are wary about being cheated, have strong incentives to offer binding warranties to guarantee (and signal) product quality. In the used-car example, if the buyer will eventually be able to detect the quality of the car, the offer of a money-back guarantee gives the seller an incentive to be truthful about quality. But contingent agreements not only provide incentives to act in certain ways, they also shift risk, including risk that the guarantor does not control. If the better-informed player is not certain ex ante, merely more certain than his counterpart, or if the state observable after the deal by both is contingent on other uncertainties unknown to or uncontrolled by either player, then contingent agreements may shift an unacceptable degree of risk to the better informed. And if the more informed player is more risk averse than the less informed player, a guarantee assigns risk inefficiently, erasing one of the gains to trade.[19]

The randomization remedy, suggested by Roger Myerson, induces honesty into market transactions by introducing a mechanism under which transactions are consummated only with some probability that varies inversely with the informed player's incentive to lie, so that the expected cost of failing to agree exceeds the expected gain from bluffing, should agreement be reached.[20] An illustration will make this clear. Suppose Seller's car is either a peach or a lemon, but Buyer does not know which. Seller can ask either a peach's price or a lemon's

[19] See, for example, Stephen A. Ross, "The Economic Theory of Agency: The Principal's Problem," in *Microeconomics: Theoretical and Applied*, ed. Robert E. Kuenne (Aldershot: Elgar, 1973), 2: 378–83, and John W. Pratt and Richard J. Zeckhauser, *Principals and Agents* (Boston: Harvard Business School Press, 1985).

[20] Roger Myerson, "Incentive Compatibility and the Bargaining Problem," *Econometrica* 47 (1979): 61–74.

price. His profit from selling a lemon at lemon's price or a peach at a peach's price is $1,000; his profit from selling a lemon at a peach's price is $6,000; he would never sell a peach at a lemon's price. Buyer would buy a lemon at a lemon's price and a peach at a peach's price, but would not knowingly pay the price of a peach for a lemon. Buyer doesn't know if the car is a peach or a lemon, but she does know (a big assumption, this) Seller's payoffs. How might Buyer induce Seller to tell the truth (or how might Seller convince Buyer to believe him and play)? If Buyer takes out a die and says "If you claim the car's a peach, I will roll the die and buy only if it comes up six," Seller has no reason to lie. If the car's a lemon, he stands only a one-in-six shot of reaping the $6,000 reward for lying, and a five-in-six chance of getting nothing; he gets $1,000 for sure if he tells the bitter truth.

To implement a randomized strategy in practice, one must find a convincing way of making agreement probabilistic, with odds contingent on the attractiveness of the offer. One way might be to require ratification by a player or body whose assent is uncertain. Another is for targets to convince would-be dissemblers that the targets' subjective degree of belief in the signal varies with what is signaled.

Randomized responses work by reducing the odds of profiting from misrepresentation, but at the cost of reducing the odds of agreement when mutually beneficial agreement is possible. In this case, to assure honest revelation, a peach stands a five-in-six chance of going unsold, even though mutually beneficial agreement is always possible at some price and both players know it. Again, the market's solution to the problem of trust comes at a serious loss of efficiency.

Third, consider market signaling. Rarely is knowledge so unverifiable that the informed can do nothing to support the veracity of the information he shares. Equally rare, however, is the ability to present incontrovertible proof of an assertion. Usually we back our claims with evidence that imperfectly signals the truth. Others are likely to make the inferences we want them to make from these signals if they believe that certain signals correlate strongly with the truth. In a setting where incentives to misrepresent exist, this correlation comes from the relative difficulty, or costliness, of sending an unrepresentative signal. The uninformed puts her trust in signals that the informed has no incentive to forge.

Michael Spence has captured many interactions in the job market with simple models of signals and screens.[21] If schooling is relatively more costly to acquire for those of low ability than for those of high

---

[21] A. Michael Spence, *Market Signaling: Informational Transfer in Hiring and Related Screening Processes* (Cambridge, Mass.: Harvard University Press, 1974).

ability (but, as students often suspect, confers no ability itself), employers could set a salary schedule based on education that would sort job seekers by ability. Over time, as the employers learn more about the relationship between signal and ability, they may update their pay scale.

Two problems arise from signaling mechanisms, both related to the uncertainty that surrounds the relationship of value to the cost of signaling. First, to the extent that signaling imposes costs on truth tellers as well, the mechanism eats up joint gain (a drawback found in each of the three remedies to asymmetric information). Second, as Spence shows, screening mechanisms may create self-confirming but false beliefs about the relationship between the signal and the unknown variable. In job markets, employers could ask for such costly signals (or offer sufficiently low wages in return for a favorable signal) that high-ability workers who face high signaling costs withdraw from the market. Or the education signal may be disproportionately more expensive to acquire for a subset of high-ability workers—women or blacks, for example. Employers' beliefs about the effectiveness of education as a screen could be (incorrectly) confirmed. Buyer may never be offered a peach, and conclude that all used cars are lemons, when in fact she set verification requirements that are too expensive to meet.

We have seen that, despite an array of sophisticated safeguards, markets cannot completely self-correct for at least one important class of adversary tactics, concealment and deception. Along with entrenched monopoly power and uncompensated externalities, such as pollution, persistent asymmetric information is a leading cause of the failure of the price system to reach Pareto-efficient allocations in production and consumption. Often these three sources of market failure work together to make the harms of adversary action especially intractable to self-correction. Economic actors are less likely to take into account the harms of deception and concealment when they fall as externalities on distant and diffuse targets, rather than on the firm's more immediate stakeholders—shareholders, workers, suppliers, customers—who can defend or retaliate in response; and economic actors with monopoly or monopsony power are less vulnerable to the responses of some classes of stakeholders to deception.

In the tool kit of regulatory interventions, economists typically reach first for reporting and disclosure rules that correct for entrenched asymmetries of information. This is so for several reasons. Disclosure rules are usually less liberty-restricting for the regulated, and more clearly autonomy-enhancing for the public, than heavier-handed regulatory solutions that prohibit, limit, or tax economic activity. Economists also appreciate how sensitive the efficiency of market equilibria is to imperfections in the market for information, and how improbable it is that self-correcting mechanisms for those imperfections will evolve. Economists as wary of government regulation as Milton Friedman single out deception and lack of openness as market failures that need to be governed by rules.[22] There is nothing, then, to the notion that the invisible hand of competition will channel *all* adversary action to good ends. Good ends in equilibrium are contingent on specific conditions obtaining, and many adversary tactics in an unregulated market violate those conditions.

Well, then, argues the adversary, regulate the market. Set rules for adversary engagement that correct for market failure. Prohibit adversary tactics that both have bad consequences and are invulnerable to self-correcting mechanisms. The job of legislatures and rule-making agencies is to do just that. In a market that regulates adversary practice well, two results obtain: when players seek their own greatest advantage by engaging in adversary action permitted under the rules, good consequences result in equilibrium; and when players refrain from taking permitted advantageous adversary action, the good equilibrium is upset, and inefficiencies result. Of course, lawmakers do not always do the job well, and sometimes the rules that regulate adversary practices in the market are too permissive or too restrictive. But even in a less-than-perfectly-regulated market, as long as the rules of the game fall within some range of tolerably decent design, players still produce better consequences by competing as vigorously as possible, using any advantageous adversary tactic permitted by the existing rules, than by attempting to compensate for imperfections in the rules by refraining from adversary action. Whether market rules are perfect or not, the good ends of economic activity are best achieved if players play to win. The invisible hand sometimes needs to be gloved, but the glove need not be a perfect fit.

These claims, as all claims about good ends, are in part factual, making assertions about how well the best of regulations can correct market failures, and about how robust good equilibrium outcomes are to regulations that are not the best. The claims imply that adversaries never need to aim at good consequences for good consequences to come about, and never need to aim at market efficiency for markets to be efficient. But a closer look at the content of some adversary practices in the marketplace calls into question the plausibility of the claims and their implications.

[22] Milton Friedman, *Capitalism and Freedom* (Chicago: University of Chicago Press, 1962), pp. 129–33.

In highly regarded guides to corporate strategy widely used in business schools, Michael Porter systematically elaborates and applies an idea that business executives and economists have always, in some sense, known: one makes money in business by creating and sustaining market failures.[23] In perfectly competitive markets, no firm earns profits in excess of the risk-adjusted market cost of capital for very long. Entrants to growth industries bid down the surpluses earned by existing firms. Cost-cutting technologies and advances in quality are copied by rival firms. Informed consumers pick their preferred mix of price, quality, and quantity from many choices, and are not influenced by advertising or brand names that do not convey accurate information. To earn for its investors above-average returns, a business must wield some monopoly power, either by differentiating its product from the competition or by sustaining a cost advantage.

The search for competitive advantage is in the first instance an enterprise that creates economic value: build a better (or less costly) mousetrap, and the world will make a beaten path to your door. But to keep rivals off the path, to perpetuate the advantage, Porter describes a series of anticompetitive adversary tactics that create monopoly power by raising barriers to entry and driving up competitors' costs, and so *destroy* economic value. Here, in some detail, are a few of what he calls defensive strategies:[24]

BLOCK CHANNEL ACCESS: A firm can raise a large barrier to competition by hindering a competitor's efforts to reach consumers through stores and other channels. "Defensive strategy should be directed not only toward a firm's own channels but also toward blocking access to other channels that may be a substitute channel or a springboard for the challenger's entry." These tactics include exclusive contracts with distributors to not carry competitors' products, and "expanding the product line to include all possible sizes and forms of a product, in order to clog the channels' shelf or warehouse space."

FORECLOSE ALTERNATIVE TECHNOLOGIES: A firm can deter competitors by patenting technological alternatives to its product, even if the firm has no intention of using this technology in its own products.

TIE UP SUPPLIERS: "Barriers increase if a firm can foreclose or limit a challenger's access to the best sources of raw materials, labor, or

---

[23] Michael E. Porter, *Competitive Strategy* (New York: Free Press, 1980), and *Competitive Advantage* (New York: Free Press, 1985).

[24] Drawn from Porter, *Competitive Advantage*, by Harold Pollack. Quotations are from pp. 490–94.

other inputs." A firm can tie up its suppliers by arranging exclusive contracts with suppliers, by buying its most important suppliers, or by "purchasing key locations (mines, forest lands, etc.) in excess of needs to preempt them from competitors."

RAISE COMPETITORS' INPUT COSTS: A firm can accomplish this by "avoiding suppliers that also serve as competitors," and so prevent competitors from achieving scale economies, or by "bidding up the price of labor or raw materials if they represent a higher percentage of costs for competitors."

ENCOURAGE GOVERNMENT POLICIES THAT RAISE BARRIERS: To gain advantage, firms can "encourage stringent safety and pollution standards" and "challenge competitors' products or practices in regulatory proceedings."

This is not a list of academic hypotheticals. Many of these tactics are easily recognizable as common business practices: laundry detergent and shampoo manufactures clog up supermarket aisles; copyrights and patents are purchased and shelved by film makers and computer manufacturers; airlines corner scarce landing gates; one auto manufacturer lobbies for a stricter bumper standard because it has a cost advantage in bumper manufacture. And then, there is Microsoft. Thousands of executives and consultants devote their careers to perfecting these anticompetitive tactics. But the list reads like a catalog of possible antitrust violations. Each is designed to create or perpetuate a market failure, and so to destroy economic value. Many of these practices have been the subject of antitrust litigation.

To be clear, Porter is not at all suggesting that companies should engage in antitrust violations. Indeed, as a matter of public policy, he has argued for strong antitrust laws and their vigorous enforcement.[25] But his advice to companies is to do everything possible within the bounds of existing antitrust rules to achieve the results that those rules attempt to prevent: securing monopoly power by deterring and driving out competition.

This conduct is not obviously wrong. We have noted a number of plausible justifications for sharp adversary tactics. But one cannot plausibly claim that anticompetitive practices are justified on the grounds of the good ends of competitive markets. It is one thing to think that self-interested actions lead to the greatest good by way of the invisible hand. It requires an optimism that competes with Dr. Pangloss to think that actions deliberately designed to undermine the mechanism of the invisible hand lead to the greatest good by way of

[25] Michael E. Porter, *The Competitive Advantage of Nations* (New York: Free Press, 1990).

the invisible hand. One can more easily believe that the Bay of Lisbon had been formed expressly for a certain Anabaptist to drown in.

This is surely so for less-than-perfectly-regulated markets. A firm that creates and exploits a market failure that is currently legal because of a legislative failure cannot plausibly claim that such action is economically efficient. But what about in the best of all possible regulatory worlds? Perfect regulation can be understood in two ways. If it is taken to mean a set of rules and policies that completely corrects for all market failures that might be brought about by adversary action, then, tautologically, all legally permissible adversary action is economically efficient action. But no such set of rules is possible that does not impose its own economic costs and introduce its own inefficiencies. Under reasonable assumptions about the marginal benefits and costs of eliminating the inefficiencies of adversary action, complete elimination of market failures caused by players almost certainly would introduce greater systemic economic inefficiencies, even before considering the noneconomic burdens and restrictions on liberty that regulation "perfect" in this sense would impose. If, instead, the best of regulatory worlds is understood as the set of rules and levels of detection and enforcement that best balances the gains of eliminating the costs and harms and liberty restrictions of adversary action against the costs and harms and liberty restrictions of the regulations themselves, then the best set of regulations will legally permit a great deal of adversary action that is economically inefficient, harmful, and liberty-restricting. There is nothing, then, to the notion that the invisible hand of competition, even in a well-regulated market, will channel all adversary action to good ends.

So good consequences in equilibrium will depend on at least some voluntary compliance with nonlegal prescriptions. This has often been argued. Kenneth Arrow suggests that honest dealing is an essential precondition for a wide range of business and professional transactions:

> Purely selfish behavior of individuals is really incompatible with any kind of settled economic life. There is almost invariably some element of trust and confidence. Much business is done on the basis of verbal assurance. It would be too elaborate to try to get written commitments on every possible point. Every contract depends for its observance on a mass of unspecified conditions which suggest that the performance will be carried out in good faith without insistence on sticking literally to its wording.[26]

---

[26] Kenneth Arrow, "Social Responsibility and Economic Efficiency," *Public Policy* 21 (1973): 314.

From the factual observation that the good ends of the market will not be realized if economic players seek to undermine market efficiency, Christopher MacMahon draws moral conclusions, and derives a morality internal to the market.[27] On his view, if economic activity is morally justified by appeal to the good ends of efficient markets, then players in the market are morally required to avoid certain deceptive and anticompetitive practices, whether or not permitted by law. We need not go so far as to argue for a blanket moral requirement at this point: there may be other moral reasons to permit even inefficient adversary action in the marketplace. What we can conclude is that the justification for efficiency-thwarting action cannot be an argument from efficiency.

Without contradiction, one can have the moral right to do a moral wrong, and a possible implication of such a moral right is that there morally ought to be a legal permission to do that moral wrong. Similarly, in asking about good and bad, rather than right and wrong, it sometimes is a good state of affairs that actors are legally permitted to bring about a bad state of affairs, *but that does not imply that it is a good state of affairs that an actor has brought about a bad state of affairs.* That *is* a contradiction, not to be confused with a noncontradictory asymmetry in the structure of practical reason between what it is good to allow and what it is good to do. Overreaching claims for the invisible hand have not grasped the importance of that asymmetry.

ADVERSARY EQUIPOISE AND THE DIVISION OF MORAL LABOR

With the logic of equilibrium mechanisms in mind, we turn now to ends-based arguments that appeal to the distinctive roles that actors are expected to play in an adversary process. The invisible hand requires for its good functioning a large number of indistinguishable, interchangeable actors: many producers who can make identical products at the same cost and who are quick to mimic new products, advances in design, and cost-saving methods of manufacture and organization, each seeking the same end of profit maximization. In contrast, appeals to the equilibrium mechanisms of a division of moral labor and of adversary equipoise invoke a differentiation and specialization of purpose and skill.

The argument from a division of moral labor claims that some good ends are best produced under a form of social organization in which

---

[27] Christopher MacMahon, "Morality and the Invisible Hand," *Philosophy and Public Affairs* 10 (1981): 247–77.

differentiated actors pursue more narrow aims, rather than aiming directly at the good end that is the purpose of the institution. Moral labor is divided horizontally among those who do the work of the institution, but it is also divided vertically between those who do the work and those who shape the work through institutional design, goal setting, rule making, and adjudication. Armies and bureaucracies appeal to a vertical division of labor to justify the restricted moral reasons and moral aims of its members. The argument from adversary equipoise adds to the possibly harmonious division-of-labor image a contest between identified opponents, and claims that good ends result from a form of social organization in which the specialized aims and efforts of one are poised against the contrary aims and efforts of others in careful balance, so that if one shirks one's adversary task, the favorable equipoise will be upset. The term equipoise is used to convey two senses: the instability of the good equilibrium and the importance of a particular player to its maintenance. Such an argument is most familiarly offered in justification of the adversary legal profession.

Appeals to equipoise between adversaries and appeals to a division of moral labor between adversaries and rule makers clearly are mutually supporting: an equipoise that indeed produces good ends is most likely under carefully constructed and monitored conditions provided by those playing regulatory parts. And the claim that an adversary may or perhaps must refrain from taking on a rule maker's aims and reasons is bolstered if the adversary's partisanship is needed to maintain equipoise.

The two arguments also are related in a deeper way. Each relies on a form of generalization about consequences to justify differentiation and particularization in institutional design. Division of labor creates the role of rule maker, who, in setting general policies that best produce the good ends of the adversary institution, is permitted or required by the institution to ignore the all-things-considered bad ends that inevitably come about in particular cases of the policy's underinclusiveness or overinclusiveness. Under a claim of adversary equipoise, the institution creates a general permission or requirement for its players to act on behalf of different and partial goods, and to ignore the all-things-considered bad ends that inevitably come about from particular adversary acts. Each of the two arguments also runs the danger of conflating these justifications of forms of *social organization*, the way a cooperative venture may or ought to be structured and regulated, with justifications of forms of *moral reasoning*, the way actors may or ought to make judgments about what to do within a cooperative venture. But it is a mistake to move too quickly from

good reasons for dividing institutional roles to good reasons for restricting moral judgment. It may be good for a free society that its
members hold a diversity of conflicting views of the good life, including many mistaken ones, and it may be good to set up institutions
that encourage or protect diverse views, including the mistaken ones.
But no one has a good reason to hold a mistaken view, even though
that would further the goal of diversity.

The moral point of view of the designer is importantly different
from the point of view of the practitioner in two ways. Though there
are good reasons for regulating social activity by rule, the individual
facing the particularity of a case typically has less reason to follow the
generalization than the rule maker has for making and enforcing it.[28]
Ordinarily, I ought to trust my own judgment that a generalization
doesn't fit a particular case more than the rule maker ought to trust
my judgment. So what justifies making a rule that in general leads to
good social outcomes or in general neutralizes bad outcomes does not
by itself justify complying with the rule. When these rules permit
person violation, a second asymmetry comes into play, the distinction
between doing and allowing. Our moral responsibility for the harms
that we bring about ordinarily is more stringent and extensive than
our moral responsibility for harms that we do not prevent. Therefore,
the fact that an adversary institution morally may permit violation
does not entail that practitioners are morally permitted to violate.

The exemplar of equipoise is the adversary system of legal representation, and especially criminal defense, in American courts of law.
The argument in defense of the trial lawyer's zealous advocacy is
perhaps the most familiar and most widely accepted bit of institutional justification in popular political culture, its likely challengers
being the argument for a marketplace of ideas in democratic politics,
the argument for divided, checked, and balanced branches of government, and, of course, the argument for a competitive economic marketplace. By the rules of the bar, defense attorneys may, indeed must
attempt to acquit those whom they know to be factually guilty if the
defendant's interests will be served, and to do so they may conceal
incriminating information and spin to juries stories they know to be
false. Civil litigators may not conceal material facts or adverse prece-
dent, but they may, indeed must make an argument about the law in
support of their client's case that they believe is a bad argument if
they think a judge or jury will believe it. There are a number of claims
offered in justification of such zealous advocacy, not all of which ap-

---

[28] For a different emphasis, see Frederick Schauer, *Playing by the Rules* (Oxford: Oxford University Press, 1991), pp. 128–34.

peal to the good ends in equilibrium of such a practice.[29] We are here interested in claims of adversary equipoise: that the institution of zealous legal advocates is, on the whole, the best way to uncover the factual and legal truth, and so the best way to achieve just outcomes. The lawyer therefore is justified in playing the role of zealous advocate, even in those cases where such zealousness will not reveal the truth or lead to a just settlement of legal disputes.

This claim, as has been noted several times before about other claims, is in part an assertion of fact, difficult to document, which may or may not be true. But whether or not it is true about the American legal profession, lawyers in equipoise are sufficiently different from those other adversaries in equipoise that take up space in the popular imagination, political actors in a divided government jousting with one another, that no inference about politics and government can be made. As always, we must be on guard against spurious analogies that ignore details of mechanism and specification. Consider two possible disanalogies.

The first disanalogy between adversary equipoise in the legal system and adversary equipoise in politics and government is that only in the legal system is there a highly developed and refined division of labor between players and referees. We have noted that the argument from adversary equipoise and the argument from a vertical division of moral labor can be mutually supporting, and nowhere is this more clear than in the U.S. courtroom, where the practice of adversary engagement is carefully constructed and carefully monitored by judges at both the trial level and on appeal. Without making any claim about how *successful* courts are at uncovering truth and achieving just outcomes, we at least can observe the efforts of designers and referees to modify the rules of engagement and their interpretation and enforcement in the direction of greater success. At the trial level, judges are continually making judgments about the admissibility of evidence and testimony and about the fairness of various procedural motions, and higher courts regularly review and interpret the rules of engagement. Occasionally, through court decisions or legislation, major changes have been made that systematically shift the adversary equilibrium: the exclusionary rule in criminal justice, and discovery in civil proceedings. Although the mechanisms of the market for political ideas and the struggle for power between political actors also are occasionally subjected to revision and adjustment, either through con-

---

[29] For example, the protection of the vulnerable from the powerful. For an excellent account of various claims, see Luban, *Lawyers and Justice*.

stitutional court cases or legislation on campaign financing and lobbying, there is nothing like the close act-by-act and statement-by-statement refereeing that a trial judge provides (or, at least, is supposed to provide). Within legal practice itself, lawyers who engage in adversary tactics as deal makers and publicists mistakenly help themselves to equipoise justifications that work, if at all, only in the highly structured arena of the courtroom. As we shall see in Chapter 10, it is also a mistake for officeholders in divided government to help themselves to the adversary permissions of lawyers before the bench (and this is so even if a law degree happens to hang on the political adversary's wall).

Second, the strength of an ends-based justification of a lawyer's adversary practices comes in part from the lawyer's status as an agent for a principal, the client. The good ends of an adversary institution—in the legal system, truth and justice—may depend on an efficient division of moral labor between client and professional, the principal choosing substantive moral purposes and the professional exercising instrumental expertise on behalf of those purposes. The stable expectations of both principal adversaries and targets about the actions of professional agents under such a division might be jeopardized if agents are permitted or required to act on their judgments about a client's moral purposes in particular cases of zealous advocacy, and such predictability is an important efficiency condition. So agents may have strong moral reasons to act as adversaries, and this is so even before considering reasons for action grounded either in obligations incurred by an agent to a principal, in an agent's permission to enable the principal's exercise of a right, or in some account of goods internal to a professional role. Principals, however, cannot help themselves so readily to this appeal to ends (and cannot help themselves to most of the other appeals at all, unless one is morally right to exercise all of one's legal rights—a clearly false proposition). The criminal defendant ordinarily cannot claim that any good social end depends on pleading not guilty when she in fact committed the crime as charged, and the civil litigant ordinarily cannot claim any good social end depends on pressing an unjust suit. Legal principals usually best serve the good ends of truth and justice by telling the truth and acting justly.

Whether an argument from good ends in adversary equipoise works for political actors depends in part on whether political advocates, candidates, and officeholders are to be understood as agents whose predictable exercise of instrumental expertise on behalf of principals is needed for good social outcomes. Although political actors are in part agents, they are not agents only, except on the thinnest conception of democratic representation in which political actors are viewed solely as delegates of the wishes of constituents.[30] But political actors are and ought to be, at least in part, principals for their own conceptions of political principles.[31] To the extent that this is so, they cannot justify a division of labor between partisan adversaries by appeal to a division of labor between instrumental agents and purposeful principals. A political candidate who airs manipulative advertisements, a lobbyist who pushes for bad legislation, or a president who evades congressional checks is more like the litigant who tries to avoid paying a just claim than like the lawyer who represents him.

Nonconsequentialist moral theories, such as contractualism, take two kinds of judgments seriously: that there is a moral distinction to be made between harms that we do and harms that we allow to happen, and that there is a moral distinction to be made, as variously put, between intending and merely foreseeing harm; between harming that is causally necessary for the agent's ends and harming that is a mere side effect; or between using others as means and merely not making them ends. One way to argue for nonconsequentialism is to show that consequentialism does not adequately account for our judgment that there is something to these distinctions (and one way to argue for consequentialism is to show that these distinctions do not hold water, and that our judgments are either mistaken or can be explained differently). If adversaries in equilibrium are to meet the test of reasonable consent, then we would expect the harms associated with adversary institutions to fall on the easier-to-justify side of these distinctions. This chapter has assessed some attempts to put invisible-handed violation on the easy side of the two lines, and argued that the attempts fail.

There is a version of the doing-allowing distinction that explains a possible asymmetry between the moral obligations of institutional rule makers and designers, on the one hand, and practitioners, on the other. There are actions that are good to allow but bad to do, and there are actions that are right to allow but wrong to do. The practitioner may fence, but may not offence, and this is so even if the rule makers of the sport are morally permitted to allow offencing to hap-

---

[30] For accounts of democratic representation, see Hanna F. Pitkin, *Representation* (Berkeley: University of California Press, 1967), and Dennis F. Thompson, *Political Ethics and Public Office* (Cambridge, Mass.: Harvard University Press, 1987), ch. 4.

[31] This should not be misunderstood as a permission to act on nonpublic reasons in one's public capacity.

pen. Each practitioner is capable of self-command and the judgments that support it. So practitioners ordinarily cannot rely on rule permissibility to underwrite moral permissibility. The practitioner is morally responsible for what she does.

Adversaries might try to shift responsibility onto the institution, and interpret the harm they do as something merely foreseen in the workings of a mechanism aimed at producing good and minimizing injury—the moral equivalent of an accident. But this attempt to redescribe intent fails. Surely the offencer intends to injure her opponent, whatever else she intends about having a good match, and uses her opponent as a means. The manipulative advertiser surely intends to deceive consumers, whatever else he may intend about market efficiency, and uses his customers as a means. To borrow from the bumper sticker: invisible hands don't violate people—people violate people.

Part IV, "Authority and Dissent," develops the view that actors in institutions have grounds for making independent judgments about the goodness and rightness of what they are called upon to do, and they have grounds for making judgments about the legitimate authority of persons and institutions that command them to do what they judge to be bad or wrong. This is so, even if the political institutions that divide labor and command obedience are justified. Forms of social organization are one thing, moral reasoning within those institutions, another. In the face of this asymmetry, a new sort of adversary relationship demands our attention: not one designed by governments, markets, or professions, but one created by the conflict between the authority of these institutions and the judgment of dissenting practitioners.

PART IV

AUTHORITY AND DISSENT

JACQUES: But without coming back on this dispute, could we not prevent a hundred more like it by means of some reasonable agreement?

MASTER: I agree to that.

JACQUES: Whereas it is agreed: Firstly, considering that it is written up above that I am essential to you, that I know it, and that I know you know that you cannot do without me, I will abuse this advantage each and every time the occasion presents itself.

MASTER: But Jacques, no such agreement was ever made.

JACQUES: Made or not, that's how it has been for all time, is now, and shall ever be. . . . It was ordained that you would have the title to the thing and I would have the thing itself. . . .

MASTER: But if that is right your lot is worth more than mine.

JACQUES: Who's arguing with you?

MASTER: Then if that is true I have only to take your place and put you in mine.

JACQUES: Do you know what would happen then? You would lose the title to the thing and still not have it. Let us stay as we are. It suits us both very well, and let the rest of our life be devoted to creating a proverb.

MASTER: What proverb?

JACQUES: Jacques leads his master. It will be said of us first but it will be repeated about a thousand others who are worth more than you or me.

MASTER: That seems to be hard, very hard.

JACQUES: My Master, my dear Master, you are shying away from a needle which will only prick you the harder. That is what has been agreed between us.

MASTER: What relevance has our consent got if it's a law of necessity?

JACQUES: A lot. Do you not think that it would be useful to know where we stand, clearly and precisely, once and for all? The only reason for our quarrels up to now is that we have not accepted, for your part, that you would call yourself master and, for my part, I would be yours.

Denis Diderot, Jacques the Fatalist and His Master

Chapter Nine

DEMOCRATIC LEGITIMACY
AND OFFICIAL DISCRETION

The lyre's strings do not constrict his hands.
And it is in overstepping that he obeys.

Rainer Maria Rilke, The Sonnets to Orpheus

IN THE STRUGGLE to make and carry out public policy, the substantive views of government officials often are not, or are not yet, supported by their superiors, or by most legislators, or by most citizens. May government officials create and exercise discretion to pursue their dissenting views of good policy (constrained only by political prudence and a reasonable interpretation of the law), or should officials faithfully serve the will or the interests of those who have formal authority over their actions or over the disputed policies?

The answer to such a broad question must be, It depends—but on what? Two considerations jump to mind: the substantive merits of the public official's views (right or wrong), and the job held by the public official (elected representative, appointed cabinet secretary, career administrator). Upon scrutiny, however, these two distinctions either do not do enough work or do too much.

If an account of justified discretion is to be of any critical use to a would-be political entrepreneur, it cannot turn on the rightness or wrongness of her substantive policy judgment: if she did not believe that she was right, she would not be dissenting. The question of justified discretion does not specify political appointees, bureaucrats, or generals, and it does not specify the executive branch, for a reason. An account of when a public official may legitimately act on her judgment of good policy in the face of the disagreement of superiors has much in common—at least, more than is commonly acknowledged—with accounts of when legislators may act on their judgments in the face of disagreement with their constituents, or when presidents can act on their judgments in the face of congressional disagreement. The ethics of official dissent, of legislative representation, and of executive authority under a separation of powers all appeal to a common consideration: if substantive *judgments* conflict, when should an actor subordinate her conduct to the *authority* of others?

I will restrict our attention to the moral point of view of the political actor who faces such a choice between judgment and authority, rather than to the standpoint of institutions or other observers of official entrepreneurship and dissent. For it may be the case that, though an official, by her lights and in her position, may or must exercise discretion, others, by their lights and in their positions, may or must try to control, suppress, or punish such discretion. This, therefore, is an exercise in actor-centered moral reasoning in the face of nearly but not ideally just political institutions, rather than a contribution to the design of ideal political institutions.[1]

I also will restrict our attention to acts of discretion that are legal under a reasonable interpretation of existing law. This not because the specter of lawbreaking renders the problem of illegal disobedience discontinuous with the problem of political discretion (I do not think it does), but simply because, although the moral obligation to obey the law has been exhaustively discussed, questions of political obligation within the bounds of the law have not received the attention they deserve. So I will not ask directly the classic question of when civil disobedience or other forms of lawbreaking are justified, although I will, by analogy, draw on well-known accounts of civil disobedience. I will also sidestep the hoary question of what is meant by "legal under a reasonable interpretation of existing law." I do not believe that I need to take a stand here on legal realism, the doctrine that, as Holmes put it, law is simply the "prophecies of what the courts will do in fact, and nothing more pretentious."[2] I will, however, wrestle with the doctrine that may be called *political* realism—the view that morally authoritative political mandates are simply whatever politics permits in fact, and nothing more pretentious.

The argument about justified official dissent and discretion proceeds in three parts, and I have already hinted at each. First, although there is truth in political realism, the moral authority of a political mandate is at least partly independent of both the formal mandate on the books (laws, rules, policy declarations) and the effective mandate (what is politically possible and sustainable). Second, political actors can, and indeed ought to, make judgments about the moral authority of political mandates, and judgments about their moral authority to act on those judgments. Third, reasonable criteria to guide the exercise of such judgment can be formulated. To find our bearings in the

---

[1] See John Rawls, *A Theory of Justice* (Cambridge, Mass.: Harvard University Press, 1971), for the distinction between ideal and nonideal theory (pp. 244–48) and for the book's only foray into nonideal theory, the account of civil disobedience (ch. 6).

[2] Oliver Wendell Holmes, who anticipated the legal realist movement, in "The Path of Law," *Harvard Law Review* 10 (1897): 461.

relatively uncharted search for these criteria, we will triangulate from two well-trodden topics in political ethics. Theories of legislative choice in the face of the opposing will of constituents will be helpful in formulating an account of administrative choice in the face of the opposing will of legislators or superiors; and theories of civil disobedience in the face of legal mandates will be helpful in formulating an account of official discretion in the face of political mandates.

THREE EXAMPLES

For concreteness, consider three episodes in the exercise of official discretion taken from American government.

Califano's Conscience

The first concerns Joseph Califano, President Jimmy Carter's secretary of health, education, and welfare. The Supreme Court ruled that the government was not required to fund abortions; Congress, in a hard fought compromise, was prepared to pay for Medicaid abortions in cases of rape, incest, and danger to the health of the woman. The prospect of writing regulations governing the funding of abortions in cases of rape and incest deeply troubled Califano, a practicing Catholic who believed that abortion is morally wrong except to save the life of the mother, and who held that, as a matter of public policy, elective abortions should *not* be funded by the government.

Califano called upon Father Richard McCormick, a Georgetown University professor, for guidance. Califano recalls McCormick's advice: "You should always keep in mind three levels of distinction here. First, there is the personal conscience and belief thing. Second, there is what the appropriate public policy should be in a pluralistic democracy. . . . And third, there is the obligation of the public official to carry out the law the nation enacts."[3] McCormick's first level corresponds to what has been called a view of the good, which may come from religion, or from other values and commitments. The move from the first to the second level requires a judgment about what public policy should be, given that people disagree about what is good. Califano opposes abortion on both levels: he believes that abortion is a

[3] Joseph A. Califano Jr., *Governing America*, excerpted in *Ethics and Politics*, ed. Amy Gutmann and Dennis F. Thompson (Chicago: Nelson-Hall, 1990), p. 260. The facts of this account are drawn from the excerpt.

moral wrong, and he believes that it should not be funded, even though others disagree with him about its wrongness.

Father McCormick introduces a third level: judgments about obedience to authority, given disagreement about the second level, about a public philosophy. When we disagree, not only about what is good, but about what to do given such disagreement, whose public philosophy is authoritative?

McCormick goes on to tell Califano that he may—indeed, *must*—carry out the responsibilities of his office and fund abortions where required by law, even though he believes the law is unjust.

Califano accepted McCormick's view of authority, and set about to interpret the congressional mandate fairly. He included pro-choicers on the rule-making staff, and resisted strong pressure from President Carter to tighten the reporting provisions for rape and incest. When Carter said he "personally" thought that a sixty-day window allowed "too much opportunity for fraud and would encourage women to lie," Califano responded, "But what counts is what the congressional intent is."[4]

Legal Aid in Rural California

The second example is drawn from a now forgotten skirmish in Lyndon Johnson's War on Poverty. David Goldman,[5] a young lawyer and community organizer, went to rural California in 1966 to start a federally funded legal services organization.[6] Cesar Chavez's new farm workers' union was then struggling to take root, despite the fierce opposition of growers and of then governor Ronald Reagan. Goldman took as his mission the use of legal action to organize and empower poor farm workers, in common cause with Chavez, thus rejecting tamer missions more acceptable to local interests.

Goldman's overseers in the White House Office of Economic Opportunity were in sympathy with the lawyer-organizer mission. When the California State Bar Association complained that the legal services organization proposed to advocate "the contentions of one side of an

---

[4] Gutmann and Thompson, *Ethics and Politics*, p. 279. Congress ultimately reversed itself, however, and stopped Medicaid funding for all elective abortions.

[5] A pseudonym.

[6] This account relies on Stephen B. Hitchner, "California Legal Services, Inc.," Parts A-D, Kennedy School of Government Case C94-75-9, -10, -11, -12; and Mark H. Moore and Malcolm K. Sparrow, "David Goldman and California Legal Services," in their *Ethics in Government: The Moral Challenge of Public Leadership* (Englewood Cliffs, N.J.: Prentice-Hall, 1990), pp. 57–63.

economic struggle now pending," an OEO official replied that that was the best one-line definition of the War on Poverty that he had heard.[7]

The formal, written mandate of Goldman's organization, however, reflected a political bargain between powerful and competing interests. The organization's lawyers were explicitly forbidden in its charter from representing any labor union, from organizing clients into collective bargaining units, and from moonlighting (to prevent any circumvention of the first two conditions).

For the most part, Goldman did not violate the letter of his mandate, although he devoted all his energy to the violation of its spirit, repeatedly reminding his staff, in their selection of cases and in decisions to settle or to go to court, that the union was the "real" client. On at least one occasion, however, Goldman clearly stepped over the line. Chavez asked a legal question about a contemplated boycott, and Goldman and staffers worked all night on the answer. When the press picked up a rumor that the poverty lawyers were advising Chavez directly, Goldman was called by a White House aide, who guardedly asked, "We don't have any problems with that, do we?" After Goldman answered "None," Washington asked no more questions.[8]

We, however, have many questions to ask David Goldman. Does he straightforwardly reject the force of Father McCormick's third level, and believe that the deals of democratic politics and the directives of political superiors have little or no moral authority if they fail the second-level test of what "public policy should be in a pluralistic democracy"? If so, who grades the test?

Does he reject the moral authority of merely *this* particular mandate, because it was forged in a bargain among competing interests in a smoke-filled room? Would his actions have been any different had his charter been deliberated openly on the floor of Congress and approved by a wide margin on principled reasons?

Does Goldman distinguish morally between the clear violation of the formal mandate (advising Chavez) and pursuing goals counter to the intent of, but that do not literally violate, those constraints—choosing cases and clients that advance the union's interests? And does he go so far as to claim that, in politics, there is no morally important formal mandate, apart from what the push and pull of political forces in fact permits or prevents?

---

[7] Hitchner, "California Legal Services," Part A, p. 16.
[8] Moore and Sparrow, "David Goldman," p. 63.

Covert Military Aid for the Nicaraguan Contras

The third example is much better known: the Reagan administration's provision of covert military aid, without the knowledge or consent of Congress, to the Contras, opponents of the Sandinista regime in Nicaragua.[9] To stop U.S. military support for the Contras, Congress had added increasingly stringent and precise conditions, known as the Boland amendments,[10] to defense appropriations bills. The most strict read: "No appropriations or funds made available pursuant to this joint resolution to the Central Intelligence Agency, the Department of Defense, or any other agency or entity of the United States involved in intelligence activities may be obligated or expended for the purpose or which would have the effect of supporting, directly or indirectly, military or paramilitary operations in Nicaragua by any nation, group, organization, or individual."[11]

In the hope that Congress would eventually restore military aid, the administration sought ways to keep the Nicaraguan resistance intact. The general strategy was to transfer the management of covert operations in support of the Contras from the Central Intelligence Agency to the White House national security adviser, who was not *specifically named in the amendment,* and to seek third-party contributions to replace U.S. government funds. Oliver North, a marine lieutenant colonel posted to the national security adviser's staff, took the main operational lead. North threw himself into the task with great energy and initiative.

North's activities were conducted on a compartmentalized, "need-to-know" basis, hidden from Congress and, for the most part, from the regular foreign-policy apparatus. Secretary of State George Shultz opposed soliciting foreign governments, so Saudi Arabia and other countries were approached without his knowledge. Using the authority of the White House, North periodically called upon ambassadors, military officers, and intelligence officers to make things happen, and they typically responded to these requests from the White House without protest, without question, and without seeking approval through their own chains of command.

The secrecy surrounding North's activities was not designed to fool the Sandinistas, who never doubted that the U.S. government was the source of its troubles, or neighboring Honduras and Costa Rica, who

---

[9] This account relies on Theodore Draper, *A Very Thin Line: The Iran-Contra Affairs* (New York: Farrar, Straus and Giroux, 1991), pp. 3–119, 290–314, 332–51, 558–79.

[10] After the chairman of the House Select Committee on Intelligence, Edward P. Boland, a Massachusetts Democrat.

[11] Draper, *A Very Thin Line*, p. 24.

tolerated the resupply effort because of, not despite, the White House connection. Rather, the target was Congress, which would have angrily rewritten Boland yet again to close any conceivable loophole.

As the administration had hoped, Congress eventually did reverse itself, and by October 1986 resumed military aid for the Contras. By year's end, however, the Iran-Contra story broke, leaving the administration's Central American policy in tatters.

Some of the activities of North and others did, of course, involve blatant violation of law, most notably episodes of straightforward lying under oath at congressional hearings. But the protagonists in the Contra affair exhibit a literalism that shows an odd *deference* to legal authority. They could have found more secure ways to get arms to the Contras that would have required undeniable violations of Boland. Instead, a strategy was adopted that was far more susceptible to exposure, but that allowed for a series of contorted legal claims: Boland does not cover the National Security Council because it is not an intelligence agency, and Boland does not cover unappropriated money.

If some Ollie South, just like North but with a law degree, had managed never to cross the very thin line of legality, the strategies of evasion of and concealment from Congress would still have sparked a political crisis of the first order. The mandate of Congress, though fickle, was crystal clear, and the administration's actions, even when legal, repeatedly denied the *moral* authority of that mandate. The most important and interesting challenges of the Contra affair are not about statutory interpretation, but about legitimate political authority.

Reactions of liberal audiences to these three stories is fairly predictable: most approve of Califano's obedience, but wish that those ambassadors and officers called upon to help North had asked more questions, and that the secretary of state who opposed him had lodged stronger, more effective protests. Most condemn Oliver North in the strongest terms, but struggle to explain and justify David Goldman (in the end, splitting on whether, all things considered, he acted rightly).

Taylor Branch, commenting in the early 1970s on the odd parallels between Daniel Ellsberg, leaker of the Pentagon Papers, and the more obscure Otto Otepka, an anti-Communist State Department official who leaked information to red-baiting allies in Congress, puzzled over liberal and conservative reactions to the two cases. The *New York Times*, for example, publisher of the Pentagon Papers, condemned Otepka for not following the rules, while the *Richmond Times-Dispatch*, which gave Otepka a hero's treatment, was scandalized by the example of Ellsberg taking matters into his own hands. Anyone who wants to encourage dissent by public officials, Branch wrote, "is obliged by honesty and consistency to take his Otepkas with his Ellsbergs."[12] To do otherwise, on Branch's view, is unprincipled hypocrisy, presumably because principled judgments about authority of the law and disobedience of it must be substantively neutral.

About the exercise of official discretion, must we take our Oliver Norths with our David Goldmans? Or can we find principled grounds to distinguish between them that do not turn—or do not turn merely—on our substantive views of good policy?

MANDATES IN BOOKS OR MANDATES IN ACTION?

Consider two extreme positions on this question, Michael Quinlan's obedient-servant ethic sketched earlier in Chapter 4 and the political-realist ethic. On the obedient-servant view, one's own beliefs about the good are never good reasons for action. Public roles are to be impersonal, public figures are to be interchangeable. Recall that on this view facelessness and namelessness are bureaucratic virtues. Public officials should obey orders and be the vessels of the will of their superiors. Discretion, though often necessary, is an evil.

Whatever one can say about the normative desirability of the obedient-servant ethic, this accountant's version of public control and accountability is grossly inadequate as a description of political life. A public administrator who wants to do nothing but obey her superiors—or a governor who wants only to respond to the will of the people—faces a serious problem: the mandates of public officials to act are ambiguous, conflict-ridden, forever changing, and shaped in part by the very actions of these intendedly obedient public officials.[13]

Political realism takes this descriptive truth—that public officials have control over the conditions of their own discretion—and turns it into a normative claim. To the political realist, asking a public official to do only what she is mandated to do makes little sense. The mandate of a public official to act is precisely what is in play. The job of an official is to press a substantive agenda as forcefully and as skillfully

[12] Taylor Branch, "The Odd Couple," *Washington Monthly*, October 1971. Reprinted in Gutmann and Thompson, *Ethics and Politics*, pp. 104–13.

[13] See Richard E. Neustadt, *Presidential Power and the Modern Presidents* (1960; New York: Free Press, 1990); Mark H. Moore, *Creating Public Value* (Cambridge, Mass.: Harvard University Press, 1995); and Donald P. Warwick, "The Ethics of Administrative Discretion," in *Public Duties: The Moral Obligations of Government Officials*, ed. Joel L. Fleishman, Lance Liebman, and Mark H. Moore (Cambridge, Mass.: Harvard University Press, 1981), pp. 93–127.

as she can. She should heed prudence, of course—she cannot do a good job if she is stopped, undone, or ruined (although she might advance her cause by resigning or being fired). But in the end, her moral authority to act is nothing more or less than what in fact the political process allows her to get away with. To a public official who thinks like a political realist, any questions about the *legitimate* exercise of discretion, about moral authority, reduce to purely *strategic* predictions about the power, attention, and will of political opponents and supporters. To paraphrase Holmes again, the obligations of public officials are simply "the prophecies of what powerful political actors will do in fact, and nothing more pretentious."

On the realist view, David Goldman fulfilled the only obligation a public official has: to advance the correct substantive political agenda. On this same view, Califano's deference to Father McCormick's third level—official responsibility to obey the law—was cowardly, because Califano did not push for the interpretation most favorable to his political agenda.

Who has the better part of the argument, the political realists or the obedient servants? There *is* a moral truth in political realism, but it is captured by a paraphrase, not of Holmes, but of Roscoe Pound, who spoke of law in books and law in action: there is a difference between formal mandates in books and legitimate mandates in action.[14] Democratic legitimacy—and not merely strategic opportunity, not merely the effective mandate—indeed is ambiguous, shifting, and in play, with government officials at all levels as players. Recall the discussions of practice positivism in Chapters 3 and 5: both the content of the positive role of the public official and the legitimacy of that positive role can be contested. But what does *not* follow from Pound's truth is the Holmesian conclusion that there are no grounds independent of political prediction on which to make judgments about democratic legitimacy. The range of morally legitimate actions is not coextensive with the zone of possible agreement in the political bargain,[15] and the reasons or considerations that count in a determination of legitimacy are different from those that determine the strength of a political coalition. Notions such as consent, representation, self-governance, publicity, transparency, reasonableness, and deliberativeness are quite separate from measures of political constraint and opportunity.

[14] Cf. Roscoe Pound, "Law in Books and Law in Action," *American Law Review* 44 (1910): 12–36.

[15] For analytic treatments of negotiation, see Howard Raiffa, *The Art and Science of Negotiation* (Cambridge, Mass.: Harvard University Press, 1982); and David A. Lax and James K. Sebenius, *The Manager as Negotiator* (New York: Free Press, 1986).

So there is more to democratic legitimacy than the intersection of rule books and political possibility. A public official may have both the formal mandate and the political support to act, yet lack the moral legitimacy to do so; and a public official may, in the face of both a formal mandate and political support for action, legitimately do otherwise. The answer to Taylor Branch is neither purely substantive nor purely procedural. Rather, public action demands independent judgment about the legitimacy of formal and effective mandates—which may very well turn on substantive, but not merely on substantive, grounds. To map those grounds is the task ahead.

JUDGMENT OR AUTHORITY: WHO IS TO DECIDE?

When an official makes a judgment about what is good public policy, she has a substantive reason to act in accord with that judgment. But a public official also faces what Joseph Raz has called second-order reasons, which direct the official to not act on her first-order substantive reasons, but rather to defer to the strength of a different sort of reason, and act in accord with the judgment of an authority, or on the outcome of a procedure.[16]

The landscape of practical and moral reason is filled with such second-order considerations: in the face of a disagreement with your boss, defer to her wishes; in the face of disagreement with a friend about which movie to go to, flip a coin. In the face of disagreement between doctor and patient about treatment, let the patient decide; in the face of disagreement about candidates, decide by majority vote.

Claims of democratic legitimacy, whether writ large as the moral authority of a regime or a form of government, or writ small as the moral authority of particular political actors to act or demand action, whether claims of authority over persons or claims of authority over actions,[17] are all varieties of second-order reasons. Liberalism is itself a form of second-order reasoning on a grand scale: in the face of disagreement about substantive conceptions of the good, seek agreement about a conception of justice that treats those who hold different views of the good fairly.[18]

A purely procedural view of justice, in which justice is nothing

---

[16] Joseph Raz, *Practical Reason and Norms* (London: Hutchinson Press, 1975), and *The Authority of the Law* (Oxford: Oxford University Press, 1979).

[17] See Raz, *The Authority of Law*, p. 19, for the importance of this distinction.

[18] See Rawls, *A Theory of Justice*.

other than the outcome of a specified procedure, may collapse into a view of legitimacy, where the justice question of "what to decide"—given substantive conflict of interests, beliefs, or values—cannot be separated from the legitimacy question of "how to decide" or "who is to decide."[19] The result of a coin flip determining who kicks off in the Super Bowl is both just and legitimate. But when second-order reasons of justice have substantive content, they may conflict with second-order reasons of legitimacy. Solutions to democratic dirty-hands problems, say in times of war or civil unrest, may be both uncontroversially unjust and uncontroversially legitimate.[20]

One can interpret political legitimacy as yet a third order of reason: in the face of disagreement about conceptions of justice, seek agreement about conceptions of legitimacy in government that treat those who hold different views of justice fairly.[21] Lawmakers may disagree about whether justice demands the funding of legal services or medical care for the poor, but agree to enact the conception favored by majority vote. (This view, however, should not be interpreted as claiming a general priority of majoritarianism over justice—majoritarianism is but one claimant among many for the mantle of political legitimacy.)

At the risk of invoking the title of a spaghetti western, I have identified three orders of reason: the good, the just, and the legitimate.[22] Table 3 locates these three orders of moral reasoning and conflict. Within each order, moral actors form judgments, identify conflicts with one another, and engage in substantive deliberation about their reasons for those judgments. If conflicting judgments persist, the search for moral resolution moves to a new order of reasons.[23]

We can now see that Father McCormick's advice to Califano contained an instance of each order of reason. Califano believes that

---

[19] For an elaboration of pure procedural justice, see ibid., pp. 85–86.

[20] For discussions of the dirty-hands problem, see Michael Walzer, "Political Action: The Problem of Dirty Hands," *Philosophy and Public Affairs* 2 (1973): 160–80; and Dennis F. Thompson, "Democratic Dirty Hands," in his *Political Ethics and Public Office* (Cambridge, Mass.: Harvard University Press, 1987), pp. 11–39.

[21] See John Rawls, *Political Liberalism* (New York: Columbia University Press, 1993).

[22] Following Raz, I will continue to use "second-order" as a general term referring to all higher orders of reasons.

[23] For simplicity of exposition, Table 3 has been presented as a sequence of steps in an ideal deliberation among moral actors. But the table is best interpreted not as a model of the process of deliberation but as a road map to locate arguments by their function in moral justification. Justification does not require all these steps or require this order. Furthermore, not all questions of justice arise out of conflicts about the good, and not all questions of legitimacy arise out of conflicts about the just.

TABLE 3
Orders of Reasons

	The Good	The Just	The Legitimate
Judgment	A1. Judgment of the good	B1. Judgment of the just, given A4	C1. Judgment of legitimacy, given A4 or B4
Conflict	A2. Conflicting conceptions of the good	B2. Conflicting conceptions of the just	C2. Conflicting conceptions of the legitimate
Deliberation	A3. Deliberation about the good	B3. Deliberation about the just	C3. Deliberation about the legitimate
Residual Conflict	A4. Residual conflict about the good	B4. Residual conflict about the just	C4. Residual conflict about the legitimate

abortion not only is a moral bad (A1), but an injustice that ought to be prohibited—in disagreement with the prevailing mandate (B4). He defers, however, to what he believes to be the legitimate authority of Congress (C1).

Judgments of legitimacy include both judgments about others' actions, and judgments about the judge's actions, given the legitimacy or illegitimacy of others. Someone else's lack of moral authority is not quite enough to justify your action or disobedience. And, as Raz pointedly notes, the (moral) right to (moral) authority is not the same as (moral) authority.[24] So judgments of legitimacy are of two sorts: the evaluative judgment about how to decide or who is to decide, given disagreement, and the prescriptive judgment about how to act, given one's evaluative judgment. Judgments of legitimacy may be evaluative but not prescriptive, in that they are not immediate calls for or justifications of action, although an evaluative finding may be a very strong reason for prescribing action.

At some point, one runs out of reasons. When words fail, the only recourse may be withdrawal, evasion or subversion, anarchy, revolution, or civil war. But moral reasoning in politics is a many-layered thing.[25]

[24] Raz, *The Authority of Law*, p. 9n. The modifier "moral" is mine.
[25] Since the logic of higher-order reasons can be extended indefinitely, we stop at

With this account of second-order reasons in mind, one can raise an objection to the emerging argument for official entrepreneurship and discretion. Granted, the truth in political realism does not destroy the grounds on which to make judgments about whether formal and effective mandates are good, whether they are just, and whether they are legitimate. But do public officials also have the grounds on which to make judgments about whether they have the authority to *act* on their judgments and exercise discretion in defiance of a formal and effective mandate that they judge to be bad, unjust, or illegitimate?

Perhaps public officials face very strong second-order reasons to not act on their judgments about defects in the goodness, justice, or legitimacy of the formal and effective mandates they face. On this view, the duties of office severely circumscribe the authority of officials to exercise judgment. John Rawls, commenting on the law and civil disobedience, might have said the same about political mandates and official dissent: "Up to a certain point it is better that the law and its interpretation be settled than that it be settled rightly. Therefore it may be protested that the preceding account does not determine who is to say when circumstances are such as to justify civil disobedience. It invites anarchy by encouraging everyone to decide for himself, and to abandon the public rendering of political principles."[26]

The logic of second-order reasons developed so far points to the reply. True, we do not have the authority to act on every justified judgment.[27] We have no choice, however, at some level, to make judgments about our authority to act. An account of second-order reasons must allow for judgments about second-order reasons, for conflicts between second-order reasons, and for third-order reasons that exclude certain second-order reasons.[28] We have nowhere else to stand but on our own two feet: moral agency requires making judgments that sometimes commit us to acting on our judgments. Rawls continues: "The reply to this is that each person must indeed make his own decision. Even though men normally seek advice and counsel,

---

three levels because the good, the just, and the legitimate have ready interpretations using ordinary political concepts. A fourth-order reason does not.

[26] Rawls, *A Theory of Justice*, p. 389.

[27] Jeremy Waldron, "Rights and Majorities: Rousseau Revisited," in *NOMOS XXXII: Majorities and Minorities*, ed. John W. Chapman and Alan Wertheimer (New York: New York University Press, 1990), pp. 44–75; T. M. Scanlon, "Who Is to Say?" (lecture at Harvard University, September 14, 1990).

[28] And perhaps for exceptions from second-order reasons. Frederick Schauer argues, against Raz, that second-order reasons are merely presumptive, not conclusive. See *Playing by the Rules* (Oxford: Oxford University Press, 1991), pp. 88–93.

and accept the injunctions of those in authority when these seem reasonable to them, they are always accountable for their deeds. We cannot divest ourselves of our responsibility and transfer the burden of blame to others. This is true on any theory of political duty and obligation that is compatible with the principles of a democratic constitution."[29]

THREE TENSIONS IN A CONSTITUTIONAL DEMOCRACY

If Rawls is right about the responsibility for autonomous judgment, if Raz is right that sometimes one can autonomously choose to defer to authority, and if there is truth in the view of political realism termed "mandates in action," then the moral authority of various political actors and institutions will depend on criteria more fluid and more substantive than any formal, hierarchical, or procedural division of moral labor can capture. A satisfactory account of justified official discretion, in a world where legitimate mandates are not read straight from the books or the organizational charts, must attend to the substantive content of democracy, and therefore engage three tensions in constitutional democratic theory: democratic justice and liberal justice; legitimate jurisdiction and legitimate reasons; and democracy as method and democracy as value.

Democratic Justice and Liberal Justice

Liberalism and democracy coexist uneasily. As Judith Shklar put it, "liberalism is monogamously, faithfully, and permanently married to democracy—but it is a marriage of convenience."[30] Nonetheless, even those who are more deeply democratic than they are liberal agree that at least some democratic, or political, liberties are either logical or contingent preconditions of democracy. Some principles (such as freedom of political expression, or universal suffrage) ought to be excluded from the democratic agenda; some issues ought not to be decided by the will of the majority.[31] This is the idea behind constitu-

---

[29] Rawls, *A Theory of Justice*, p. 389.

[30] Judith N. Shklar, "Liberalism of Fear," in *Liberalism and the Moral Life*, ed. Nancy Rosenblum (Cambridge, Mass.: Harvard University Press, 1989), p. 37.

[31] For the democratic view, see, for example, Michael Walzer, "Philosophy and Democracy," *Political Theory* 9 (1981): 379–99; John Hart Ely, *Democracy and Distrust: A Theory of Judicial Review* (Cambridge, Mass.: Harvard University Press, 1980); and Robert A. Dahl, *Democracy and Its Critics* (New Haven: Yale University Press, 1989). Amy Gutmann identifies two principles that democracies are prevented from violating on

tionalism. True, as a practical matter we turn to majorities to ratify constitutions establishing basic liberties, but the moral authority of such constitutions flows from the fact that they are more or less just, that they more or less enumerate the right rights, and not the other way around. The moral authority of at least some political principles does not depend on their being recognized by majority rule. Liberals and democrats disagree about whether questions of liberal, or substantive, justice (such as freedom of religion, or the provision of basic medical care) also trump, or take priority over, the wishes of the majority.[32] So an evaluation of Califano, Goldman, and North may turn on whether their actions on behalf of innocent fetuses and indigent mothers, disenfranchised migrants and legal representation, freedom fighters and presidential privilege, are in the service of democratic justice, liberal justice, or are not matters of justice at all.

Legitimate Jurisdiction and Legitimate Reasons

How, or by whom, are these trumps to be played? Some indeed are matters of what might be called jurisdiction. Some actors—typically, legislators—are morally precluded from taking certain positions on some *issues*, such as a law that institutes slavery, or that establishes a state religion.[33] A fuller account of democratic legitimacy would specify as well, or instead, the *reasons* upon which majorities may legitimately decide. On some questions of liberal and democratic justice, the trump attaches to the sorts of arguments that may legitimately support decisions, rather than to the sorts of issues that may legitimately be on the legislative agenda. So, for example, if there is anything like a moral right to minimal health care, the legal enactment and specification of this moral right may legitimately be in the jurisdiction of legislatures to decide. The majority's reasons for and

---

democratic grounds: nonrepression and nondiscrimination. See "How Liberal Is Democracy?" in *Liberalism Reconsidered*, ed. Douglas MacLean and Claudia Mills (Lanham, Md.: Rowman and Allanheld, 1983), pp. 25–50. But see Frederick Schauer, "Who Decides?" in *Democracy and the Mass Media*, ed. Judith Lichtenberg (Cambridge: Cambridge University Press, 1990), pp. 202–28, for the suggestion that if the principle of free speech is grounded in an argument for democracy, majority rule has a larger role to play in its articulation.

[32] For the liberal view, see Rawls, *A Theory of Justice*, and Ronald Dworkin, *Taking Rights Seriously* (Cambridge, Mass.: Harvard University Press, 1978).

[33] Oddly, in the abortion debate, both supporters of fetal rights and supporters of women's rights agree that abortion ought to be off the democratic table—they disagree about from which side to remove it. Fetal rights activists hold that no majority can legitimately vote to permit the killing of babies; abortion rights activists hold that no majority can legitimately vote to outlaw abortion.

against enactment, and for and against any particular specification, are limited, though, in that the legislators must engage in good faith the claims of liberal or democratic justice, rather than decide on the grounds of what is in the best interests of the majority. The criterion of legitimate reasons requires that questions of justice be decided on *some* conception of justice.[34]

Therefore, a liberal like Ronald Dworkin and a democrat like Michael Walzer may disagree about whether or not majorities have legitimate jurisdiction over some issue of liberal justice, but still agree that the mandate in question is short on legitimacy—Dworkin on the familiar ground of legitimate jurisdiction, Walzer on the ground of legitimate reasons.

Note that legitimacy does not collapse into substantive judgment: deciding on the right sort of reasons may still produce the wrong sort of answer. Some legitimate conceptions of justice are mistaken. A mandate that inflicts an injustice still meets the criterion of legitimate reasons if it was decided through a good-faith effort at seeking justice. So, to pursue the example of medical care, a dissenter may judge a legislative decision refusing to fund organ transplants for poor people to be a liberal injustice. But if the legislature took seriously the question of whether there is some sort of substantive right to health care, and, in a good-faith effort to ask what justice requires, decided that there is no such right, or that any such right does not extend to the funding of transplants, then the dissenter must judge the legislature to have decided upon legitimate reasons. If, instead, the question of what justice requires of a public health policy is decided by appeal to the interests of healthy or wealthy majorities in legislative districts, then the issue will have been decided on illegitimate reasons (though the content of the decision may coincide with what substantive justice requires).

A finding by a dissenter that a political mandate has not been decided in the legitimate jurisdiction or on legitimate reasons is, of course, still a judgment. But it is a judgment about legitimacy, not a judgment about the good or the just.

[34] For an account of democratic legitimacy that excludes fewer issues from the legislative agenda than does standard liberalism, in exchange for more principled restrictions on the way legislatures ought to talk about these issues, see Amy Gutmann and Dennis F. Thompson, "Moral Conflict and Political Consensus," *Ethics* 101 (1990): 64–88, and *Democracy and Disagreement* (Cambridge, Mass.: Harvard University Press, 1996). Gutmann and Thompson emphasize principles of public deliberation—consistency and mutual respect, for example—but substantive principles might govern legislative reasons as well: protect minorities, benefit the least advantaged, strengthen democratic institutions, and so on.

Democracy as a Method and Democracy as a Value

The notion that democracy is a formal decision-making method and the notion that democracy is a value, a practice that has intrinsic worth, stand in uneasy tension.[35] I have suggested throughout that the truth in the mandates-in-action view requires that we pay attention to the values realized in the actual practice of real democracies, rather than merely to the satisfaction of formal procedural requirements. In the construction of the political mandate in question, have citizens in fact participated in self-governance in meaningful and rewarding ways? Have their views been fairly noted? Have legislators and administrators opened their deliberations to public scrutiny and criticism? Are the reasons and motives behind the mandate sufficiently transparent? Are officials accountable for their decisions and actions? On the view presented here, these determinations about the value of the content of democratic practices count in an assessment of the legitimacy of a mandate, and the strength of a dissenter's allegiance to such mandates varies in part with this substantive evaluation. If democratic value, not merely procedure, matters, Oliver North can look to the circumstances that produced Boland. Is the amendment a considered policy judgment of Congress or a petulant flexing of muscle by the intelligence committees? Do legislators support Boland on substantive grounds, or was it ransom for passage of the defense appropriations bill?

Now that we have developed some analytic understanding of judgment and authority, and have taken a brief look at some of the enduring puzzles of constitutional democracy, we can embark on the search for criteria to guide the exercise of official discretion. The strategy: to triangulate between two well-understood topics in political ethics. A double analogy to legislative choice and civil disobedience will teach us about official discretion. First, the analogy to legislators.

LESSONS FROM LEGISLATIVE ETHICS

An account of when a public official may legitimately act on her judgment of good policy in the face of disagreement of superiors has much in common with an account of when legislators can act on their

---

[35] Cf. Joseph A. Schumpeter, *Capitalism, Socialism, and Democracy* (1942; London: Allen and Unwin, 1976); Walzer, "Philosophy and Democracy"; Gutmann, "How Liberal Is Democracy?"

judgments in the face of disagreement with their constituents. Questions of official dissent and the ethics of representation both appeal to a common consideration discussed earlier: if substantive judgments conflict, when to subordinate one's conduct to the authority of others?

The political realist's view helps to point out that the distinction often drawn between elected and unelected officials is overdrawn. Appointed officials and civil servants face many of the same political, policy-making, and quasi-legislative challenges, opportunities, and responsibilities that legislators do. When we look to the actual circumstances of the jobs, and the degree of democratic responsiveness they require, rather than the mere formal criterion of standing for office, we find that important measures of actual democratic accountability are matters of degree. The act of raising one's hand to cast a vote in a legislature, that unique act of "lawmaking," is always a small and often a relatively unimportant part of a legislator's day. The tasks of drafting legislation, building coalitions of support inside and outside of Congress, trading and deal making, and fixing the problems of particular citizens are not reserved, in law or practice, to members of the legislature: those are games anyone with a long enough rolodex or a fat enough wallet can play, inside government or out. And the formal consensual link of elected officials to an electorate does not necessarily translate into the actual consent of the governed. The administrator of the Environmental Protection Agency in practice is more accountable to voters, and has more of an independent political base, than a Senate committee chair from a small one-party state who holds sway over national banking or trade policy by dint of seniority, not popular election.

Why am I pointing this out? Because the ethical responsibilities of elected officials is a topic that has engaged the attention of political philosophers for a very long time. To the extent that the truth in realism permits us to assimilate the problem of official discretion to the problem of representation, we can draw on insights from legislative ethics.

If legal realism is true about anyone, it is true about legislators—the law is what lawmakers collectively say it is. And if political realism is true about anyone, it is true about legislators—legitimate political mandates are simply what politicians collectively say they are. When voting, elected officials are always, in a strictly formal sense, acting with democratic legitimacy. But just as plainly, we want a way to evaluate the democratic performance of legislators. We want to say more than that, by definition, legislators act democratically. We should have independent moral grounds to evaluate the legitimacy of the actions of elected officials.

Surely a legislator must have such independent grounds for evaluating her own action. Imagine a senator opposed to the death penalty, whose constituents are for it, asking herself: what is the right way, all things considered, to vote? Not simply, what is the best policy, but what does democracy demand, given that my constituents do not share my conception or application of justice? The answer cannot be to prophesy her own decision, so that whatever she decides has equal legitimacy. Surely the senator has grounds to judge some decisions more legitimate than others.

This question is as old as democratic representation itself. Should legislators be responsive to the express wishes of the electorate—that is, be delegates of the will of the people?[36] Should legislators act in the interests, though not on the wishes, of the electorate—as trustees of the interests of the people? Or should legislators act independently and impartially, as principals for political-philosophical principles?[37]

Although this question is posed classically as a choice of role, the problem is understood more usefully as a contingent choice for particular issues and situations. In part, the choice should depend on the democratic tensions and conditions discussed earlier. What sort of issue is at stake? Do legislators and constituents disagree about the good, or do they disagree about the just? Are democratic freedoms or liberal freedoms at stake? Is legitimacy itself at issue? Does the legislature have legitimate jurisdiction over the issue, or is this a matter that individuals or the courts should decide? Are citizens and legislators invoking legitimate reasons for their positions? Has the political process been democratically valuable, or merely a formal method for decision?

A legislator faces a stronger second-order reason to defer to the wishes of constituents if citizens have engaged in an informed and valuable process of democratic deliberation over an issue that falls within the legitimate jurisdiction of majoritarian politics. As the quality of actual democratic discussion and participation degrades, legislators have more reason to assert trusteeship over citizens' interests. On questions of justice that fall within the jurisdiction of majoritarian politics, a legislator has more reason to defer to the views of constituents if those views are grounded in legitimate reasons, in some conception of justice. She has more reason to invoke her own principled reasons when the opposing view is not grounded in a principled reason. On questions of

---

[36] If so, which people—residents of their district, the majority of voters, their party, their supporters, all citizens?

[37] For extended treatments of legislative ethics, see Hanna Fenichel Pitkin, *The Concept of Representation* (Berkeley: University of California Press, 1967); and Dennis F. Thompson, "Legislative Ethics," in *Political Ethics and Public Office*, pp. 96–122.

justice that should not to be decided by majority rule, there is no second-order reason of authority to defer to constituents.[38]

In the death penalty example, the senator should examine her reasons for opposing the death penalty. Is execution, in her considered judgment, a grave violation of basic liberties, or merely a bad policy—because it is ugly, or uncharitable, or ineffective as a deterrent? If she believes the death penalty to be an injustice, is it the sort of injustice that no democracy can legitimately inflict and still be a democracy, or is this the sort of injustice that can arise from a legitimate mistake about realizing justice? If the latter, have citizens in fact made such a legitimate mistake, or are their reasons for supporting the death penalty based on economy, brutality, or prejudice, but not on a mistaken or misapplied conception of justice? Note that every step requires a judgment by the senator, and some of these judgments will turn on substantive and contested questions of political philosophy—the deeply democratic Walzer may answer differently than the deeply liberal Dworkin. But the answer does not turn immediately on the rights and wrongs of the death penalty: higher-order reasons have their due.

Lessons from Civil Disobedience

The exercise of official discretion need not, and usually does not, involve lawbreaking, and officials face duties that citizens do not. Still, we usefully can enlist the underlying logic of civil disobedience in our search for criteria of discretion. Ronald Dworkin offers one of the clearest accounts of civil disobedience and its justification, the main lines of which are easily put forward. I will follow the structure, but not always the content, of his argument.

Dworkin makes two important distinctions of interest to us: between justice-based and what I will call common-good-based disobedience; and between persuasive and nonpersuasive strategies.[39] Jus-

---

[38] Although there may be first-order reasons: she may believe that it is for the best that voters learn from their mistakes, or believe that it is for the best to win reelection.

[39] For clarity, I substitute the label "common-good-based" for what Dworkin calls "policy-based." I do not include here what Dworkin calls integrity-based civil disobedience and what Rawls calls conscientious refusal. The liberal demand for public, political principles may prevent a public official—in contrast with a citizen—from disobeying on integrity grounds alone. But note that quiet, nonthreatening, nondisruptive resignation on integrity grounds alone is almost always justified; and that the source of many agent-centered integrity objections is the belief that the government's decision is unjust from a public, political, or impartial point of view as well. A Christian Scientist who finds himself in the Public Health Service surely is justified in resigning out of

tice-based disobedience counters what the actor believes is a violation of the rights of some minority by the majority. Common-good-based disobedience counters what the actor believes is bad for all—a mistake by the majority about what is in the public interest. Persuasive strategies are intended to work by changing the majority's mind about what justice demands or about what is in the common good. Nonpersuasive strategies are intended to work not by provoking any deliberation or reflection but by driving up the cost to the majority—in financial expense, inconvenience, or fear—of continuing the unjust or unwise course.

A justification of justice-based civil disobedience appeals to the notion, explored earlier, that some issues ought to be excluded from the democratic agenda, and not decided by the will of the majority. Justice-based disobedience questions the jurisdiction of democracy over some issues. A justification of persuasive civil disobedience appeals to the notion of perfecting democracy, rather than finding the jurisdictional limits of democratic authority. Persuasive strategies defy formal democratic authority in the service of the ideal of democratic deliberation, in the service of the *value* of democracy. The persuasive disobedient aims to remind the majority that it is not living up to its own sense of the good or the just.

Civil disobedience may be grounded in the common good or in justice or both, and may adopt a persuasive or a nonpersuasive strategy or both. For example, southern blacks who defied Jim Crow by sitting at segregated lunch counters were practicing persuasive, justice-based civil disobedience: persuasive, because their actions were symbolic and expressive in a way that provoked reflection in the majority; justice-based, because they were fighting for civil liberties that no majority may legitimately violate. Dworkin characterizes European protest against the deployment of U.S. cruise missiles as common-good-based and nonpersuasive: common-good-based, because if nuclear deterrence is wrong, it is a wrong the majority inflicts on itself, not on a minority; nonpersuasive, because the protesters intended to drive up the political costs of deployment to European leaders, rather than to change hearts and minds.

Dworkin argues that the type of civil disobedience most difficult to

---

conscience, but probably is not justified in disobeying. A public health physician who defies the prohibition on abortion counseling upheld in *Rust v. Sullivan* because the prohibition violates the professional commitments of doctors, and because those professional commitments are grounded in the justice claims of patients, has both reasons of integrity and reasons of justice to disobey. If instead, the doctor's objections spring from her own private commitments to patients, so that she does not object to other doctors abiding by *Rust*, the grounds for defiance (rather than resignation) are weaker.

justify is nonpersuasive common-good-based disobedience, because, over an issue that ought to be decided democratically, such disobedience both rejects the legitimate authority of democratic rule and does nothing to improve the quality of democratic deliberation.

In this theory of civil disobedience we can find the seeds of a more general account of judgment and authority that guides us in answering our questions about official dissent and discretion in a democracy. Dworkin points us in the right direction in matching the basis of the dissenter's disagreement (common good or justice) to the strategies of influence that such disagreement justifies (persuasive or nonpersuasive). We need not, however, subscribe to Dworkin's strict division of labor between legislatures and courts over matters of justice and the common good. We have already noted that majorities can have jurisdiction over at least some questions of justice if their answers are grounded in legitimate reasons.

To Play or Not to Play? Four Conditions of Democratic Legitimacy

We are now ready to sketch out four conditions that morally matter to a dissenter deciding to exercise discretion in the face of or in the absence of a political mandate.

The Basis of Dissent

The first condition, the basis of dissent, identifies the type of disagreement between the dissenter and the source of the political mandate. Is the disagreement about the good—a common-good-based dissent? Is the disagreement about how to proceed given unresolved disagreements about the good—a justice-based dissent? Or is the disagreement about how to proceed given unresolved disagreements about the just—a legitimacy-based dissent? We have distinguished two sorts of justice-based dissent: the claim that the political mandate involves a liberal, or substantive, injustice (abortion) and the claim that the political mandate involves a democratic, or political, injustice (disenfranchisement of migrant farm workers).

We have seen that, contrary to Dworkin's view, fixing upon the basis of dissent does not determine the question of democratic authority: basis does not settle the question of legitimate jurisdiction, or of legitimate reasons, or of democratic value. Having identified the grounds of one's substantive disagreement with a political mandate, one must still take the measure of the moral authority of the wrong-headed view.

Legitimate Jurisdiction

Does the source of the political mandate have jurisdiction over the issue at hand? Given Pound's truth, the truth in the mandates-in-action view, this is never merely a factual or formal question of procedure, a neat division of labor. Richard Neustadt trenchantly observes that the American constitution dictates no separation of powers, but separated institutions sharing powers.[40] In this way, too, work legitimate jurisdictions, which are fluid, overlapping, and demanding of moral interpretation. Whether the source of a political mandate has legitimate jurisdiction is a kind of higher-order moral question. If the answer is no, the dissenter has more reason to exercise discretion in opposition to the political mandate.

Legitimate Reasons

Has the political mandate been decided on the relevant reasons? Have questions of the good been decided by appeal to conceptions of the good? Have questions of justice (in the face of unreconciled disagreements about the good) been decided by appeal to conceptions of justice? Have questions of legitimacy (in the face of unreconciled disagreements about the just) been decided by appeal to conceptions of legitimacy? Again, if the answer is no, the dissenter has more reason to exercise discretion in opposition to the political mandate.

Democratic Value

Is the politics that created the mandate democratically valuable in the ways we have explored, or is the mandate a product of a politics that is democratic only in a formal sense? In judging the moral authority of mandates, public officials should attend to the actual conditions of the democratic process, and to the democratic values realized by it, not merely to the existence of formal democratic features. The more the values of democracy are realized, the more officials should defer to the authority claims of democracy's mandates; when democracy is merely a formal process, the case for observing merely the formal rules of law and politics is strengthened.

[40] Neustadt, *Presidential Power*, p. 26.

How to Play? The Strategies of Discretion

We saw that justification in the theory of civil disobedience turns in part on the strategies or means used to influence the actions of others. Similarly, a complete account of official discretion will match the strategies of dissent to the conditions of democratic legitimacy. Consider three classes of discretionary strategy that a public official might employ: persuasive strategies, incentive strategies, and deceptive strategies.

Persuasive Strategies: Reasons and Publicity

Persuasive strategies seek to change, in good faith, the beliefs, values, and interests of other political players through deliberation or symbolic action. Persuasive strategies are necessarily public, in the sense that they act openly on the rational faculties of some relevant audience. Secretary of State George Shultz attempted, in a limited way, to offer President Reagan reasons not to seek third-party funding for the Contras. One of David Goldman's intentions in publicizing the plight of the migrant farm workers through lawsuits widely covered in the press was to win the hearts and minds of Californians. But not every public strategy is a persuasive one: a political entrepreneur can publicly seek influence over mandates through honest political bargaining and coalition building.

Incentive Strategies: Offers and Threats

Incentive strategies shift the location of the zone of possible agreement in the political bargain, either by improving one's alternative to agreement or by worsening the alternatives of those with formal mandates, and by making offers, trades or threats to reach a favorable point in the zone.[41] The strategy works by altering the costs and benefits to political authorities of thwarting discretionary action. Had Secretary of State Shultz threatened to resign if the Contra affair proceeded (a threat he employed successfully before to halt the use of polygraph tests on State Department officials) he would have been pursuing an incentive strategy. The success of David Goldman's legal aid campaign in rural California rested in part on an incentive strategy, making opposition to the farm workers' union increasingly more costly to growers. But Califano refused President Carter's instruction

[41] See Raiffa, *Art and Science of Negotiation*, and Lax and Sebenius, *Manager as Negotiator*.

to employ an open, stop-me-if-you-can strategy in writing regulations for funding abortions.

Deceptive Strategies: Lies, Secrets, and Manipulation

Deceptive strategies work by inducing beliefs about facts or values in the sources of political authority that the discretionary agent believes to be false. Lies and secrets are assaults on the autonomy of their intended public, and so are presumptively problematic in democratic politics. Oliver North and company clearly embarked on a deceptive strategy, seeking to hide from Congress the administration's continued military support of the Contras. David Goldman's covert direct aid to Cesar Chavez was also an example of a deceptive strategy of dissent (in contrast with his mandate-defying lawsuits, which were open to public scrutiny).

MATCHING STRATEGIES TO CONDITIONS OF DEMOCRACY

We are now prepared to offer some guidance to the entrepreneurial public official. Let us match, in a rough way, the three strategies of discretionary action to the four conditions of democratic legitimacy outlined earlier, and illustrate by returning to the three examples with which we began. These suggestions have the virtues of specificity and provocativeness, but the vice of probable error. I offer my reasons, but if you find them wanting, you are welcome to propose improvements. Obviously, there can be no knockdown proof for these tests. A sound suggestion will appropriately match discretionary strategies with the conditions the strategies seek to remedy (in the way that, on Dworkin's view of civil disobedience, persuasive strategies perfect democracy when dissent is common-good-based), or exploit the weaknesses in a mandate's legitimacy (in the way that nonpersuasive strategies of civil disobedience are justified when majorities lack jurisdiction), and otherwise be fittingly proportional (so that the slightest defect in democratic legitimacy does not permit the gravest political fraud).

When Should a Dissenter Forsake All Entrepreneurial Action, and Confine Her Dissent to Formal Channels?

If the democratic process has done everything one can expect of it, short of producing a substantive outcome that matches one's view of good policy, to then deny the moral authority of such a mandate is to deny authority simply. Unless the most extreme catch-me-if-you-can political realism is true, there must be some conditions under which the substantive judgment of public officials gives way to authority.

Consider one reasonable set of such conditions: when an official dissents on common-good grounds, not justice grounds, from a mandate decided on legitimate reasons, through a process rich in intrinsic democratic values, by authorities who have jurisdiction over the issue in question.

For example, suppose the residents of a town overwhelmingly dislike a prominently displayed public sculpture purchased with public funds, and the reasons that they articulate appeal legitimately, though perhaps mistakenly, to aesthetics.[42] The issue is widely debated in town meetings and city council hearings, where experts and citizens of all stripes come forward, and a nonbinding referendum is held, in which the art is roundly rejected. But the town's arts director favors the sculpture, arguing that the public has not yet developed an appreciation for postmodern works. If, after carefully considering the views of the public and the opposing view of the town's arts director, the town council instructs the arts director to return the sculpture to its sculptor, on what grounds can the arts director exercise discretion to postpone, obstruct, or reverse the decision? If democratic authority is ever a dispositive second-order reason, it is so here.[43]

In contrast, by Joseph Califano's lights, he may, and perhaps must, exercise *more* entrepreneurial discretion than he does in drafting guidelines for funding abortion. On his view, abortion, even in the case of rape, is a grave liberal injustice to the fetus that the government ought not to permit, let alone fund. The strongest case Califano can make for congressional authority is that Congress has, within its jurisdiction, legitimately but mistakenly interpreted the demands of liberal justice. At the least, Califano can help the democratic majority realize its own political principle of respect for persons by persuasively confronting it with what he believes is the right conception of justice—perhaps through further public hearings, perhaps through public protest, perhaps by noisy resignation.[44]

---

[42] There are many legitimate reasons for making decisions about art, but surely reasons of aesthetics are among them. Note, however, that some reasons for making common-good-based decisions are illegitimate reasons. A city council that rejects a proposal because of ethnic prejudice against the artist, or that directs a commission to a campaign supporter, is deciding for illegitimate reasons.

[43] This account is loosely based on events in Tacoma, Washington. Cf. "Tacoma Neon Wars," Kennedy School of Government Case C15–87–764, -765, -766.

[44] And Califano need not be so charitable about congressional authority. True, the Supreme Court, which shares jurisdiction over the question of legitimacy, ruled, for legitimate reasons, that Congress has substantive jurisdiction over funding questions. But Califano believes that such reasoning by the Court is mistaken: permitting and

Which Conditions of Democratic Legitimacy Call for a Persuasive Strategy?

Entrepreneurship that influences political mandates through deliberation and openness, that appeals to public reason, is always less problematic than nonpersuasive, coercive, secretive, or deceptive strategies. Honest persuasion seems particularly fitting in opposing mandates that rest on legitimate but mistaken reasons. Honest persuasion appears to be the only justifiable strategy for a common-good-based dissenter when there are only minor defects in the conditions of legitimacy. Such justification appeals to the notion that public and persuasive entrepreneurship challenges democratic authority on behalf of democracy itself, to perfect democracy by improving the quality of deliberation and realizing democratic values.

On this logic of perfecting democracy, an official entrepreneur may exercise public, persuasive discretion even when matters of justice are not at stake. The legislator may vote her best judgment on trade bills and highway bills, as well as on the death penalty, so long as her dissenting performance is public and accountable in a way that contributes to the deliberation and political education of her constituents.

More controversial: on this view, even if justice is not implicated, the secretary of state may continue to protest a foreign-policy initiative after a presidential decision has been reached, and may do so publicly, so long as the path of influence is largely persuasive, rather than coercive or threatening.

More controversial still: on this view Reagan and his national security apparatus may take public, persuasive dissenting action to convince the congressional majority that it erred in Boland, even if such action strains a good-faith interpretation of the amendment. For example, if the Contras required funds to document Sandinista support for other Latin American insurgencies, or some other evidence that might reasonably be expected to change congressional views, then the White House would be justified in engaging in an open, third-party fund raiser to finance such documentation.

When Is Political Bargaining a Justified Strategy for a Dissenter?

The case for a nonpersuasive (but still nondeceptive) strategy of discretion, with its offers and threats, its coalitions and exchanges, is

funding abortion ought not to be within the jurisdiction of the legislature. Turning Raz around, in Califano's judgment, Congress has been granted legitimate jurisdiction, though it does not have the right to such jurisdiction.

strongest when the source of the political mandate lacks legitimate jurisdiction, or when the mandate has been decided for illegitimate reasons, or when the democratic value of the mandating process is low. Each of these conditions signals some serious weakness in the democratic legitimacy of the political mandate. The less legitimacy and value one finds in a particular episode of policy making, the more one is justified in acting like a political realist. Here, proportionality is called for: the slightest defect in participation does not justify the most heavy-handed coercive threat, but one can treat such mandates as in play.

Now we can see why David Goldman's political entrepreneurship (although not necessarily his deception) is justified. The issue in question is one of democratic, political justice—the most egregious violations of which even deep democrats acknowledge no majority may legitimately inflict. Goldman need not go so far as to claim that legal aid for migrant farm workers is such a precondition of democracy, whose denial falls outside the jurisdiction of majorities. Though that is doubtful, the restricted political mandate of California legal aid was brokered for illegitimate reasons, which do not appeal to some conception, right or wrong, of democratic justice. And clearly, the political process that produced Goldman's mandate scores low in the democratic values of deliberation and participation. Valuable, and not merely formal, democracy is particularly important to establish the legitimate authority of mandates about justice that fall within the jurisdiction of majority rule, because minorities and individuals must rely solely on their own political voices, not on the institutional protection of the courts. So, a valuable democracy both directly strengthens the authority of political mandates and improves the chances that majorities will decide on legitimate reasons.

In the face of a mandate democratic only in a formal sense, about an issue of democratic justice, decided on illegitimate reasons, Goldman justifiably took the role of a principal player, not a fiduciary agent, in the pull and tug of politics, and showed merely formal deference to a merely formal authority. If he used his entrepreneurial skills to raise the political costs of stopping him, he did not offend against any second-order reason of authority that comes from pluralist, interest group politics. Here, another truth in realism: realist politics in fact cannot generate mandates that have more legitimate authority than conceded by the ethic of political realism.

This should not be interpreted either as a tit-for-tat reciprocity argument (do unto others as others do unto you) or as a contingent obligation (do only if others do). Rather, the justification for a nonpersuasive strategy of discretion appeals to the nature of the political mandate's legitimate authority: if such a mandate has moral authority, it has it only by virtue of the satisfaction of some formal procedure, not because it is a substantive expression of reasoned principle or of some "general will," however that is understood. Therefore, second-order reasons of authority that arise out of some modus vivendi bargain are different reasons, with different force, than are second-order reasons of authority that arise out of a valuable, deliberative democratic process.

When Are Manipulative or Deceptive Strategies Justified?

Since manipulation, lies, and many sorts of secrets corrode the principle of publicity on which deliberative democracy depends, these strategies can be justified only when there is precious little, democratically speaking, to lose (when formal political mandates lack legitimate jurisdiction and legitimate reasoning and democratic value) or, perhaps, when there is much democratically to gain (when very important matters of democratic justice hang in the balance).

The most charitable tale we can tell about the deceptive discretion practiced by Oliver North in the Contra affair is that, far more than a common-good-based dispute over the wisdom of military involvement in Latin America, it was a legitimacy-based dispute, a struggle between branches of government for moral authority over the making of foreign policy. On this view, the Reagan White House had made a judgment of legitimate jurisdiction and found Congress wanting. On the scheme developed so far, such a judgment (if made in good faith) would justify a public but nonpersuasive incentive strategy. One scenario: flout Boland's meaning through public appeals to foreign allies and domestic supporters to arm the Contras.

Under this charitable interpretation, can the case also be made for a secret and deceptive strategy? I think not. There was much, democratically, to lose. Congress, even if mistaken about its assertion of jurisdiction, was making a claim based on legitimate reasons, and the process of congressional decision making—both about the substance of the Nicaraguan issue and, more generally, about authority over war powers—was moderately rich in the democratic values. And nothing, democratically, would be gained by the covert defiance of congressional authority, in contrast with public defiance. In any case, this charity is undeserved: the Contra affair, at bottom, was not a sincere claim of legitimate authority by the president, but a slinky evasion of the legitimate authority of Congress.

OBJECTIONS AND REFINEMENTS

In conclusion, consider three sorts of objection to this account of official discretion and democratic legitimacy. The answers to these objections will help to place and clarify the view put forth here, and point to further work.

Gresham's Law and the Externality Condition

The conditions of ideal democracy almost never hold in practice. The criteria for justified discretion would allow persuasive dissent in virtually all circumstances, and would allow nonpersuasive, open dissent in the normal circumstance of actual democratic decision making, where presidents, cabinet secretaries, and legislators act on a mix of reasons, some legitimate and some not, in response to a mix of influences, some principled, some not, sometimes deliberating, sometimes trading and maneuvering, sometimes under public scrutiny, sometimes not. Political mandates will almost always suffer from some defect in democratic legitimacy or value, so the moral authority of those mandates will almost always be attenuated, commanding only a formal deference, thereby approving official entrepreneurship within merely formal constraints. The criteria of official discretion allow too much.

Furthermore, this permissiveness sets in motion a spiral of democratic degradation. The more that some dissenters exercise nonpersuasive discretion, the more other actors will respond in kind: sources of the dissenters' mandates, to control discretion; subordinates of dissenters, because the legitimacy of *their* received mandates is devalued by their superiors' nonpersuasive strategies. Like Gresham's Law of bad money driving out good, nonpersuasive political practices drive out persuasive political practices, and, in equilibrium, all political mandates result from hard bargaining over interests, not democratic deliberation about public principles.[45]

Here we return to theories of *civil* disobedience for instruction, this time from Rawls.[46] Rawls is concerned that excessive civil disobedience might undermine respect for the rule of law and a just constitution, so he adds to his account what amounts to an externality condition: those who would be civilly disobedient ought to consider whether their actions, justified on all other grounds, will damage the

---

[45] Cf. Bernard Williams, *Morality: An Introduction to Ethics* (1972; Cambridge: Cambridge University Press, 1993), p. 96, on a Gresham's Law in utilitarianism.

[46] Rawls, *A Theory of Justice*, pp. 373–75.

future capacity of democratic institutions to seek justice. Surprisingly, Rawls does not mean this to be a Kantian generalization of the form, "Disobey only if you will that others in similar circumstances disobey," but rather a hard-nosed, pragmatic judgment about the actual consequences of one's actions in a particular case.

In this form, the externality condition can be readily endorsed as a criterion for official discretion as well: if the democratic consequences of your entrepreneurship are sufficiently bad, refrain. Whether the competitive dynamics of the collective action problem are such that no nonpersuasive discretion is ever justified requires further investigation. But note that the externality condition, for Rawls and for us, asks for a first-order, substantive judgment about consequences, and not deference to a second-order reason of legitimate authority.

"Who Is to Say?" and the Humility Condition

This account asks public officials to make judgments at every turn: judgments about the good, the just, and the legitimate; judgments about liberal justice and democratic justice; judgments about the legitimacy of jurisdiction and the legitimacy of reasons; judgments about the intrinsic value of a democratic process and, now, about future consequences for democratic processes. But reasonable people will disagree at each step about these judgments. Who is to say whose judgments are authoritative?

The answer given earlier still holds: if guidance is to be given to a political actor questioning the legitimate authority of her mandate, then there is nowhere else for her to stand but in her own shoes. She cannot, without judgment, defer to the very authority whose legitimacy she questions. We have tried to develop a sufficiently rich set of conditions sufficiently distant from the original substantive conflict, so that the would-be entrepreneur must look beyond the initial disagreement for justification. But there can be no justification of authority without judgment about authoritative claims.

Note well that nothing in this account challenges deference to the division of *expert* labor: others, because of their positions, or knowledge, or wisdom, may be much better judges of all the conditions of legitimacy discussed so far; and, by serendipity or wise institutional design, those who are legitimate authorities by virtue of a division of moral labor may as well be such expert judges—but expertise, by itself, conveys no moral authority.

A would-be dissenter would be foolish and morally irresponsible not to seek out the best available help in making judgments about substance and legitimacy, and may judge that deferring to the judgment of an expert is more accurate than making all judgments herself. But this sort of deference is to expert, not to moral, authority. The moral irresponsibility of one who neglects expert opinion is a failure to judge, not a failure to obey.

One of the more ugly attributes of political entrepreneurs like Oliver North is a confidence, an arrogance, a militant righteousness about their cause. Humility, a recognition of the fallibility of one's judgment, is a rare and noble virtue in public life. Democratic dissenters, because they act against the judgments of the many, must practice a special sort of humility, seek whatever wisdom is available, and safeguard against overconfidence or special pleading in their own judgments by taking cooler counsel.

Is This a Partisan View of Democracy?

No political theory can be neutral with respect to everything and still say something. But is this account of official discretion committed to a particularly narrow interpretation of democratic principle? What must one accept about democracy for one to accept the criteria of discretion presented here?

The scheme depends on commitment to a democracy that is both deliberative and liberal: deliberative, in that, to at least some degree, under some circumstances, the preferences and political views of citizens can and ought to change through reasonable discourse; liberal, in that the liberties of individuals are valuable, and that at least part of the value of individual liberties does not depend on valuation by others—and in particular, does not depend on valuation by a majority of citizens. Because this version of democracy is liberal, the demands of justice and the will of democracy can conflict; because it is deliberative, under some conditions (perhaps difficult to specify and difficult to attain) the outcomes of democratic deliberation and the demands of justice could converge. This conception of democracy is broadly consistent with the views of writers as diverse as Mill, Rawls, and Habermas.

Much is made here of the contrast between legitimate political mandates and merely formal political mandates. For this distinction to do work, it requires an account of meaning and interpretation, which I have not begun to provide. But I do not believe it requires any particular account of meaning and interpretation. It certainly does not require anything like the doctrine of original intent, with which I have little sympathy. As with the difference between the more liberal Dworkin and the more democratic Walzer about jurisdiction over liberal justice, one's view about meaning and interpretation could lead to different substantive results. So be it.

Taylor Branch wondered whether we have to take our Otepkas with our Ellsbergs; we wondered about having to take our marine colonels with our poverty lawyers. The answer is no: we can find principled grounds to distinguish one act of official discretion from another, principled grounds that have gained some distance from our perhaps partial judgments about the rights and wrongs in the underlying political conflict. But we and dissenters may disagree in our judgments about legitimate authority as well, perhaps for the same political-philosophical reasons that give rise to the substantive dispute in the first instance. When it comes to legitimacy, it's judgment all the way down.

Chapter Ten

MONTAIGNE'S MISTAKE

My fellow Americans:

I have an announcement to make to you tonight of the greatest national importance. As you know, the Senate has voted this afternoon to remove me from the Office of the Presidency. That, of course, is their right under the Constitution of the United States of America. . . . They have the right to express their opinion, as does any American, without Presidential interference or pressure of any kind from the Executive branch. That is what is known as the separation of powers. . . .

However, according to the doctrine of the separation of powers, the Executive branch has an equal voice in the management of government, along with the Legislative and Judicial branches. That, after all, is only fair. . . . Moreover, the President, which I am, has the sole responsibility for safeguarding the security of the nation. That responsibility is spelled out in the oath of office. . . . President Washington, whose picture you see here, took that oath. So did President Lincoln, pictured here. And so did our great President Dwight David Eisenhower, whose grandson has just completed serving his country in the United States Navy and is married to my daughter Julie, whom you see pictured here. My other daughter, Tricia, is pictured here, in her wedding dress. . . .

And that is why I have decided tonight to remain in this Office. My fellow Americans, though I respect the sincerity and integrity of those Senators who voted earlier in the day for my removal, I find, after careful study and grave reflection, that to accept their decision would be to betray the trust placed in me by the American people, and to endanger the security and the well-being of this nation. . . .

. . . My fellow Americans, I understand that there are going to be those in Congress who will not respect the decision I have announced here tonight, as I respected theirs, arrived at earlier in the day. . . . There are even going to be some who will use my words to attempt to create a national crisis in order to reap political gain for themselves or their party. And, most dangerous of all, there are some elements in this country, given to violence and lawlessness as a way of life, who may attempt to use force to remove me from Office. . . .

In order to discourage those who would resort to violence of any kind, in order to maintain law and order in the nation and to safeguard the welfare and well-being of law-abiding American citizens, I have tonight, in my constitutional role as Commander-in-Chief, ordered the Joint Chiefs of Staff to place the Armed Forces on stand-by alert around the nation. The Department of Justice and the Federal Bureau of Investigation have also been advised to take all necessary steps to ensure domestic tranquility. The National Guard has already been notified and throughout the fifty states . . .

Philip Roth, "The President Addresses the Nation"

THE EXPLORATION of ethics for adversaries playing divided roles has so far been divided into several connected but distinct arguments. In this concluding chapter I hope to show through an extended illustration how the parts fit.

MARBURY V. NIXON

Consider the celebrated episode in contemporary American political history that has become known as the Saturday Night Massacre.[1] In the fall of 1973, Richard Nixon was a president under an ever tightening siege, facing criminal investigation for his part in the break-in of the Democratic National Committee headquarters in the Watergate office complex, and for the administration's subsequent cover-up of that affair. Former presidential counsel John Dean had already testified before the Senate about widespread abuses of power and "dirty tricks" in the Nixon White House; Chief of Staff H. R. Haldeman and Domestic Policy Advisor John Ehrlichman had already resigned in disgrace.

The Saturday Night Massacre drama circles around the public officials appointed after the deeds in question, who struggled against one another to scrutinize or deflect scrutiny from the misadventures of the Nixon White House. Alexander Haig, an Army general and a top aide to Henry Kissinger, was chosen by Nixon to be White House chief of staff. Nixon, pressured to restore trust in a Justice Department compromised by its desultory probe into Watergate thus far, nominated to the post of attorney general the widely respected secretary of defense, Elliot Richardson, calling him a man of "unimpeachable integrity." In his confirmation hearings before the Senate Judiciary Committee, Richardson proposed to appoint a Watergate special prosecutor, prom-

[1] The factual account is drawn from "The Saturday Night Massacre" (A-D), Kennedy School of Government Case C14-77-150, -542, -543, -544.

ised not to dismiss the prosecutor without "overwhelming evidence" of serious misconduct, and promised to resign rather than comply with a presidential order to dismiss in the absence of such evidence. Richardson named Archibald Cox, a Harvard law professor who once taught Richardson, to head the inquiry. Cox and Richardson agreed upon a charter granting the prosecutor the power to subpoena evidence and to contest assertions of executive privilege, guaranteeing "the greatest degree of independence that is consistent with the Attorney General's statutory accountability," and assuring that the prosecutor would not be removed from office except for "extraordinary improprieties." Only then did the demanding Senate committee confirm Richardson.

Cox and Nixon came to an impasse over tape recordings of Oval Office conversations. The prosecutor subpoenaed a number of the tapes. Asserting executive privilege, a constitutional protection of the confidentiality of presidential communication with advisors, the president refused to comply, despite both district and appellate court decisions requiring him to do so.[2]

The prospect of Nixon's continued refusal, even in the face of a Supreme Court ruling, portended a crisis in constitutional legitimacy. If Nixon were to insist that presidents, not courts, have the last word on what is protected by executive privilege, then for the first time since 1803 the authority of judicial review itself would be put into play. A power claimed for the courts in *Marbury v. Madison*,[3] Chief Justice John Marshall's ingenious pronouncement about the proper division of *constitutional* labor, judicial review survives through the continued acquiescence of the executive and legislative branches. To save the Nixon presidency, partisans would be tempted to support

---

[2] *Nixon v. Sirica*, 487 F.2d 700 (D.C. Cir. 1973).

[3] "It is emphatically the province and duty of the judicial department to say what the law is." 5 U.S. 137, 177 (1803). *Marbury* also contains the first recognition of some sort of executive privilege: "It is not wonderful that in a case such as this, the assertion, by an individual, of his legal claims in a court of justice . . . should at first be considered by some, as an attempt to intrude into the cabinet, and to intermeddle with the prerogatives of the executive. It is scarcely necessary for the court to disclaim all pretentions to such a jurisdiction. An extravagance, so absurd and excessive, could not have been entertained for a moment." 5 U.S. 169. But when Thomas Jefferson asserts presidential privilege to withhold letters in the trials of Aaron Burr, Marshall, sitting on circuit, issues subpoenas, showing that in his view the judiciary has the power to rule on the limits of the privilege. See *United States v. Burr*, 25 F. Cas. 30 and 187 (CC Va. 1807). For a constitutional history of executive privilege, see Paul A. Freund, "The Supreme Court, 1973 Term—Foreword: On Presidential Privilege," *Harvard Law Review* 88 (1974): 13. For recent developments, see the Mike Espy case, *In re: Sealed Case*, 326 U.S. App. D.C. 276 (1997).

Nixon's claims to interpretive authority over questions of executive privilege, and so undermine the effective authority of judicial review. Nixon was threatening to upset an eight-score-and-ten-year-old tacit agreement, with no established avenue of appeal, short of the upheaval of impeachment. And even if Congress were to find the president's refusal to comply with a Supreme Court order a high crime or misdemeanor, what would stop the president from challenging Congress's legitimate jurisdiction over such a finding on the same grounds on which the Supreme Court's jurisdiction was challenged? How many infantry divisions has the Senate's sergeant at arms?

To avoid such a constitutional confrontation, Richardson sought to broker a compromise between president and prosecutor. Nixon, however, resolved to rid himself of the persistent Cox. Acting on behalf of the president, Haig tried to maneuver Richardson into firing the special prosecutor. After a tense week of brinkmanship, Richardson was ordered to direct Cox to accept verified transcripts in lieu of the tapes presently in dispute and to forbid Cox from subpoenaing any further tapes. Haig expected Richardson to carry out the order, Cox to reject the imposed terms, and Richardson to dismiss Cox.

But Haig miscalculated. On Saturday, October 20, Richardson resigned, rather than carry out Nixon's order. When Haig ordered Deputy Attorney General William Ruckleshaus to fire Cox, Ruckleshaus, who had also made promises to the Senate committee, refused and resigned as well. Solicitor General Robert Bork, next in command, finally complied, and signed Cox's dismissal papers.

The ensuing public uproar over the president's interference with the Watergate prosecution—the White House logged nearly a half million calls and telegrams of protest—hastened Nixon's downfall. Although Nixon succeeded in ridding himself of Cox, the ferocious public reaction forced the president into obeying the appeals court order anyway (thereby backing off from the constitutional showdown). Three days after the Justice Department departures, Nixon's lawyer declared in open court, "This president does not defy the law."[4] The actions of Cox and Richardson made them overnight

---

[4] The lawyer was Charles Wright. See "The Saturday Night Massacre" (D), p. 17. When further subpoenas by Cox's successor, Leon Jaworski, were contested, the Supreme Court definitively upheld the application of *Marbury*. "In the performance of assigned constitutional duties each branch of the Government must initially interpret the Constitution, and the interpretation of its powers by any branch is due great respect from the others. . . . Notwithstanding the deference each branch must accord the others, the 'judicial Power of the United States' vested in the federal courts by Art. III, § 1, of the Constitution can no more be shared with the Executive Branch than the Chief Executive, for example, can share with the Judiciary the veto power, or the Con-

heroes. The actions of Haig and Bork remain controversial, but have, as we will see, eloquent and unexpected defenders.

Many pages have been written reconstructing the events, dissecting the protagonists' intentions, and interpreting the constitutional import of this affair. I will not attempt to reproduce those efforts. Here, the story is pressed into service to illustrate and test arguments offered by adversaries in support of a division of moral labor. Alexander Haig lent all of his strategic and moral energies to do the bidding of Richard Nixon. Elliot Richardson tried to protect Cox and, in the end, resigned rather than comply with a presidential order. Robert Bork, upon assuming the duties and authority of Richardson's office, immediately obeyed the president. Can Haig and Richardson, who worked at cross-purposes pursuing conflicting moral ends, both be justified in their actions? Can Richardson and Bork, one who resisted the will of the president, the other who complied, both be justified in their actions? Must we take our Haigs and Borks with our Richardsons?

For these to be hard questions, we need to suppose some facts about the law in force at the time: that the president has the formal legal authority to direct the attorney general to dismiss the special prosecutor;[5] that directing the dismissal of a prosecutor while under investigation by that prosecutor is not on its face an illegal obstruction of justice; and that Haig and Bork, whatever their suspicions, had

---

gress share with the Judiciary the power to override a Presidential veto. . . . We therefore affirm that it is the province and duty of this Court 'to say what the law is' with respect to the claim of privilege presented in this case." *United States v. Nixon*, 418 U.S. 683, 704–5 (1974).

[5] The protagonists, including Cox, appeared to hold this view at the time. He prophetically told the press Saturday morning, "I'm not saying that no one can fire me. Of course, eventually there are ways of firing me. I don't know what the Attorney General will do. Now, eventually, a President can always work his will. You remember when Andrew Jackson wanted to take the deposits from the Bank of the United States and his Secretary of the Treasury wouldn't do it; he fired him, and then he appointed a new Secretary of the Treasury, and he wouldn't do it, and he fired him. And finally he got a third who would. That's one way of proceeding." See "The Saturday Night Massacre" (D), p. 6. The influential Yale constitutional scholar Alexander Bickel had argued that since the prosecutor was the creature of the attorney general who was the creature of the president, Nixon could even replace Cox with the president's own lawyer if he wanted to. See *The New Republic*, September 29, 1973, pp. 13–14. But a district judge later issued a declaratory judgment that Bork had violated the regulations of the Justice Department in dismissing Cox while the special prosecutor's charter was in effect, and that the charter could not be abolished by Bork without the special prosecutor's consent. See *Nader v. Bork*, 366 F. Supp. 104 (D.D.C. 1973). The ruling was vacated on appeal because of mootness—the special prosecutor's office had already been reestablished under Leon Jaworski and Cox was not seeking reinstatement—so the argument for this sweeping limitation on an agency's power to change its own regulations was not tested in higher courts.

no direct evidence about Nixon's prior wrongdoing or present intentions that would render their participation in this dismissal an illegal obstruction of justice.

HAIG V. RICHARDSON

First, consider Haig and Richardson. The simplest answer, requiring no appeal to the morality of roles under a division of moral labor, is that, indeed, both *cannot* be justified: one of the two is simply mistaken about the moral consequences of his actions, about the prerogatives of a president under a constitutional separation of powers, or about the facts and application of constitutional principle in this case. On this interpretation, Haig believes, rightly or wrongly, that the president must appear strong and decisive, in part because of the military crisis in the Middle East (Egypt launched the Yom Kippur War days earlier, and Israel had just gained the upper hand); and Haig does not recognize any overwhelming importance in prosecutorial independence. Richardson, wrong or right, does not agree with Haig about the international urgency, or he does not see why Nixon must press the Cox issue in the midst of an international crisis; and he does see supreme importance in the prosecutor's independence. On this account, the reasons of the two do not flow from their different roles, but from their different assessment and valuation of consequences. So, although it may be a psychological or sociological fact that Haig's or Richardson's role in their organizations *cause* one or the other to hold actual beliefs and valuations, occupying a role here does not give one or the other a *reason* for action.[6] The prediction that actors situated in different roles will be caused to hold different beliefs and values might give designers reasons to set up divided institutions, but that is a different matter.

Consider, however, a plausible adversary argument: the different positions they find themselves in *do* give them different moral reasons for action—role-relative reasons—so that each ought to have done as he did. Though the republic be led by a liar and crook, the president requires a loyal chief of staff, and Haig is that chief. Though the president requires a faithful staff, the attorney general is charged with duties to uphold the rule of law, and Richardson is that attorney general.

---

[6] For the difference between causes and reasons for belief, see Jon Elster, *Ulysses and the Sirens* (Cambridge: Cambridge University Press, 1979), p. 130. See also Gerald A. Cohen, "Beliefs and Roles," *Proceedings of the Aristotelian Society* 41 (1966–67): 17–34, reprinted in *The Philosophy of Mind*, ed. J. Glover (Oxford: Oxford University Press, 1976), pp. 53–66.

These role-relative prescriptions are justified by appealing to the over-all good, in equilibrium, of the institution in which chiefs of staff push one way, and attorneys general, the other.

To put a sharper edge on the argument: suppose we hold a scheme of separated powers (or, as Richard Neustadt pithily puts it, separated institutions sharing powers)[7] to be the best check against the tyrannies of majorities or minorities about which James Madison warned. Then, if a president is to hold his own against competing, possibly tyrannical institutions of government, he must have some capacity to work his will—*even if that will be tyrannical*. Justified by a system whose end is to prevent abuses of power, Haig must attempt to carry out even the abusive purposes of his president, so long as, in general, the institution of separated institutions properly anticipates and counters such abuse.

Henry Kissinger offers some such justification of Haig's actions, in this (perhaps artful) account:

> Only those who lived through the fervid atmosphere of those months can fully appreciate the debt the nation owes Al Haig. By sheer willpower, dedication, and self-discipline, he held the government together. He more than anyone succeeded in conveying the impression of a functioning White House. . . .
>
> To be sure, only a man of colossal self-confidence could have sustained such a role. His methods were sometimes rough; his insistence on formal status could be grating. But the role assigned to Haig was not one that could be filled by choirboys. He had to preserve the sinew of America for its indispensable mission of being the last resort for the free, the hope of the oppressed, and the one country that with all of its turbulent vitality could be relied upon to walk the path of mercy.

Then, from under this heap of aspartame, Kissinger draws an incisive argument from a division of moral labor: *"It is not necessary that in an hour of crisis America's representatives embody all of these qualities as long as they enable our country to do so."*[8] It is not necessary, claims Kissinger, for Haig *himself* to act in the service of freedom, nonoppression, or mercy. Haig does not have to deliberate upon a wide range of moral reasons for action, including the reason of preserving the institutions of democracy and the rule of law, protecting them from presi-

<hr>

[7] Richard E. Neustadt, *Presidential Power and the Modern Presidents* (1960; New York: Free Press, 1990), p. 26.

[8] Henry Kissinger, *Years of Upheaval* (Boston: Little Brown, 1982), p. 1197 (emphasis added). Compare Georges Danton, arguing for the establishment of the Revolutionary Tribunal: "Let us be terrible, so that the people will not have to be." Simon Schama, *Citizens: A Chronicle of the French Revolution* (New York: Random House, 1989), p. 707.

dential tyranny. *Those* concerns fall to Richardson, to Cox, or—so long as the consequences of the actions of government players generally favor those ends—to no one in particular. So long as, in equilibrium, such democratic institutions would be preserved, and such tyranny averted, Haig may—indeed must—be the president's partisan, concerned only with advancing the political power of the president. Or so Kissinger appears to argue.

By now, however, we have discovered that claims for role-relative adversary permissions under a division of moral labor are difficult to justify. Consider, one by one, some of the arguments that have been employed so far.

Act Redescription

Giffard claims to carry out a prosecution, not to compass the death of a man; Sanson claims to perform executions, not serial killings; lawyers claim to represent their clients, not lie. Haig could claim that he practices public service: he carries out the presumptively lawful instructions of the democratically elected leader of a legitimate government. Now, there is no need to dispute this description of Haig's actions. We need only hold that this description does not eat up prepractice act descriptions, and so short-circuit the need for moral evaluation. Political hardball is not acidball.

Which prepractice descriptions of Haig's actions call out for moral evaluation? One might think that, since the presidency, the constitution, and the special prosecutor's office are themselves conventional institutions, Haig's actions with respect to those institutions have no meaning outside of the practice of his public service role. But this is not so. We have seen that practices can be nested—a contract can also be a promise. Though there is no apt natural description of Haig's efforts—"keep a quantity of magnetized ribbon away from the tall fellow in a bow tie called Cox" clearly is inadequate—there are apt conventional descriptions that make no essential reference to the constitutive rules of Haig's official role. Haig helps a president whom he must at least suspect is guilty of misconduct avoid being called to account. He does so by interfering with a properly conducted criminal investigation and by bullying the attorney general into dismissing a prosecutor without cause. He risks destabilizing legitimate and just legal institutions by plotting with Nixon to threaten defiance of judicial review. These are all apt descriptions of what Haig does.

Haig might concede that descriptions persist, but claim that "performing his official duties" is among the apt descriptions. The role he occupies contains the requirement to carry out the lawful commands of the president; the role is indirectly moralized in that he has acquired a moral commitment to perform the role, and the role is not in itself immoral. So, though there are multiple apt descriptions of what he does, the normatively controlling description is that he is performing the requirements of a role that he is morally obligated to practice.

Role requirements can overwrite moral permissions, and become moral requirements. But role requirements cannot overwrite moral prohibitions and mint moral permissions. Haig's appeal to the requirements of his role will work only if the actions he performs are not morally prohibited under some other apt description. So, if his efforts on behalf of Nixon amount to person violation, and if the person violation cannot be justified by appeal to a valid defense, then invoking role requirements is to no avail. A role that requires morally unjustified person violation is not a morally justified role, and one cannot acquire a moral obligation to practice it.

Actor Redescription

Can Haig successfully argue that only Nixon is the author of the act, not Haig, and that the artificial person "White House Chief of Staff," not the natural person "Alexander Haig," personates the president? No. Both the artificial person Executioner of Criminal Judgments of Paris and the natural person Charles-Henri Sanson kill on the scaffold. That the members of the Revolutionary Tribunal are the authors of the Terror does not diminish Sanson's authorship. There is no law of conservation of moral agency, such that if an act is attributable to you, it cannot be attributable to me as well. If Nixon is aptly described as threatening the stability of just and legitimate institutions, and if Haig believes or reasonably should believe that this is what Nixon is doing, then Haig does not merely perform his role: he too threatens the stability of just and legitimate institutions. The institutions of American government constitute the office of White House chief of staff, and that office, understood as an artificial person, acts in carrying out at least the lawful directives of the president. But any act performed in role is attributable to the natural person occupying it as well. The reverse is not always so: not every act performed by a natural person also counts as an act of the role that person occupies. Under practice positivism, it is up to the conventional rules of the practice to define which natural acts count also as official acts. Not all of the president's meals are state dinners, and not every offense committed by an occupant of an office is an act of the office (though there are good pragmatic reasons for holding governments strictly liable for such offenses). But the main point stands: like act descriptions, actor descriptions persist.

If Haig's efforts on Nixon's behalf do not violate persons, then we need ask only if Haig's role serves good, or good enough, ends. Does the adversary institution of separated powers, within which presidents expect a loyal and partisan White House staff, do a decent job, overall, in governing well and protecting against tyranny? The test is not the most stringent one of whether Haig's role is the very best way. Unless act consequentialism is the correct moral theory, one is not morally required to maximize the good, and one is permitted to undertake projects and commitments that do not aim to maximize the good. But the tests for justified person violation *are* stringent.

Fair Play

Much turns, then, on whether Haig violates persons. Does he? Whom? The treatment of the natural persons of Richardson and Cox are a minor part of any account of the rights and wrongs of the Saturday Night Massacre, but, even so, neither man appears to have a serious *personal* complaint. Both arguably were deceived and threatened. Richardson reported being manipulated and treated shabbily. But even if they are violated by adversary tactics, the violation appears to meet the criteria of the fair-play principle. Richardson and Cox are voluntary and informed players in the game of adversary politics whose rules permit sharp tactics within the bounds of the law. They need not have been motivated by the honor and glory that rewards occupants of high office to have freely and knowingly accepted such benefits. At least some sharp tactics are necessary for the success of the profession of politician in a democracy. If political leaders are to be effective at gaining and maintaining power and in pushing through programs in the face of opposition, they need ways to induce compliance in dissenting and fractious subordinates. Among such ways are pander, trickery, and threat within the bounds of the law. One asymmetry about adversary institutions noted earlier is that the permissibility of dissent does not entail the impermissibility of its control and punishment. If some version of political realism is correct, then Haig, Richardson, and Cox may try to outfox each other without wronging each other. Though there of course will be winners and losers in such a game—Richardson's courage ended his promising political career, while Haig's loyalty led in time to the post of secretary of state—the ex ante expected distribution of personal burdens and benefits to players of rough politics is not obviously unjust in any systematic way to the players. As Richardson mused to Cox in the final days, "it is better to lose your job than to have your head cut off."[9] If we are to find serious unjustified person violation, we will need to look beyond the personal stakes of political professionals to the citizens of the United States.

Political Illegitimacy as Person Violation

Does Haig wrongfully violate American citizens? Without a political philosophy in hand, we cannot decide—but this should come as no surprise. I have been claiming that the occupants of roles must judge the legitimacy of their roles, and cannot defer *that* judgment to an authority. The British public servant Quinlan, like the British private servant Stevens, must look outside the role to the principles the role serves. Political roles must look to political principles.

Recall that persons are violated when their moral agency is either damaged or denied. Surely there are ways of limiting political liberty that either deny or damage moral agency—indeed, serious political oppression insults in both ways. The illegitimate exercise of political power denies the moral agency of citizens by disregarding their claims to a fair share of the exercise of collective self rule. This is disrespectful in the way that other forms of deception, coercion, or force are disrespectful: the will of citizens is treated like an obstacle to be overpowered or undermined, and not as a source of valid claims. Persistent or severe political illegitimacy can damage moral agency as well by cultivating in persons the dispositions of tyrannized or paternalized subjects, not of free and self-ruling citizens. It is hyperbolic to claim that Haig damages the capacity of citizens to exercise moral agency in that way. But it is not hyperbolic to claim that undermining the effective authority of the courts and blocking a proper investigation of suspected political crimes denies the moral agency of citizens, because arguably such moves are illegitimate exercises of political power.

We must distinguish two different strategies that Haig might pursue:

1. Helping Nixon to contest Cox's subpoena in the courts on the ground that the tapes are protected by executive privilege;

[9] Archibald Cox, *The Court and the Constitution* (Boston: Houghton Mifflin Company, 1987), p. 17.

2. Helping Nixon to dismiss Cox on the ground that the president, not the Supreme Court, has the final word on whether the tapes are protected by executive privilege.

The first strategy is permissible under a wide range of accounts of legitimate government. Haig may depend on the division of moral labor this far: the claim of executive privilege will be settled by judges whose legitimate authority is not in dispute, so Haig needn't decide for himself questions of constitutional law before showing up for work at the White House.

In contrast, the claim that Nixon has the final word on the mandate of the man who is investigating him is a claim Haig must judge for himself. As a moral agent capable of self-command, Haig is responsible for making judgments about the legitimacy of Nixon's commands, and the second strategy is permissible only under accounts of legitimate authority that are formal, procedural, and minimal. I have argued that the correct conception of political legitimacy has substantive content, and is not purely formal or procedural, and is not minimal. If I am right, actions taken by public officials that are legal under the laws of a just and legitimate political society can nonetheless be illegitimate. Even an ideal constitution would not make all illegitimate acts illegal, so legitimacy and legality are not coextensive. One substantive criterion is the duty not to undermine just and legitimate institutions. The political strategy of threatening to challenge the authority of the courts if Cox does not back off undermines two important institutions of constitutional democracy: judicial review and rule of law.

Justifying Person Violation

If Haig does engage in person violation, can he successfully invoke any of the defenses that permit it? In general form, the test is that it would be reasonable for American citizens, from the appropriate ex ante perspective, to consent to Haig's infringement of their political liberties, even though such infringement would violate their persons ex post.

Doesn't any political strategy that is lawful under a just and legitimate constitution meet this test? No. The test is more demanding, even on the problematic view that citizens have genuinely consented to be subject to a just and legitimate constitution, and even on the unproblematic view that it is reasonable for citizens to consent to be subject to a just and legitimate constitution. Consenting to legally permit violation is different from consenting to be violated. We may all agree that hate speech should be constitutionally protected, but still not consent to be the target of hate speech. Agreed-upon legal permissions are not by themselves moral permissions. To meet the test of ex ante reasonable consent, Haig will need to invoke one of the more specific defenses of person violation.

Self-Defeat

Violations are permitted when a constraint against violation is self-defeating. If Haig does not play chicken with the authority of the Supreme Court, will Nixon violate political liberties more severely? One can sketch a nightmare scenario, like the dark satire that begins this chapter, in which Nixon will take far more drastic measures against his enemies if Haig fails to block Cox's inquiry. I have no evidence that Nixon had one thought too many on this subject ("I could impose martial law . . . but that would be wrong"), or that Haig knew about such thoughts. The point is hypothetical: *if* Haig had reasonably feared a Sunday Morning Putsch, *then* his part in the Saturday Night Massacre would have met the test of self-defeat: he would have violated the political liberties of the American people for the sake of their collective moral agency, to prevent a much graver violation.

Any Hands and Pareto Inferiority

Haig might claim, along with players in marketlike adversary practices, that if he doesn't plot to fire Cox, someone else will. Even if this is true, we noted in Chapter 7 that the any-hands argument, which would not pass a test of ex ante reasonable acceptance, should not be conflated with the argument from Pareto-inferior nonviolation, which would pass the test, or at least might. If I violate someone who will be violated anyway in order to prevent others from violation, I do so for reasons that arguably do not disrespect the violated. Ex ante, all are afforded more protection from violation from such a policy, and, ex post, none is afforded less. But if I violate someone who will be violated anyway merely because I will benefit, from no point of view do I act for the sake of protecting the victim's or any one else's moral agency. The any-hands argument does not express respect for persons.

In addition, the factual assumption of the any-hands claim, that if you don't do it someone else will, often is false. I have argued that specifying the mechanism that leads to equilibrium outcomes is important, and that one should not glibly analogize from perfectly competitive markets. Some small number of senior officials could, by their refusal, put serious obstacles in Nixon's way. Bork, for example, probably is mistaken to think that Nixon will continue to fire Justice Department officials until one is found to dismiss Cox. If this is so, it does make a difference what Haig and Bork do.

RICHARDSON V. BORK

Consider now the question of Richardson and Bork. The two surely thought one another to be justified. Bork showed nothing but admiration and respect for Richardson and his decision. Bork's compliance was defended by Richardson, at the time and in later years. Richardson enthusiastically endorsed Bork for a seat on the Supreme Court, calling him a man of "integrity, courage, and uncommon intellectual honesty."[10] But Richardson saw himself, and was seen by others, as an honest, courageous man of integrity precisely because he *refused* to fire Cox. How are we to make sense of Richardson praising, in those same terms, the man who *did* fire Cox?

One explanation, which again requires no appeal to roles, is straightforwardly based on the strategic consequences of the actions Richardson and Bork might take on that October Saturday. The best way to advance the cause of justice and protect the Watergate investigation, given Nixon's determination, is for the two, planning and acting in concert, to do as they did: Richardson refusing to be the instrument of Nixon's will in a way that alerts the public to Nixon's continued abuses of power; Bork becoming the instrument of Nixon's inexorable will, so that the Justice Department and the Watergate prosecution will still have trustworthy senior leadership in a time of crisis. On this view, because they *share* moral reasons and ends, they can agree upon the most effective division of *strategic* labor to act on those reasons and bring those ends about.

Consider, however, an interpretation closer to Richardson's own understanding: that the two men faced *different* moral reasons, and so were justified in seeking different ends. Richardson defended Bork's compliance, at the time and in later years, on the ground that, while Richardson had made a promise to the Senate during his confirmation hearings not to fire Cox, Bork had made no such promise. Richardson

---

[10] "Nomination of Robert H. Bork to be Associate Justice of the United States Supreme Court: Hearings before the Committee on the Judiciary, United States Senate, 100th Congress, First Session" (1987), p. 1646.

therefore had assumed an obligation that Bork had not. On this account, if not for the promise, Richardson may, and perhaps must, fire
Cox himself.

One of the most straightforward ways in which two moral actors in
similar situations can face different reasons for action is when one has
made a promissory commitment and the other has not, so if Richardson were not an actor in a public role, his explanation would be
unremarkable. But the force of Richardson's promise on public officials in role is puzzling. What is the nature of this promise, that it
binds Richardson but not his office, and therefore, not Bork, the acting
attorney general?

Perhaps the promise is personal—made by Richardson as a natural
person only—and therefore is not a moral reason for Bork. But if so,
why is Richardson justified in making it and keeping it? Richardson is
to join the president's administration, where he will be charged with
executing the president's policies. What business does he have in limiting his freedom of action, thereby altering the balance of power between the executive and legislature? And once made, why should this
promise have weight for Richardson in the face of the role obligations
of Richardson-as-attorney general? Some promises ought not to be
made, and some promises, though made, ought to be broken, either
because they commit the actor to bad ends or they conflict with pre-
existing or more important obligations. The promise surely has no
legal force. In the adversary system of separated institutions sharing
power, the senators have but one way to legally bind the attorney
general, and that is by duly enacted legislation.

If the promise is to have *moral* force against a presidential directive, what sort of promise must it be? Perhaps the promise is really
between Nixon and the Senate, made with Nixon's consent or on
Nixon's behalf as part of an agreement to secure Richardson's confirmation. This, a kind of political promise, is akin to a campaign
platform or other statements by public officials to secure democratic
consent for their leadership and projects. But then why does it not
commit the office of Nixon's attorney general, and fall on Bork? Or,
alternatively, why is Richardson's own integrity so deeply implicated,
but no one else's, when his boss finds it politically expedient to interfere with the prosecutor's independence, though he promised that he
would not? It is an oddly formalistic ethic that sees one's own integrity at stake in keeping a very narrowly interpreted political promise,
but not the integrity of others if the spirit of such a promise is violated. In any case, the senators do not appear to have understood the
commitment demanded of Richardson as an agreement with Nixon,
but with Richardson. And therefore, on one plausible view of the morality of roles, the senators were asking for a commitment that Rich-

ardson, acting in role, ought not to have made and ought not to have kept.

On this view, Richardson appeals to personal integrity where it has little or no moral force, misunderstands the moral reasons why, nonetheless, he should refuse to fire Cox, and therefore does not recognize that Bork should refuse as well. The reasons that they both should defy Nixon can be found either in an expansive understanding of the role of attorney general, which includes responsibilities to the rule of law and the constitution that are independent of and prior to responsibilities to the president; or else, in an appeal to impartial, political principles outside the role of attorney general, principles that give reasons to anyone. Either way, the promise to the Senate is otiose: it merely acknowledges an obligation, professional and political, that already binds both Richardson and Bork.

We come, then, to two surprising results. Richardson, though still a hero, misunderstands the grounds he has for dissent. The reasons for refusing to do the bidding of Nixon and Haig are public and political. Therefore, the action he chooses, resignation, does not best match the best reasons, and so does not send the clearest message. Resignation is the appropriate response to a conflict between personal and professional obligations, or to a reasonable disagreement about the common good. The message of resignation is that this public official can no longer execute this government's policies in good faith, so person and office must part ways. Someone else, with different contingent obligations or different reasonable views, *could* in good faith do the job, for the legitimacy of the government or its policies are not in question. But if the order to dismiss Cox is an illegitimate violation of the political liberties of the American people, and if one of the most important professional duties of the head of the Justice Department is to protect those liberties, measures stronger than a parting of ways are called for in response. In keeping with the account of official discretion against merely formal authority presented in the preceding chapter, Richardson does not face a forced choice between serving obediently and stepping aside so another can serve obediently. He owes Nixon's formal authority no more than formal deference (and perhaps not even that). Surely he may employ an incentive-based strategy within the bounds of formal law aimed at thwarting Haig and Nixon. The most effective time to have done this was in the days before the fateful Saturday, when a clear and public restatement of Cox's charter—and Richardson's resolve to uphold it—might have altered Nixon's calculations:

> WASHINGTON POST: Sir, if the President orders you to dismiss the special prosecutor, will you comply?

ATTORNEY GENERAL: The very suggestion that the President would give such an order is preposterous. This administration is unalterably committed to respecting the prosecutor's independence. As you well know, the charter of the special prosecutor does not permit removal without overwhelming evidence of extraordinary improprieties.

Even though he failed to show such early resolve, Richardson still might have resisted Saturday's order in lawful ways. Resistance almost certainly would have led to his own dismissal, but would have signaled, more clearly than resignation, the illegitimacy of Nixon's directive. Delay might as well have given the public more time to pressure Nixon to rescind. Part of what makes this affair dramatically suspenseful is that Nixon's directive was not, under law, self-executing: the attorney general needed to do the deed. This opens the possibility that timely execution by the attorney general need not be instantaneous. Richardson might have publicly asked Nixon to clarify that he intended to countermand Cox's charter; he might have announced that the Justice Department needed time to study the legality of Nixon's directive; he might even have sought guidance from the court; he might simply have waited until the next business day after the long holiday weekend to do anything at all. More astute political strategists than I no doubt could come up with more clever ways to protect Cox lawfully or signal Nixon's misconduct. The point is that Richardson is morally permitted to act strategically here.

May Richardson disobey Nixon's lawful command outright, and not pay the president even formal deference? Nixon would have immediately fired him, of course, and turned to another to do the deed, so disobedience would not help Cox. But it would, in a persuasive and conscientious way, present to the American people the correct interpretation of what was at stake: that Nixon was not merely acting badly, but unjustly and illegitimately; that the political liberties of the people can be and have been seriously undermined by lawful acts; and that political leaders who undermine just and legitimate institutions, even when they do so lawfully, commit grave political injustices that call for extraordinary remedy. As the criminal and congressional probes progressed, most Americans did eventually come to this understanding, but Richardson could not have known at the time of his own resignation that Nixon would fail in his attempts to deny access to the tapes and to stop the special prosecution. Do Richardson's reasons for dissent, properly understood, meet the test for justified official disobedience?

I believe that they do in all respects but one. Although there is no conceptual or practical contradiction in disobeying a formally lawful order to protest disrespect for the rule of law, there is a danger that one's disobedience itself may be misunderstood as showing disrespect for the rule of law.[11] Since disobedience is addressed to the sense of justice (and legitimacy) of citizens, subtlety of justification is a defect. On Rawls's account, for example, economic injustice should not normally be protested by civil disobedience, because the appeal to the public's conception of justice is unclear, and, therefore, one may fail to convince others of one's good faith.[12] Since some version of lawful defiance that does not risk this misunderstanding appears to be open to Richardson, there he should go.

If Richardson's reasons for dissent are public and political, they are reasons for Bork as well. Hence, the second result: Bork is wrong to fire Cox on the grounds that he made no promise, and Richardson is mistaken to think that Bork for that reason acts rightly.[13] Upon reflection, the tragic conflicts of obligation that the Saturday Night Massacre appears to present to its protagonists resolve without remainder. Haig and Bork are not caught in a Sophoclean dilemma. Insofar as they think that they face different role-relative obligations, they simply commit errors in judgment.

NECESSARY OFFICES?

The adversary professions appeal to a division of moral labor that, in demanding both person neutrality and role relativity, restricts the set of reasons upon which role players should act. In so doing, this division of labor claims to permit the violation of persons in ways that otherwise would be wrong. This argument, despite its appearance of sophistication and its pose of knowing worldliness, is much weaker than supposed. The truth is more simple: institutions and the roles they create ordinarily cannot mint moral permissions to do what otherwise would be prohibited. They cannot because the filtering of rea-

[11] This point was made to me by both Peter DeMarneffe and Alan Wertheimer.

[12] John Rawls, *A Theory of Justice* (Cambridge, Mass.: Harvard University Press, 1971), p. 372.

[13] We cannot, however, lightly dismiss the view sketched earlier, that Bork and Richardson, faced with the same obligations, justifiably divided their strategic labor. After Nixon ordered that the functions of the office of the special prosecutor be absorbed by the Justice Department and Haig sent FBI agents to "secure" the office files, Bork urged Cox's staff to stay on the job and announced to the press that the investigators could still take the president to court to obtain evidence. He then oversaw the reestablishment of the special prosecutor's office and the appointment of Jaworski. There is a dispute among Cox's top deputies about the importance, timeliness, and motivation of Bork's actions. See "Nomination of Robert H. Bork," Testimony of Henry Ruth, pp. 1712–70; Statement of Philip A. Lacovara, pp. 1738–50.

sons and the redescription of actions and actors that adversary roles demand do not properly have a grip on the judgments of role players who are also persons simply, and so who face all the reasons for action that apply to persons simply. Constituted act descriptions do not preempt natural act descriptions, and artificial actor descriptions do not preempt natural actor descriptions. Act and actor redescription in part fails because the redescription of targets fails: the victims of adversary action, though they too might play roles, do not lose their claims to be treated with the dignity and respect that befit persons simply. Descriptions persist.

The adversary professional claims that a policy of acting upon restricted reasons can itself meet an all-reasons-considered test. Some practices of partiality—friendship, romantic love, parenthood—can be justified on impartial grounds because they realize goods that are valuable when impartially considered. Why not the partiality of a lawyer, business competitor, or political operative? Because what the adversary professional seeks to justify is not merely the pursuit of a plurality of goods, but the violation of persons—mainly through deception and manipulation, but also at times through coercion, force, or violence. If persons are to be treated with respect then their violation must be reasonably acceptable to them. It is unlikely that a proposal to permit the violation of one to realize other goods for others would meet such a test. And in an adversary practice governed by general rules, the rules will permit person violation even in particular instances where the goods of the practice are not realized. When the generalization fails to apply and one is to be violated for no good end, what acceptable reason can be given to the victim?

There is an important asymmetry here between justifying forms of social practice and justifying the moral judgments of actors playing roles within a social practice. The competition that results from different actors acting upon partial reasons may result in good consequences or realize important values, and that might be a good enough reason for rule makers and institution builders to allow or even promote partiality of a sort that makes room for the violation of persons. But from the point of view of an actor guided by practical reason, much of the partiality permitted or demanded by adversary institutions cannot be a reasonable aim. Rather, partiality is realized only as a by-product of different actors making different imperfect judgments about the best reasons that apply to them. Even this asymmetry between designer and practitioner is vulnerable to reflection, because if morality requires a certain transparency, the stability of a practice must not depend on actors being ignorant of its structure.

There remains the question of legitimate authority. If practice positivism is correct, roles simply are what they are, not what they ought to be. Why are professionals not subject to the authority of their professions, and so obligated to comply with the role that is? Because practice positivism by itself says nothing about the moral authority of a positive practice. Some legal positivists are moved by an extra clause: the law is what it is, not what it ought to be, *and the law that is must be obeyed*. But this extra clause is in need of its own argument, for it does not follow simply from the idea of legal positivism or practice positivism. Precisely because roles are conventional, they are only indirectly moralized. Role obligations are not in themselves moral obligations, and role permissions are not in themselves moral permissions. Surely we can become obligated in various ways to do what we otherwise do not have good enough moral reason to do—that is, moral requirements can overwrite moral permissions. But we cannot acquire a moral obligation to do what we are morally forbidden to do. Just as a promise to become a contract killer is void ab initio, a promise to become a contract liar—whether for a political candidate, a corporate litigant, or a soapsuds manufacturer—is void ab initio. Or, to be more precise, *if* a lie of a certain sort is morally wrong, then a promise to lie cannot make it right.

If our professions were simply institutionalized villainy, the fact that they were institutions would count for nothing. But since most of our professions aim at goods and purposes worthy of the commitment of a reflective practitioner, they are not without legitimacy, even when their rules are imperfect. That is why criteria of justified professional dissent and disobedience are needed. Judgments about the legitimate authority of a role can and must always be made from a standpoint outside the role, within one's own shoes. Constitutive rules do not rule out self-command.

In what way, then, should we take roles seriously? The answer is clear: though roles ordinarily cannot permit what is forbidden, they can require what is permitted. Professional roles are powerful obligators. Nothing that I have said here should be taken to argue for the weakening of the moral commitments that tie professionals to their legitimate and just professional role obligations. But neither consent nor some version of the fair-play principle can bind an actor to an illegitimate or unjust role. Montaigne is wrong: lawyers and financiers, politicians and public servants, *are* responsible for the vice and stupidity of their trades, and *should* refuse to practice them in vicious and stupid ways.

SOURCES AND CREDITS

Epigraphs have been drawn from the following sources. Where permission to reprint is needed, I am grateful to the noted copyright-holder for kindly granting it.

Part I: Michel de Montaigne, "Of the Useful and the Honorable," in *The Complete Essays of Montaigne*, 3:1 (1588), trans. Donald M. Frame (Stanford: Stanford University Press, 1958), p. 600, except that I have rendered *rolles* as "roles" where Frame has "parts."

Chapter 2: Anon., "Complaints of the Public Executioner against Those Who Have Exercised His Profession without Having Served Out Their Apprenticeship" (1789), in Daniel Arasse, *The Guillotine and the Terror*, trans. Christopher Miller (1987; London: Penguin Books, 1989), app. 3, pp. 188–89.

Part II: W. S. Gilbert and Arthur Sullivan, *The Mikado, or The Town of Titipu* (1885), ed. Bryceson Treharne (New York: G. Schirmer, n.d.), p. 62.

Chapter 3: Henry David Thoreau, "Resistance to Civil Government" (1849), in *The Writings of Henry D. Thoreau: Reform Papers*, ed. Wendell Glick (Princeton, N.J.: Princeton University Press, 1973), p. 75. Reprinted posthumously under the title "Civil Disobedience."

Chapter 4: Montaigne, "Of Husbanding Your Will," in *Essays*, 3:10 (1588), trans. Frame, p. 773, except that I have rendered *rolle* as "role" where Frame has "part."

Chapter 5: Damon Runyon, "Situation Wanted" (1936), in *Guys and Dolls: The Stories of Damon Runyon* (New York: Penguin Books, 1992), pp. 304–5. Copyright © 1992 by Sheldon Abend. Used by permission of Viking Penguin, a division of Penguin Putnam Inc.

Part III: Kurt Vonnegut Jr., "All the King's Horses" (1953), in *Welcome to the Monkey House* (New York: Delacorte Press, 1968), pp. 91–92. Copyright © 1961 by Kurt Vonnegut Jr. Used by permission of Delacorte Press/Seymour Lawrence, a division of Bantam Doubleday Dell Publishing Group, Inc.

Chapter 6: Montaigne, "Parley Time is Dangerous," in *Essays*, 1:6 (1580), trans. Frame, p. 18.

Chapter 7: Judith N. Shklar, "The Liberalism of Fear," in *Liberalism and the Moral Life*, ed. Nancy Rosenblum (Cambridge, Mass.: Harvard University Press, 1989), p. 30.

Chapter 8: Voltaire, *Candide* (1759), trans. and ed. Robert M. Adams (New York: W. W. Norton, 1966), pp. 9–10.

Part IV: Denis Diderot, *Jacques the Fatalist and His Master* (1778), trans. Michael Henry (London: Penguin Books, 1986), pp. 160–62.

Chapter 9: Rainer Maria Rilke, *The Sonnets to Orpheus* (1922), trans. Stephen Mitchell (New York: Simon & Schuster, 1985), 1:5, p. 27.

Chapter 10: Philip Roth, "The President Addresses the Nation," *New York Review of Books*, June 14, 1973, p. 11. Copyright © 1973 by Philip Roth. Reprinted with the permission of the Wylie Agency, Inc.

Portions of the following chapters draw on my previously published or forthcoming work, as noted. Where I do not hold the copyright, permission to revise and reprint has been kindly granted by the publisher.

Chapter 2: "Professional Detachment: The Executioner of Paris," *Harvard Law Review* 109 (1995): 458–86. Copyright © 1995 by The Harvard Law Review Association.

Chapter 3: "Doctor, Schmoctor: Practice Positivism and Its Complications," in *The American Medical Ethics Revolution*, ed. Robert Baker, Stephen Latham, Arthur Caplan, and Linda Emanuel (Baltimore: Johns Hopkins University Press, forthcoming). Copyright © 1999 by Arthur Isak Applbaum.

Chapter 4: "The Remains of the Role," *Governance* 6 (1993): 545–57. Copyright © 1993 by Blackwell Publishers.

Chapter 5: "Are Lawyers Liars? The Argument of Redescription," *Legal Theory* 4 (1998): 63–91. Copyright © 1998 by Cambridge University Press. Reprinted with the permission of Cambridge University Press.

Chapter 6: "Rules of the Game, Permissible Harms, and the Principle of Fair Play," in *Wise Choices: Games, Decisions, and Negotiations*, ed. Richard J. Zeckhauser, Ralph L. Keeney, and James K. Sebenius (Boston: Harvard Business School Press, 1996), pp. 301–23. Copyright © 1996 by Arthur Isak Applbaum.

Chapter 7: "Are Violations of Rights Ever Right?" *Ethics* 108 (1998): 340–66. Copyright © 1998 by The University of Chicago. All rights reserved.

Chapter 9: "Democratic Legitimacy and Official Discretion," *Philosophy and Public Affairs* 21 (1992): 240–74. Copyright © 1992 by Princeton University Press. Reprinted by permission of Princeton University Press.

INDEX